Guide to
English Proficiency,
Logic & Quantitative Reasoning for
JIPMER

With 7 Past & 10 Practice Papers

- **Corporate Office :** 45, 2nd Floor, Maharishi Dayanand Marg, Corner Market,Malviya Nagar, New Delhi-110017
  Tel. : 011- 49404757/ 49404758/ 49404768

By

Disha Experts

Typeset by Disha DTP Team

DISHA PUBLICATION

ALL RIGHTS RESERVED

For further information about the books from DISHA,
Log on to **www.dishapublication.com** or
email to **info@dishapublication.com**

INDEX

English Proficiency

VOCABULARY

1. Choose the word which correctly explains the meaning of underlined word in the sentence: His <u>depravity</u> is responsible for the situation, we are facing now.   **[Evening 2019]**
(a) mockery
(b) indolent
(c) wickedness
(d) unmalicious

2. Harsh is jovial. Jovial in this context means: **[Morning 2019]**
(a) Bully
(b) Pessimistic
(c) Optimistic
(d) Angersome

DIRECTIONS (Qs. 3-5): In the questions given below, a sentence is given with an **bold** word followed by four options. Select the option that is nearest in meaning to the **bold** word.
[Morning 2018]

3. The food was available in **profusion**.
(a) plentiful
(b) scarcity
(c) dearth
(d) deficiency

4. She spends her money **lavishly**.
(a) carefully
(b) foolishly
(c) generously
(d) madly

5. The judge **delivered** his verdicts at 1 PM.
(a) liberated
(b) pronounced
(c) surrendered
(d) transferred

6. Antonym of Cajole is :
[Morning 2019]
(a) Nestle
(b) Secede
(c) Bully
(d) Moisten

7. Antonym of "barbarous" is :
[Evening 2019]
(a) civilized
(b) dignified
(c) magnified
(d) cruel

DIRECTIONS (Qs. 8-10): In the questions given below, a sentence is given with an **bold** word followed by four options. Select the option that is opposite in meaning to the **bold** word.
[Morning 2018]

8. She is very serious by **temperament**.
(a) stupid
(b) grave
(c) trivial
(d) sober

9. He has a **fine** ear for music.
(a) smooth
(b) coarse
(c) closed
(d) small

10. There is no **likeness** between her and her sister.
(a) disaffinity
(b) unlikeliness
(c) unlikelihood
(d) dissimilarity

DIRECTIONS (Qs. 11-12) : Select the word which is most nearly the same in meaning as the given words.   **[2017]**

11. Demise
     (a) Result
     (b) Default
     (c) Death
     (d) Apprehension
12. Disparity
     (a) Distaste   (b) Dissimilarity
     (c) Criticism (d) Distinction

DIRECTIONS (Qs. 13-14) : Out of the four alternatives, choose the one which best expresses the zmeaning of the given word.   **[2016]**

13. Instigate
     (a) Initiate   (b) Incite
     (c) Force   (d) Cause
14. Varacious
     (a) Quick   (b) Angry
     (c) Hungry   (d) Wild

DIRECTIONS (Qs. 15-16) : Choose the word opposite in meaning to the given word.   **[2015]**

15. Epilogue
     (a) Dialogue   (b) Prelude
     (c) Post script (d) Epigram
16. Indiscreet
     (a) Reliable   (b) Honest
     (c) Prudent   (d) Stupid

DIRECTIONS (Qs. 17-18) : Groups of four words are given. In each group, one word is correctly spelt. Find the correctly spelt word.   **[2015]**

17. (a) Parapharnelia
     (b) Parsimonious
     (c) Peccadilo
     (d) Peadialriis
18. (a) Tussel   (b) Tunnle
     (c) Tumble   (d) Trable

DIRECTIONS (Qs.19-21): In the questions given below, a sentence is given with an underlined word followed by four options. Select the option that is nearest in meaning to the underlined word.   **[Morning 2018]**

19. Only a health problem would <u>deter</u> him from seeking re-election.
     (a) discourage
     (b) allow
     (c) help
     (d) enlighten
20. In the last match, Indian team made a <u>mammoth</u> total.
     (a) meager   (b) small
     (c) huge   (d) tough
21. I was filled with <u>jubilation</u> to see you.
     (a) joy   (b) anger
     (c) animosity (d) humour

DIRECTIONS (Qs.22-24): In the questions given below, a sentence is given with an underlined word followed by four options. Select the option that is opposite in meaning to the underlined word.   **[Evening 2018]**

22. She is busy doing a <u>tedious</u> task.
     (a) stupid   (b) boring
     (c) exciting   (d) dull
23. He is <u>delighted</u> to receive the first prize.
     (a) excited   (b) sad
     (c) cheerful   (d) joyful
24. Please <u>delineate</u> the lecture to me.
     (a) recite   (b) distort
     (c) write   (d) give

DIRECTIONS (Qs. 25-29) : Choose the word/group of words which is the most nearly SAME in meaning as the word/ group of words.   **[2014]**

25. SINCERE

    (a) Open   (b) Earnest

    (c) Dissolute   (d) Upright

26. ENCOURAGE

    (a) Animate   (b) Urge

    (c) Stimulate (d) Dissuade

27. SELF-SUFFICIENT

    (a) Adequate

    (b) Dependent

    (c) Overflowing

    (d) Self-reliant

28. FOCUS

    (a) Adjust   (b) Concentrate

    (c) Meditate (d) Circulate

29. SUPERFICIAL

    (a) Artificial   (b) Shallow

    (c) Complete (d) Profound

DIRECTIONS (Qs. 30-34) : In the following questions, out of the four alternatives, choose the one which best express the meaning of the given word. **[2013]**

30. GAINSAY

    (a) Advantage

    (b) Proposal

    (c) Contradict

    (d) Suggestion

31. PROFOUND

    (a) Profuse   (b) Boundless

    (c) Deep   (d) Fathomless

32. FLAK

    (a) Adventure (b) Advice

    (c) Criticism (d) Praise

33. HOODLUM

    (a) Pioneer   (b) Criminal

    (c) Devotee (d) Scholar

34. SPASMODIC

    (a) Continuous

    (b) Gradual

    (c) Intermittent

    (d) Spontaneous

DIRECTIONS (Qs. 35-39) : In the following questions, choose the word opposite in meaning to the given word. **[2013]**

35. FILTHY

    (a) Stainless (b) Shining

    (c) Sterilised (d) Clean

36. CROWDED

    (a) Deserted (b) Lonely

    (c) Empty   (d) Barren

37. VAGUE

    (a) Known   (b) Published

    (c) Popular (d) Definite

38. SUPERVISE

    (a) Overlook (b) Misdirect

    (c) Neglect (d) Forget

39. MAGNANIMOUS

    (a) Selfish   (b) Naive

    (c) Generous (d) Small

DIRECTIONS (Qs. 40-44) : In the following questions, out of the four alternatives, choose the one which can be substituted for the given words/ sentence. **[2013]**

40. Word for word reproduction.

    (a) Copying (b) Mugging

    (c) Verbatim (d) Photostat

41. A person who collects coins.

    (a) Philatelist

    (b) Numismatist

    (c) Narcissist

    (d) Fatalist

42. That which is perceptible by touch
   (a) Tangible
   (b) Tenacious
   (c) Contagious
   (d) Contingent

43. One who possesses many talents.
   (a) Versatile   (b) Gifted
   (c) Exceptional   (d) Nubile

44. A person who studies the formation of the Earth.
   (a) Meteorologist
   (b) Anthropologist
   (c) Geologist
   (d) Seismologist

FILL IN THE BLANKS

DIRECTIONS (Qs. 45 - 46) : Pick out the most effective word from the given words to fill in the blank to make the sentence meaningfully complete.

[Evening 2019]

45. Mohini is an independent and innovative thinker, it is best to grant her a good deal of __________ with regard to the direction of her research.
   (a) leverage   (b) interest
   (c) assistance   (d) money

46. The __________ of meat in your refrigerator does not necessarily indicate that you are a vegetarian.
   (a) presence   (b) absence
   (c) amount   (d) colour

DIRECTIONS (Qs. 47 - 49) : *Pick out the most effective word from the given words to fill in the blank to make the sentence meaningfully complete.*

[Morning 2019]

47. His actions had __________ pain and suffering on thousands of people.
   (a) affected   (b) imposed
   (c) inflicted   (d) deplored

48. The Government will __________ all resources to fight poverty.
   (a) collect   (b) exploit
   (c) harness   (d) muster

49. The children __________ crackers to celebrate the victory of their team.
   (a) burst   (b) fired
   (c) shot   (d) released

DIRECTIONS (Qs. 50-54) : In the following passage there are blanks, each of which has been numbered. These numbers are printed below the passage and against each, four words are suggested, one of which fits the blank appropriately. Find out the appropriate word in each case. **[2017]**

Working under the psychometric approach, both scientists and practitioners have placed undue emphasis upon a unitary concept of intelligence as reflected in the single I.Q. They seem to have ......(50)...... too much attention of the products of intelligent behavior rather than the processes used to acquire .....(51)......products. Such attention to product rather than to process tends to mark qualitative differences in the processes by .....(52).... individuals interact with their environment and to .....(53).... attention away from the possibility of qualitative changes in the nature of these processes ....(54)... the curse of cognitive development.

50.   (a) gives   (b) gave
   (c) forced   (d) given

51.   (a) those   (b) these
   (c) that   (d) raw

52. (a) how   (b) way
    (c) speech   (d) which

53. (a) draw   (b) seek
    (c) force   (d) drag

54. (a) at   (b) plan
    (c) during   (d) follow

DIRECTIONS (Qs. 55-59) : Fill up the blanks in the passage given below with the most appropriate word from the options given for each blank. **[2016]**

The ... (55) ... age is the age of machines. From the ... (56) ... the industrial Revolution began in Europe. Man's life has been changing ... (57) ... many ways. At first the change was ...(58)... Now machines have become ... (59) ... of our daily lives.

55. (a) modern   (b) new
    (c) civilised   (d) present

56. (a) birth   (b) time
    (c) beginning   (d) start

57. (a) into   (b) to
    (c) in   (d) with

58. (a) slow   (b) steady
    (c) fast   (d) stagnant

59. (a) component
    (b) part
    (c) necessity
    (d) support

DIRECTIONS (Qs. 60-64) : In the following questions, sentences are given with blanks to be filled in with an appropriate word. Four alternatives are suggested from each questions. Choose the correct alternative out of the four. **[2015]**

---

60. The little girl .... for the light switch in the dark.
    (a) groped   (b) grappled
    (c) gripped   (d) groveled

61. The summit meeting provided him the much......shot in the arm.
    (a) required   (b) desired
    (c) needed   (d) urgent

62. We must........the tickets for the movie in advance.
    (a) draw   (b) buy
    (c) remove   (d) take

63. The State Transport Corporation has ....a loss of ₹ 5crore this year.
    (a) obtained   (b) derived
    (c) incurred   (d) formulated

64. .... and you know who among them is the culprit.
    (a) look   (b) deep
    (c) sight   (d) gaze

DIRECTIONS (Qs. 65-69) : Pick out the most effective word/phrase from the given words to fill in the blank to make the sentence meaningfully complete. **[2014]**

---

65. He knelt at his side and comforted him with .... words.
    (a) harsh   (b) silent
    (c) kind   (d) cruel

66. A man who is perpetually ...... which of the two things he will do first, will do neither,
    (a) confused   (b) forced
    (c) orders   (d) hesitating

67. We cannot .... of life without suitable environment.
    (a) live   (b) buy
    (c) extract   (d) think

68. He thought the boy .... to benefit the blacksmith.
    (a) wants   (b) wanting
    (c) desire   (d) harm

69. The fisherman gladly .... up the baby and took it home.
    (a) loaded   (b) picked
    (c) dragged   (d) pushed

PARAJUMBLES

70. Arrange the phrases in order to make a meaningful sentences:
When he.....   **[Evening 2019]**

P : did not know

Q : he was nervous and

R : Heard the hue and cry at midnight.

S : What to do

(a) RQPS   (b) QSPR

(c) SQPR   (d) PQRS

DIRECTION (Q. 71) : In question below, each passage consist of six sentences. The first and sixth sentence are given in the begining. The middle four sentences in each have been removed and jumbled up. These are labelled as P, Q, R and S. Find out the proper order for the four sentences.   **[2017]**

71. S1 : In the middle of one side of the square sits the Chairman of the committee, the most important person in the room.

P : For a committee is not just a mere collection of individuals.

Q : On him rests much of the responsibility for the success or failure of the committee.

R : While this is happening we have an opportunity to get the 'feel' of this committee.

S : As the meeting opens, he runs briskly through a number of formalities.

S6 : From the moment its members meet, it begins to have a sort nebulous life of its own.

The Proper sequence should be

(a) RSQP   (b) PQRS

(c) SQPR   (d) QSRP

DIRECTIONS (Qs. 72-74) : In the following questions, a sentence has divided into four parts. Arrange these parts to make the sentence meaningful
[2015]

72. In favour of English,

P : has chances of securing employment

Q : We may say that

R : in all parts of India and in foreign coutnries

S : an English knowing Indian

(a) QSPR   (b) SPQR

(c) SRQP   (d) QRPS

73. The hungry man

P : and said

Q : replied in the negative

R : that he only wanted a meal

S : to his question

(a) SQPR   (b) QSPR

(c) SPRQ   (d) QPRS

74. It is

P : that people read fewer books today

Q : that they did

R : even about a decadce ago

S : a matter of grave concern

(a) PSRQ   (b) SPRQ

(c) PSQR   (d) SPQR

DIRECTIONS (Qs. 75-79) : Rearrange the following sentences to make a meaningful paragraph and then answer the questions given below them.
[2014]

A. A classroom discussion can be initiated in order to answer this very question.

B. An electric current could not be made to traverse distilled water

C. Yet when salt and distilled water were mixed, then the solution became a liquid through which electricity could pass with ease.

D. Neither would solid salt offer free passage to electricity.

E. How could one explain this strange behavior of solution.

F. And, as the current passed through this solution, a deep seated decomposition took place.

75. Which of the following will be the FIFTH sentences?

(a) A   (b) C
(c) B   (d) E

76. Which of the following will be the FOURTH sentence?

(a) A   (b) B
(c) F   (d) E

77. Which of the following will be the LAST (SIXTH) sentence?

(a) C   (b) A
(c) B   (d) E

78. Which of the following will be the THIRD sentence?

(a) C   (b) D
(c) F   (d) A

79. Which of the following will be the FIRST sentence?

(a) A   (b) D
(c) B   (d) C

DIRECTIONS (Qs. 80-84) : In the following questions, the first and the last parts of the sentence are numbered 1 and 6. The rest of the sentence is split into four parts named P, Q, R and S. These parts are not given in their proper order. Rearrange these parts in their proper order and find out which of the given four combination is correct?

[2013]

80. (1) In reply to a question
(P) that securing extradition
(Q) operating from the UK soil remained
(R) of anti-India elements
(S) The spokesman said
(6) New Delhi's first priority.
(a) PRQS   (b) QSPR
(c) RQSP   (d) SPRQ

81. (1) The first component is
(P) and vocational training
(Q) so as to enable them
(R) the provision of further technical
(S) so both rural and urban youth
(6) to secure employment in industry and the services sector.
(a) PRSQ   (b) RPSQ
(c) RSQP   (d) SRPQ

82. (1) The move to revert to a six-day week
(P) among the employees
(Q) while the leaders represented to the Chief Minister
(R) that they be taken into confidence
(S) led to an animated decision
(6) before any decision was taken.
(a) QPSR   (b) RSPQ
(c) SPQR   (d) SQPR

83. (1) It was obvious
(P) made by him
(Q) submitted at the meeting
(R) from the comments
(S) on the draft proposals
(6) that he was not satisfied with them.
(a) PSRQ   (b) QRSP
(c) RPSQ   (d) SQRP

84. (1) The Minister of state for power
(P) in conservation of electricity in industries
(Q) has written to his counterparts in State Governments

(R) to implement the official directive

(S) on bringing about improvement

(6) by introduction of energy efficient equipment.

(a) QPSR   (b) QRSP
(c) SPQR   (d) SQPR

SPOTTING ERRORS

85. Which statement is grammatically correct?   **[Morning 2019]**

(a) He have tried to control his anger despite bully nature

(b) He had tried to control his anger despite bully nature

(c) He would tried to control his anger despite bully nature

(d) He could tried to control his anger despite bully nature

86. Which of the following is grammatically correct?

[Evening 2019]

(a) He took out his shoes.

(b) It is a most beautiful painting in the art gallery.

(c) Many villagers do not know how to write his name.

(d) Please put off the television and do your homework.

87. Which is grammatically correct?

[Evening 2019]

(a) He hardly had those kinds of shoes.

(b) He hadn't hardly those kind of shoes.

(c) He hardly had those kind of shoes.

(d) He hadn't hardly these kinds of shoes.

DIRECTIONS (Qs. 88-90) : Read each sentence to find out whether there is any error in it. The error, if any, will be in one part of the sentence. The alphabet number of that part is the answer. If there is no error, then the answer is (d).

[2017]

---

88. We (a)/ saw a elephant (b)/ In the zoo. (c)/ No error (d)

89. It is (a)/ a most (b)/ beautiful painting of the gallery. (c)/ No error (d)

90. Mr Gaurav Sharma (a) is coming to (b)/ dinner. (c) No error (d)

DIRECTIONS (Qs. 91-95) : Read each sentence to find out whether there is any grammatical error or idiomatic error in it. The error, if any, will be in one part of the sentence. The number of that part is the answer. If there is no error, the answer is (d) i.e., 'No error (Ignore errors of punctuation, if any).   **[2016]**

---

91. He is neither in (a) favour of arms race or in favour of (b)/simple nuclear disarmament. (c)/ No error (d)

(a) a   (b) b
(c) c   (d) d

92. Naturalization is the process by which (a)/ a immigrant becomes a citizen (b)/ of his new country. (c)/ No error (d)

(a) a   (b) b
(c) c   (d) d

93. A high fat diet not only increases the risks (a)/ of heart ailments (b) / however also that of other disorders. (c)/ No error (d)

(a) a   (b) b
(c) c   (d) d

94. When two vowel (a) / sounds occurs in direct succession, (b)/ the transition between them is often difficult to make. (c)/ No error (d)

(a) a   (b) b
(c) c   (d) d

95. The solutions is to avoid the impasse altogether, (a)/ by taking a (b) / slightly different route. (c) / No error (d)

(a) a   (b) b
(c) c   (d) d

DIRECTIONS (Qs. 96-100) : In each sentence below three words have been printed in bold which are number (a), (b) and (c). One of these words may be misspelt or inappropriate in the context of the sentence. Find out the wrongly spelt or inappropriate word. The number of that word is the answer. If all the words are correctly spelt and are appropriate the answer is (d) i.e., all correct **[2015]**

96. The **importanse** (a) given to content-oriented approach has affected the **methodology** (b) of this project. (c) All correct (d)
    (a) a   (b) b
    (c) c   (d) d

97. Almost all **risk-taking** (a) work **involve** (b) decision making under **uncertainty**. (c) All correct (d)
    (a) a   (b) b
    (c) c   (d) d

98. In **developing** (a) countries there is **increasing** (b) concern for fostering human **potential**. (c) All correct (d)
    (a) a   (b) b
    (c) c   (d) d

99. I want to **express** (a) my **appreciation** (b) of the help offered by my former **colleages**. (c) All correct (d)
    (a) a   (b) b
    (c) c   (d) d

100. The **research** (a) reported in this **valume** (b) assumes **importance**. (c) All correct (d).
    (a) a   (b) b
    (c) c   (d) d

DIRECTIONS (Qs. 101-105) : Which of the phrases (a), (b) and (c) given below each sentence should replace the phrase printed in bold in the sentence to make it grammatically correct? If the sentence is correct as is given and no correction is required, mark (d) as the answer **[2014]**

101. Your doctor may explain the importance of a **proper and balanced** diet in the human body.
    (a) an proper and balanced
    (b) a proper or balance
    (c) a prosperous and balance
    (d) No correction required

102. English today **is closer to been** a world language than any other language has been in history.
    (a) is closer for been
    (b) is closer upon being
    (c) is closer to being
    (d) No correction required

103. In almost every occupation on **needs simple a** understanding of electricity.
    (a) needed simple an
    (b) need a simple
    (c) needs a simple
    (d) No correction required

104. When ice and water **existed together on** the same volume, the temperature remains constant.
    (a) exist together in
    (b) will exist together on
    (c) existed together in
    (d) No correction required

105. Scientific method as a rote item in the syllabus **had little valued.**
    (a) had belittled value
    (b) has little value
    (c) have little value
    (d) No correction required

DIRECTIONS (Qs. 106-109) : In the following questions, a part of the sentence is printed in bold. Below are given alternatives to the bold part at (a), (b), (c) which may improve the sentence. Choose the correct alternative. In case no improvement is needed, your answer (d). **[2013]**

106. Ravi has got many friends because he has got **much money.**

(a) Enough money
(b) A lot of money
(c) Bags of money
(d) No improvement

107. You must try **making him to understand.**
(a) Make him understand
(b) To making him understand
(c) To make him understand
(d) No improvement

108. He has cooked that meal so often he can do it with his **eyes closed.**
(a) Mind blank
(b) Eyes covered
(c) Hands full
(d) No improvement

109. Not a word **they spoke** to the unfortunate wife about it.
(a) They had spoken
(b) Did they speak
(c) They will spea;k
(d) No improvement

IDIOMS & PHRASES

DIRECTION (Q. 110) : Choose the word that best defines the given phrase.
[Morning 2019]

110. Building castles in the air
(a) Making impossible plans
(b) Making tall promises
(c) Building skyscrapers
(d) Structures without strong foundation

DIRECTIONS (Qs. 111-114): In each of the questions given below, a/an idiom/phrase is given in **bold** which is then followed by four options which then try to decipher its meaning as used in the sentence. Choose the option which gives the meaning of the idiom/phrase most appropriately in context of the given sentence. **[Morning 2018]**

111. The kids had **a field day** at the carnival.

(a) a very tough day
(b) a very boring day
(c) a very enjoyable time
(d) an unpleasant day

112. It's time to go home, let's **call it a day**.
(a) finish the work fast
(b) to stop doing something
(c) move fast
(d) do or die

113. I am **feeling a bit under the weather**.
(a) feeling slightly ill
(b) feeling great
(c) attracted towards the nature
(d) feeling disgusted

114. Scoring 10 runs in 16 balls was a **cake walk** for the batsman.
(a) a very tough task
(b) a boring task
(c) an unachievable tasks
(d) an easy task

DIRECTIONS (Qs.115-118): In each of the questions given below, a/an idiom/phrase is given in underline which is then followed by four options which then try to decipher its meaning as used in the sentence. Choose the option which gives the meaning of the idiom/phrase most appropriately in context of the given sentence. **[Evening 2018]**

115. They finally saw eye to eye on the business deal.
(a) agreeing with someone
(b) starting argument
(c) move fast
(d) stiff competition

116. They really cut corners when they built this tank, it's leaking.
(a) to do great work
(b) to do something badly or cheaply
(c) to do something very fast
(d) to destroy resources

117. I go to my uncle <u>once in a blue moon</u>.
(a) regularly
(b) usually
(c) when someone calls someone
(d) an event that happens infrequently

118. She agreed for the picnic <u>at the drop of a hat</u>.
(a) instantly
(b) to take too much time
(c) lazily
(d) effortlessly

DIRECTIONS (Qs. 119-123) : In the following questions, four alternatives are given for the idiom/phrase printed in bold in sentence. Choose the alternative which best express the meaning of the idiom/phrase. **[2016]**

119. We have to **keep our finger crossed** till the final result is declared
(a) keep praying
(b) feel suspicious
(c) wait expectantly
(d) feel scared

120. The members of the group were **at odds** over the selection procedure.
(a) acting foolishly
(b) in dispute
(c) unanimous
(d) behaving childishly

121. The popularity of the yesteryears' superstar is **one the wane.**
(a) growing more
(b) at its peak
(c) growing less
(d) at rock -bottom

122. His father advised him to **the fair and square in** this dealings lest he should fall into trouble.
(a) considerate (b) upright
(c) careful (d) polite

123. There is **no love lost** between the two neighbours.
(a) close friendship
(b) intense dislike
(c) a love-hate relationship
(d) cool indifference

DIRECTIONS (Qs. 124 - 126) : Read the following passage carefully and answer the questions given below:
[Evening 2019]

We shall go on the end, we shall fight in France, we shall fight on the seas and oceans, we shall fight with the growing confidence and strength in the air, we shall defend our island, whatever the cost may be, we shall fight on the beaches, we shall fight on the landing grounds, we shall fight in the fields and in the streets, we shall fight in the hills. We shall never surrender, and even if this island or a large part of it was subjugated and starving, then our empire beyond the seas would carry on the struggle, until the New World steps forth to the rescue and the liberation of the Old.

124. On the basis of the passage which of the following statements may be said to be correct?
(a) The speaker is encouraging his men for the conquest of France
(b) The speaker is an aggressive and maniacal war-monger
(c) The speaker is not satisfied with the conquest of the island
(d) The speaker is a patriot urging the defence of his motherland

125. The speaker in the passage wants to go on fighting because
- (a) he is a raving lunatic
- (b) he is in a state of utter despair
- (c) he expects help from other quarters
- (d) he is the leader of a suicide squad

126. Which of the following pair of the phrases helps best to bring out the intension of the speaker?
- (a) "Go on to the end", "shall never surrender"
- (b) "Growing confidence", "subjugated and starving"
- (c) "Subjugated and starving", "fighting and landing around"
- (d) "Fighting in the streets", "subjugated and starving"

DIRECTIONS (Qs. 127-129) : Read the following passage carefully and answer the questions given below it.

[Morning 2019]

Recently, a newspaper article mourned the total disappearance of the common house sparrow.

This was a comment on the city's perceptible move towards edging out the flora and fauna of the city. In the rapid urbanization, multi-storied apartments grew and large scale felling of trees became necessary. Last week, however, seven pairs of these sparrows were spotted in a suburb. Possibly the greenery of this place has created a new habitat for these birds which like their proximity to human beings, and have made a comeback. A systematic development of trees and shrubs all over the city could woo the absentee house sparrow to our midst.

127. In the passage the term "urbanisation" has been used to refer to
- (a) the destruction of the greenery in the city
- (b) construction of concrete structures on a large scale
- (c) a change over from the rural life to the city life
- (d) the movement of people from villages to cities

128. The phrase "absentee house sparrow" refers to
- (a) the sparrow that makes infrequent visits
- (b) the sparrow that has forgotten its habitat
- (c) the sparrow that has gone away from the urban areas
- (d) the sparrow that has become extinct

129. According to the passage, the birds have made a comeback to the suburb because they
- (a) have been hunted down by the village people
- (b) Love to be amidst human beings
- (c) get food only where human beings live
- (d) they have been deliberately brought back by biologists

DIRECTIONS (Qs. 130-134) : Read the following passage carefully and answer the questions given below it. **[2017]**

In this work of incessant and feverish activity, men have little time to think, much less to consider ideals and objectives. Yet how are we to act, even in the present, unless we know which way we are going and what our objectives are? It is only in the peaceful atmosphere of a university that these basic problems can be adequately considered.

It is only when the young men and women, who are in the university today and on whom the burden of life's problems will fall tomorrow, learn to have clear objectives and standards of values that there is hope for the next generation. The past generation produced some great men but as a generation led the world repeatedly to disaster. World Wars IInd are the price that has been paid for the lack of wisdom on man's part in this generation.

I think that there is always a close and intimate relationship between the end we aim at and the mean adopted to attain it. Even, if the end is right, but the means are wrong, it will vitiate the end or divert us in a wrong direction. Means and ends are thus intimately and inextricably connected and cannot be separated.

That indeed has been the lesson of old taught us by many great men in the past, but unfortunately it seldom remembered.

130. People have little time to consider ideals and objectives because
    (a) they consider these ideals meaningless
    (b) they do not want to burden themselves with such ideas
    (c) they have no inclination for such things
    (d) they are excessively engaged in their routine activities

131. The burden of life's problems' in the fourth sentence refers to
    (a) the incessant and feverish activities
    (b) the burden of family responsibilities
    (c) the onerous duties of life
    (d) the sorrows and sufferings

132. The world Wars IInd are the price that man paid due to
    (a) the absence of wisdom and sagacity
    (b) his not caring to consider the life's problems
    (c) his ignoring the ideals and objectives of life
    (d) his excessive involvement in feverish activities.

133. According to the writer the adoption of wrong means even for the right end would
    (a) not let us attain our goal
    (b) bring us dishonour
    (c) impede our progress
    (d) deflect us from the right path

134. The word 'vitiate' used in the second paragraph means
    (a) negate   (b) debase
    (c) tarnish   (d) destroy

Answers

1	(c)	24	(b)	47	(c)	70	(a)	93	(a)	116	(b)
2	(c)	25	(d)	48	(c)	71	(d)	94	(b)	117	(d)
3	(a)	26	(a)	49	(a)	72	(a)	95	(a)	118	(a)
4	(c)	27	(d)	50	(d)	73	(b)	96	(a)	119	(c)
5	(b)	28	(b)	51	(b)	74	(d)	97	(d)	120	(b)
6	(c)	29	(b)	52	(d)	75	(d)	98	(b)	121	(c)
7	(a)	30	(c)	53	(d)	76	(c)	99	(c)	122	(b)
8	(c)	31	(c)	54	(c)	77	(b)	100	(b)	123	(b)
9	(b)	32	(c)	55	(a)	78	(a)	101	(d)	124	(d)
10	(d)	33	(b)	56	(b)	79	(c)	102	(c)	125	(c)
11	(c)	34	(c)	57	(c)	80	(d)	103	(c)	126	(a)
12	(b)	35	(d)	58	(a)	81	(b)	104	(a)	127	(b)
13	(b)	36	(a)	59	(b)	82	(c)	105	(b)	128	(c)
14	(c)	37	(d)	60	(a)	83	(c)	106	(b)	129	(b)
15	(b)	38	(b)	61	(c)	84	(b)	107	(c)	130	(d)
16	(c)	39	(a)	62	(b)	85	(b)	108	(d)	131	(c)
17	(b)	40	(c)	63	(c)	86	(d)	109	(b)	132	(a)
18	(c)	41	(b)	64	(a)	87	(c)	110	(a)	133	(d)
19	(a)	42	(a)	65	(c)	88	(c)	111	(c)	134	(b)
20	(c)	43	(a)	66	(d)	89	(b)	112	(b)		
21	(a)	44	(c)	67	(d)	90	(d)	113	(a)		
22	(c)	45	(a)	68	(a)	91	(a)	114	(d)		
23	(b)	46	(b)	69	(b)	92	(b)	115	(a)		

6. **(c)** The word cajole means to persuade someone to do something by sustained coaxing or flattery. Bully is the nearly opposite meaning.

45. **(a)** Leverage means to use (something) to maximum advantage.

46. **(b)** Absence is the most appropriate word because a contrast is made here.

47. **(c)** Inflicted which means make (someone) do something unpleasant; e.g. "The teacher inflicted his rage on the students. Other options do not correspond.

48. **(c)** Harness means exploit the power of.

49. **(a)** Burst. If you are bursting crackers then you are setting off fireworks.

110 (a) Build castles in the air or build castles in Spain- to daydream; to make plans that can never come true. So, (a) is the correct choice.

124. (d) The speaker is a patriot who is urging to fight against France for saving his motherland at any cost.

125. (c) The speaker wants a change, for which he is expecting his people (countrymen) and people from other quarters to come forth and fight for it.

126. (a) The phrase "Go on to the end, shall never surrender" means turning all odds to save his motherland from France.

127. (b) Urbanisation refers to construction of concrete structures on a large scale.

128. (c) Absentee house sparrow here refers to the sparrow that has gone away from the urban areas.

129. (b) According to the passage, the birds have made a comeback to the suburb because they love to be amidst human beings.

Logic & Quantitative Reasoning

1. A group of friends are sitting in an arrangement one each at the corner of an octagon. All are facing the centre. Mahima is sitting diagonally opposite Rama, who is on Sushma's right. Ravi is next to Sushma and opposite Girdhar, who is on Chandra's left. Savitri is not on mahima's right but opposite Shalini. Who is on Shalini's right
    [Morning 2019]
    (a) Ravi   (b) Mahima
    (c) Girdhar   (d) Rama

2. Out of 100 families in the neighbourhood, 50 have radios, 75 have TVs and 25 have VCRs. Only 10 families have all three and each VCR owner also has a TV. If some families have radio only, how many have only TV?
    [Morning 2019]
    (a) 30   (b) 35
    (c) 40   (d) 45

3. Choose the answer figure which completes the problem figure matrix: **[Morning 2018]**

    Problem Figure

    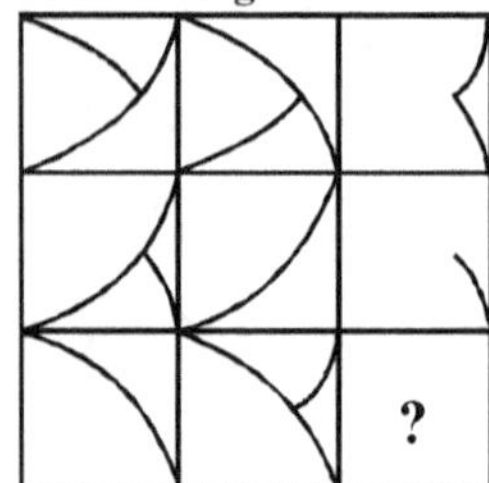

    Answer Figures

    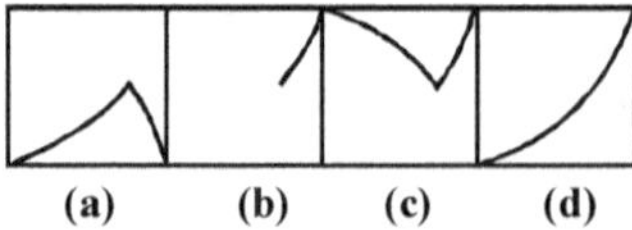

    (a)   (b)   (c)   (d)

4. Statements:
    I. All goats are kites.
    II. Some goats are rolls
    Choose the conclusion that follows the given statements:
    [Morning 2018]
    (a) All kites are goats.
    (b) All rolls are kites.
    (c) Some rolls are kites.
    (d) No kites are rolls.

5. Rajneesh is 5 ranks ahead of Aman in a class of 46 students. If Aman's rank is twelfth from the last, what is Rajneesh's rank from the start?
    [Morning 2018]
    (a) 29   (b) 31
    (c) 28   (d) 30

6. Bateson sees a gentleman and says "He is my brother's daughter's father". Then what is Bateson to that gentleman?
    [Morning 2019]
    (a) Grandfather
    b) Uncle
    (c) Son
    (d) Brother

7. Pointing to Kamal, Sheeba said, " His mother's brother is the father of my son Akilesh". How is Kamal related to Sheeba?
    [Morning 2018]
    (a) Niece   (b) Nephew
    (c) Aunt   (d) Sister-in-law

8. Which number comes opposite to 5 ?   **[Evening 2019]**

    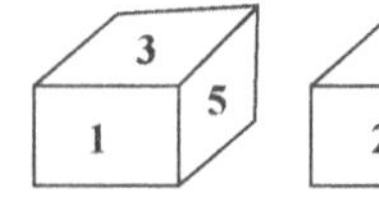 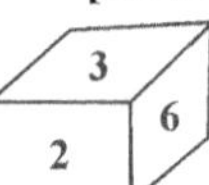

(a) 2   (b) 4
(c) 6   (d) 1

9. Which digit will appear on the face opposite to the face with number 4? **[Morning 2018]**

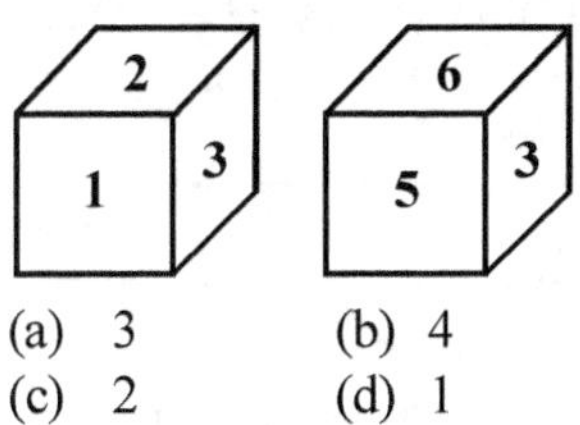

(a) 3   (b) 4
(c) 2   (d) 1

10. Identify the figure that completes the pattern **[Evening 2018]**

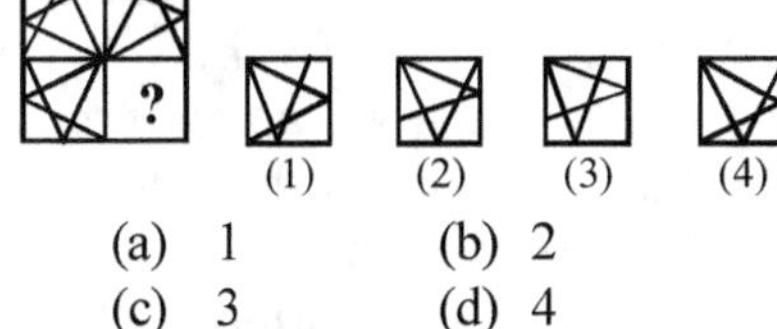

(a) 1   (b) 2
(c) 3   (d) 4

11. M is taller than Q and L. Q is only taller than N. L is taller than Q but shorter than M. Then who is the tallest and the shortest? **[Morning 2019]**

(a) L & Q
(b) Q & N
(c) M & N
(d) None of these

12. In a row of people Manu is 7th from bottom end of row. Shrey is 10 ranks above Manu. If shrey is 8th from top, then how many people are there in this row? **[Morning 2019]**

(a) 25   (b) 26
(c) 24   (d) 23

13. There are 20 children in a row. Tarun is 4th from right end Shekhar is 5th from left end. How many students are there b/w Tarun and Shekhar? **[Evening 2019]**

(a) 9   (b) 11
(c) 13   (d) 15

14. There are 5 birds – Pigeon, little Pigeon, Crow, big Crow, Parrot. Each one is flying one after another. Big Crow is ahead of Pigeon but is after Parrot. Crow is between Pigeon and little Pigeon. Find which bird is flying in the last? **[Evening 2019]**

(a) Pigeon   (b) Crow
(c) Parrot   (d) Little Pigeon

15. Five professionals live in 5 flats placed one above the other. Engineer has to go upstairs to meet his MLA Friend. Doctor is equally friendly to all. He goes upstairs as frequently as he goes downstairs. IAS Officer lives above the flat of Chemist and he has to go upstairs to meet Doctor friend. Starting for ground floor, arrange these professionals **[Evening 2019]**

(a) Chemist → IAS Officer → Doctor → Engineers → MLA
(b) IAS Officer → Chemist → Doctor → Engineers → MLA
(c) MLA → Chemist → IAS Officer → Doctor → Engineers
(d) MLA → Engineers → IAS Officer → Doctor → Chemist

16. In a class Harsh is 10th from the top and Harshita is 20th from the bottom. Naveen is 11 ranks above Harshita and 21 ranks below Harsh. How many students are there in the class? **[Morning 2018]**

(a) 60   (b) 61
(c) 62   (d) 58

17. Mohan, Ritika, Janvi, Priya and Riya are friends. Janvi runs faster than Ritika but slower than Priya. Mohan is the slowest runner and Riya runs faster than Priya. Who runs the fastest among the five? **[Evening 2018]**
(a) Priya   (b) Riya
(c) Ritika   (d) Mohan

18. Akram is the son of Shahid. Shahid's sister, Julie has a son Zeeshan and a daughter Yana. Zeba is the sister of Zeeshan's mother. How is Yana related to Zeba? **[Evening 2018]**
(a) Mother
(b) Grand-daughter
(c) Sister
(d) Niece

19. **Statements**: In a one day cricket match, the total runs made by a team were 200. Out of these 160 runs were made by spinners. **[Evening 2018]**
Conclusions:
I. 80% of the team consists of spinners.
II. The opening batsmen were spinners.
(a) Only conclusion I follows
(b) Only conclusion II follows
(c) Either I or II follows
(d) Neither I nor II follow

20. In this question, select the related letters from the given alternatives. **[Morning 2019]**

$$\frac{M}{AC} : \frac{N}{AD} :: \frac{O}{AE} : ?$$

(a) $\dfrac{P}{AF}$ (b) $\dfrac{Q}{AB}$
(c) $\dfrac{P}{AC}$ (d) $\dfrac{R}{AD}$

21. Find the missing number
QPRS : TUVW : : JIKL : ? **[2017]**
(a) NMOP   (b) NMPO
(c) MNPO   (d) MNOP

DIRECTIONS (Qs. 22 & 23) : Find the odd letter pair from the given alternatives. **[2017]**

22. (a) Wool   (b) Feather
(c) Hair   (d) Grass

23. (a) Sport : Ground
(b) Cinema : Screen
(c) Drama : Stage
(d) Rubber : Erase

24. A series is given, with one term missing. Choose the correct alternative from the given ones that will complete the series.
CAT, DBT, ECT, ? **[Morning 2019]**
(a) DCT   (b) FDT
(c) FCT   (d) FAT

25. Select the worng term 0, 2, 10, 36, 68, 130 **[Evening 2019]**
(a) 68   (b) 2
(c) 36   (d) 10

26. Complete the given series
5, 11, 23, 43, ? **[Morning 2018]**
(a) 72   (b) 63
(c) 73   (d) 83

27. Complete the given series by replacing "?" **[Morning 2018]**
: H17I, K23L, N29O, ?
(a) P35R   (b) Q25R
(c) P17R   (d) Q35R

28. Complete the given series
46, 55, 71, 96, ? **[Evening 2018]**
(a) 142   (b) 132
(c) 162   (d) 192

29. P 3 C, R 5 F, T 8 I, V 12 L, ? **[Even ing 2018]**
(a) X17M   (b) X16O
(c) Y17O   (d) X17O

DIRECTIONS (Qs. 30 & 31) : Find the missing number/letter from the given alternatives.   **[2016]**

30. BMO, EOQ, HQS, ?
    (a) SOW   (b) LMN
    (c) KSU   (d) SOV

31. 4117, 5138, 6159, 71710, ?
    (a) 71382   (b) 76599
    (c) 81911   (d) 81798

32. Find the missing number.

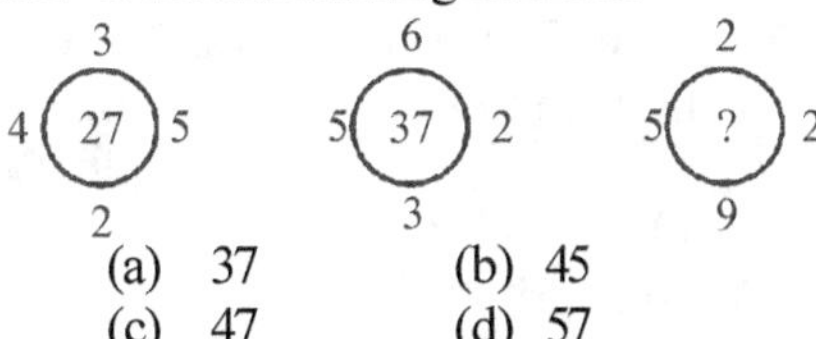

    (a) 37   (b) 45
    (c) 47   (d) 57

33. Find the missing number
                [Morning 2018]

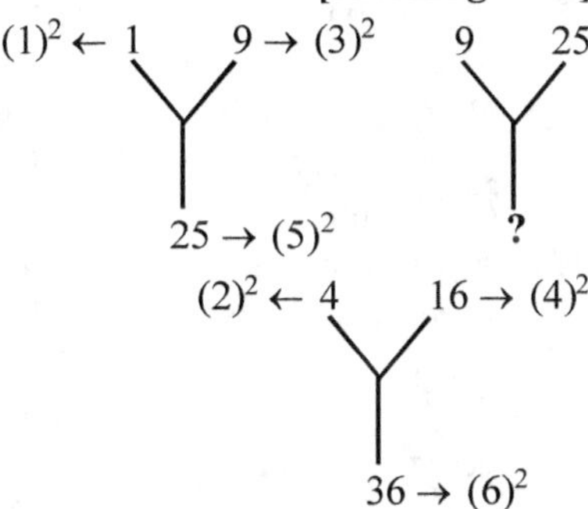

Similarly,

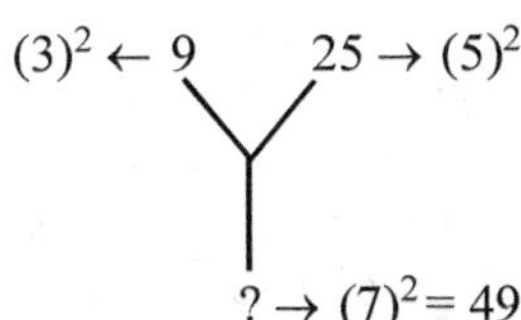

    (a) 49   (b) 64
    (c) 8   (d) 27

34. Find the missing number
                [Evening 2018]

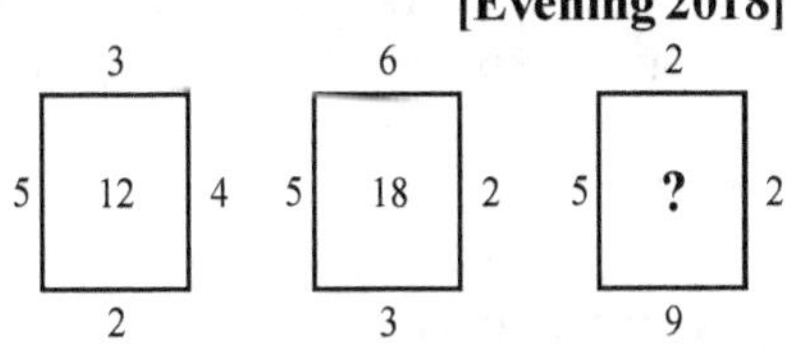

    (a) 18   (b) 19
    (c) 16   (d) 20

DIRECTIONS (Qs. 35 & 36) : In each of the following questions, select the missing number from the given alternatives.   **[2016]**

35.

2	7	9
7	3	4
9	8	?
126	168	216

    (a) 8   (b) 3
    (c) 6   (d) 36

36.

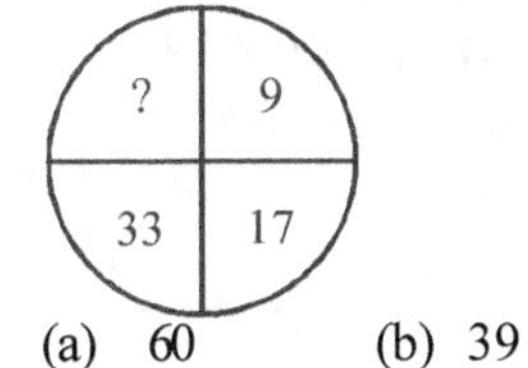

    (a) 60   (b) 39   **[2016]**
    (c) 55   (d) 65

37. Fill in the blanks
    HI – HH – JHHIJ –
                [Evening 2019]
    (a) JHI   (b) IIH
    (c) JHJ   (d) JIH

38. Which one set of letters when sequentially placed at the gaps in given letter series shall complete it?   **[2016]**
        m_st_u_t__st
    (a) ummmu   (b) umsmu
    (c) muumm   (d) ttssuu

39. Find the word which cannot be formed from the letters used in the given word.   **[2016]**
    GERMINATION
    (a) ORNAMENT
    (b) TERMINAL
    (c) IGNITE
    (d) GERMAN

40. If **HYDROGEN** is coded as **YHCQPHFM**. Then **DRY HEN** will be coded as what
                [Morning 2019]

(a) RDXGFO
(b) DRXGFO
(c) ODRXGF
(d) None of these

41. If in a coded language DISTANCE is written as IDTSBOEG, IMPRESSION is written as MIRPFTUKRQ then how the word EXAMINATION will be written in that coded language.

[Evening 2019]

(a) XEMAJOCVLRR
(b) RXEMAJOCVLR
(c) EMAJOCVLRRX
(d) XEMAJOCVLSS

42. 3 8 9 → run very fast
9 6 4 → come back fast
4 8 7 → run and come
Find code of come and run.

[Evening 2019]

(a) 473   (b) 794
(c) 874   (d) 647

43. In a certain code language, "RUST" is coded as "5642" and "TEAM" is coded as "2783". What group of letters can be formed for the code "364275"

[Morning 2018]

(a) MUESRT   (b) MUSTER
(c) MUSAER   (d) MUSSAR

44. If "MANAGER" is coded as "3141756" and "SEER" is coded as "8556". Then what will be the code for "RANGES"?

[Evening 2018]

(a) 614267   (b) 612547
(c) 614758   (d) 615768

45. In a certain code, MODEL is written as 513 # 2 and DEAR is written as 3 # % 8. How is LOAD written in the code ?   **[2016]**

(a) 23%   (b) 21%3
(c) 25%3   (d) 21#3

46. From the given alternative words, select the one which can be formed using the letters of the given word EXAMINATION.   **[2017]**

(a) ANIMAL
(b) EXAMINER
(c) NATIONAL
(d) ANIMATION

47. If ACNE can be coded as 3, 7, 29, 11, then BOIL will be coded as

[2017]

(a) 5, 29, 19, 27
(b) 5, 29, 19, 25
(c) 5, 31, 21, 25
(d) 5, 31, 19, 25

48. If the Ist November falls on Monday, what day will the 25th of November will be?   **[2016]**

(a) Tuesday   (b) Thursday
(c) Wednesday (d) Friday

49. A person walks 9 km to the South. From there he walks 5 km to the North. After this he walks 3 km to the West. In which direction and how far is he now from the starting point?   **[Morning 2019]**

(a) 4 km South
(b) 4 km North
(c) 5 km North West
(d) 5 km South West

50. Sherly starting from a fixed point goes 15 m toward North and then after turning to his right he goes 15 m. Then he goes 10, 15 and 15 metres after turning to his left each time. How far is he from his starting point?   **[Evening 2019]**

(a) 15 metres
(b) 5 metres
(c) 10 metres
(d) 20 metres

51. Raman walks 5 km towards south and then turns to the right. After walking 3 km, he turns to the left and walks 5 km. Now in which direction is he from the starting place? **[Morning 2018]**
(a) West (b) East
(c) South (d) North

52. Y is in the East of X which is in the North of Z. If P is in the South of Z, then in which direction of Y, is P? **[Evening 2018]**
(a) North
(b) South
(c) South-west
(d) North-east

53. When the bus reaches Shivani's house, it faces South. After starting from Shivani's house to the school, in turns twice to its left and once to its right. In which direction it is running now? **[2017]**
(a) North (b) West
(c) East (d) South

54. A men travels 12 km West, then 3 km towards South and then 8 km towards East. How far is he from the start? **[2017]**
(a) 23 km (b) 20 km
(c) 15 km (d) 5 km

55. A and B are standing at a distance of 20 km from each other on a straight East-West road. A and B start walking simultaneously Eastwards and Westwards respectively and both cover a distance of 5 km. Then, a turns to his left and walks 10 km. B turns to his right and walk 10 km at the same speed. What will be the distance between them? **[2016]**
(a) 10 km (b) 30 km
(c) 20 km (d) 25 km

56. If February 1, 2004 is Wednesday, what day is March 3, 2014? **[2017]**
(a) Monday (b) Sunday
(c) Saturday (d) Frinday

57. Age of a father is four times of his son's age. After 20 years, father's age will be twice of son's age. Find out 5 years ago how much time was the age of father in comparison of his son's age. **[Evening 2019]**
(a) 4 times
(b) 5 times
(c) 6 times
(d) 7 times

58. There are three baskets of fruits. 1st basket has twice the number of fruits in the 2nd basket. 3rd basket has three-fourth of the fruits in the first. The average of the fruits in all the baskets in 30. What is t he number of fruits in the first basket? **[2016]**
(a) 20 (b) 30
(c) 35 (d) 40

59. If + means –, – means ×, × means ÷ and ÷ means +, then $48 \times 4 \div 7 + 8 - 2 = ?$ **[2017]**
(a) 3 (b) –5
(c) 35 (d) 16

Answers

1	(a)	11	(c)	21	(c)	31	(c)	41	(a)	51	(c)
2	(b)	12	(c)	22	(d)	32	(c)	42	(c)	52	(c)
3	(c)	13	(b)	23	(b)	33	(a)	43	(b)	53	(c)
4	(c)	14	(d)	24	(b)	34	(a)	44	(c)	54	(d)
5	(d)	15	(a)	25	(c)	35	(c)	45	(b)	55	(a)
6	(d)	16	(b)	26	(c)	36	(d)	46	(d)	56	(c)
7	(b)	17	(b)	27	(d)	37	(d)	47	(d)	57	(d)
8	(c)	18	(d)	28	(b)	38	(b)	48	(b)	58	(d)
9	(a)	19	(d)	29	(d)	39	(b)	49	(d)	59	(a)
10	(d)	20	(a)	30	(c)	40	(a)	50	(c)		

1. (a)

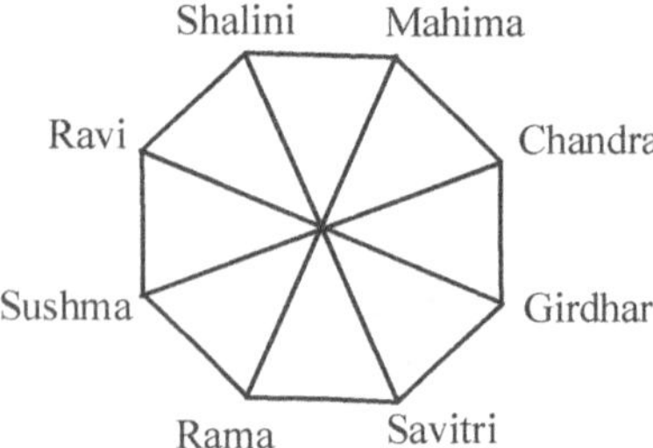

Ravi is to the right of Shalini.

2. (b) According to question,
Total number of families = 100

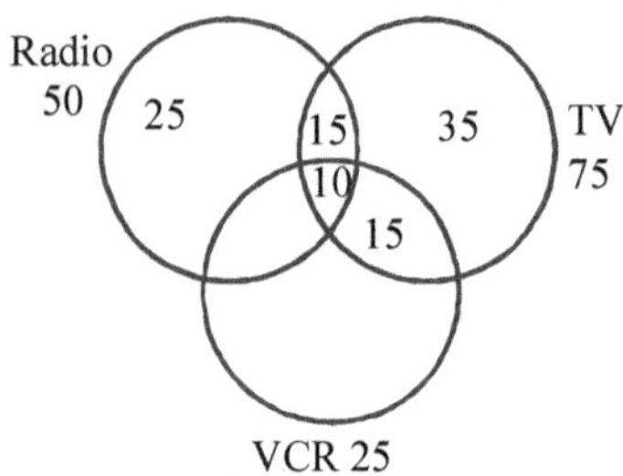

So, only 35 families have only TVs.

6. (d) Bateson's brother's daughter's father will be Bateson's brother.

8. (c) Based on the given positions, numbers on opposite faces are (1–2), (3–4) and (5–6).
Hence, opposite to 5 is 6.

11. (c) Arrangement of four person according to their height :

$$M > L > Q > N$$

$\uparrow$ (tallest) $\uparrow$ (shortest).

Tallest → M and Shortest → N.

12. (c) Manu's rank from bottom end = 7th

Shrey's rank from bottom end = $(7 + 10) = 17^{th}$

Shrey's rank from top end = 8th

∴ Total number of people
$= (17 + 8 - 1) = 24$

13. (b) Total number of children = 20

Tarun's position = 4th (from right end).

Shekhar's position = 5th (form left end).

Hence, number of children between Tarun and shekhar
$= 20 - 4 - 5 = 11$.

14. **(d)** Five birds are flying in a line. like this :

Parrot > Big Crow > Pigeon > Crow > Little Pigeon
  ↑   ↑
(First)   (Last)

Hence, little Pigeon is flying in the last.

15. **(a)** One of the possible arrangement is like this :

MLA   –   Fifth floor
Engineers
Doctor
IAS Officer
Chemist   –   First floor.

20. **(a)** As,

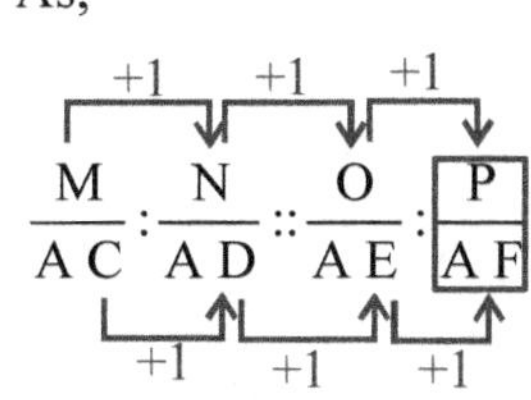

$$\frac{M}{AC} : \frac{N}{AD} :: \frac{O}{AE} : \boxed{\frac{P}{AF}}$$

24. **(b)**

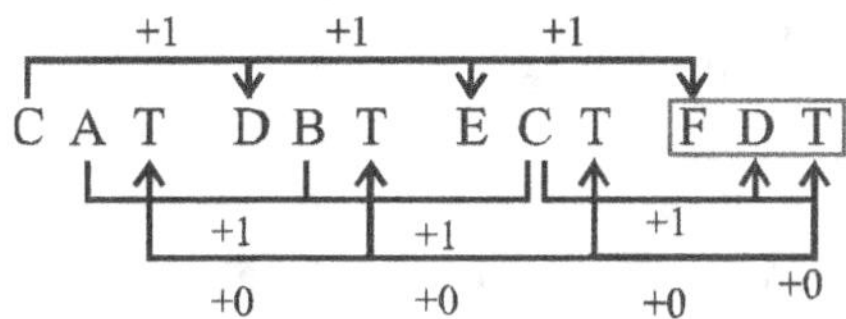

25. **(c)**

$$0, \quad 2, \quad 10, \quad \boxed{36}^{\,30} \quad 68, \quad 130,$$

$(0)^3 + 0 \quad (1)^3 + 1 \quad (2)^3 + 2 \quad (3)^3 + 3 \quad (4)^3 + 4 \quad (5)^3 + 5.$

Hence, wrong number is '36'.

32. **(c)** First Figure

$3 + 5 + 2 + 4 = 14$

$\Rightarrow 14 + 13 = 27$

Second Figure

$6 + 2 + 3 + 5 = 16$

$\Rightarrow 16 + 21 = 37$

Third Figure

$2 + 2 + 9 + 5 = 18$

$\Rightarrow 18 + 29 = \boxed{47}$

37. **(d)** The series is like this:

H I J̲ H, H I̲ J H, H I J H̲

Here, 'HIJH' is repeating.

40. **(a)**

$$\begin{array}{ccccccc} H & Y & D & R & O & G & E & N \end{array}$$

$$\begin{array}{ccccccc} Y & H & C & Q & P & H & F & M \end{array}$$

Similarly,

$$\begin{array}{cccccc} D & R & Y & H & E & N \end{array}$$

$$\begin{array}{cccccc} R & D & X & G & F & O \end{array}$$

41. **(a)**

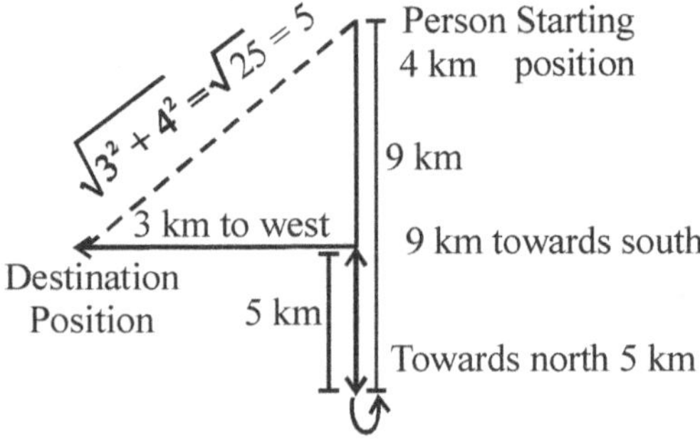

Hence,

42. **(c)** As code of 'run and come' is '487' so, code of 'come and run' is '874'.

49. **(d)**

Person is in south-west direction & 5 km from the starting point.

50. **(c)**

$\therefore \quad AF = AE - EF = 25 - 15 = 10$ metres

57. **(d)** Let son and father's present ages are x and 4x years respectively.

ATQ, $4x + 20 = 2(x + 20)$.

$4x - 2x = 40 - 20$

$2x = 20 \Rightarrow x = 10$.

Son's age = 10 years

Father's age = $4 \times 10 = 40$ years.

Now, 5 years age, ratio of their ages

$$\frac{40-5}{10-5} = \frac{35}{5} = 7 \text{ times}$$

CHAPTER 1

GRAMMAR

Grammar is the key to attaining success in a competitive examination. If you want success in a competitive exam, it is important to have a good command of grammar and its applications. No matter how hard you prepare for your competitive exams, you can never be too sure of your success.

Before sitting for an examination, it is important to evaluate yourself, where you stand and how much chances of your success are. In the English section of a competitive exam, the kind of questions likely to be asked can be categorised in three parts

(1) Fill in the blanks;

(2) Identifying errors in sentences and

(3) Correcting the sentences.

The questions can be dealt with easily and you can score well if you get your basics clear and right.

NOUN

A Noun is a word used as a name of a person, place or thing.

There are five kinds of Noun –

(a) Proper Noun   (b) Common Noun

(c) Collective Noun   (d) Abstract Noun

(e) Material Noun.

Following are certain rules of grammar regarding nouns that would be useful in a competitive exam:

1. Proper nouns are sometimes used as common nouns.

   For example :

   (a) Amitabh is **Gandhiji** of our class. (Incorrect)

   (b) Amitabh is the **Gandhiji** of our class, (Correct)

Following are rules regarding the number of the noun :

2. Some nouns have the same form both in singular as well as in plural.

   For example :

   (a) A deer **was** caught.

   (b) Deer **were** caught.

   For example :

   (a) He paid eight **hundred** rupees for this pair of shoes.

   (b) India again won the **series**.

3. Nouns denoting large numbers are used both in singular and plural form

   For example :

   (a) Three **hundred** people attended the function.

   (b) **Hundreds** of people attended the party.

4. Tell which sentence is correct:
    (a) Since long no news **has** been heard.
    (b) Since long no news **have** been heard.
    Sentence a is correct. The reason is that **some nouns are always used as singular though they look like plural nouns.** That's why we should never use the plural verb with these words. Other similar words are politics, mathematics, physics, gallows, means, billiards, ethics, summons, innings.
5. Tell which sentence is correct:
    (a) The spectacles that you are wearing **are** really nice.
    (b) The spectacles that you are wearing **is** really nice.
    Sentence a) is correct. The reason being that **some noun words are always used in the plural form.**
6. Tell which sentence is correct:
    (a) The cattle **was** grazing in the field.
    (b) The cattle **were** grazing in the field.
    Sentence (b) is correct. The reason being that **some nouns are always used as plurals though they look like singular**. Other nouns like this are public, people, folk, mankind, poultry, sheep, police, gentry, peasantry, bulk, majority, etc.
7. Tell which sentence is correct.
    (a) This project will lead to lots of **expenditures**
    (b) This project will lead to lots of **expenditure**.
    Sentence (b) is correct. The reason is that **some nouns are always used as singular**. **Preceding adjectives or the verb form indicates the singularity or plurality**. Other nouns are expenditure, furniture, information, machinery, issue, offspring, alphabet, scenery, poetry.
8. Meaning of some nouns in plural form is very **different** from the meaning of nouns in singular form. Hence, that form should be used which will convey the right meaning.
    For example:
    (a) I opened the letter and read its **contents**.
    (b) Her mouth was fixed in a smile of pure **content**.
9. Please go through the following singulars and plurals as plural forms are commonly known but their **singular forms are** not commonly known.

Singular Form	Plural form
Agendum	Agenda
Alumnus	Alumni
Index	Indices
Phenomenon	Phenomena
Criterion	Criteria
Radius	Radii
Formula	Formulae
Memorandum	Memoranda

10.   Some noun words have **two plurals with different meanings**. So, that plural form should be selected which will convey the right meaning.
For example :
(a)   I have one **brother** and one sister (meaning- children of the same parents).
(b)   Why should only select **brethren** be allowed to attend the meeting? (meaning - members of the same society, organisation)
(c)   I took off my shoes and **clothes** (meaning- things that people wear).
(d)   Cotton, Nylon, Silk are different kinds of **cloths** (meaning- kinds or pieces of cloth).

Other nouns having two plurals with different meanings are:

Singular	**Plural with different meaning**
Die	Dies - stamps
	Dice - small cubes used in games
Genius	Geniuses-persons of great talent
	Genie - spirit
Quarter	Quarter - fourth part
	Quarter(s) - lodging
Manner	Manner - Method
	Manners - Correct behaviour
Pain	Pain - Suffering
	Pains - Careful efforts
Spectacle	Spectacle - sight
	Spectacles - eye-glasses
Penny	Pence - indicate amount of money
	Pennies - number of coins

Following are rules regarding gender of the noun :

11.   Collective nouns, even when they denote living beings, are considered to be of the **neuter gender**.
For example :
(a)   Mr. Smith had a herd of cows. He kept a herdsman to look after **her**.
(b)   Mr. Smith had a herd of cows. He kept a herdsman to look after **it**.

Sentence b) is correct. Though herd consists of cows (females), herd is not a feminine noun as it a collective noun.

12.   Young children and the lower animals are also referred to as of the **neuter gender**.
For example :
(a)   The baby loves **his** toys. (Incorrect)
(b)   The baby loves **its** toys. (correct)
(c)   The mouse lost **his** tail when the cat pounced on him. (Incorrect)
(d)   The mouse lost its tail when the cat pounced on it. (correct)

We are often uncertain regarding the gender of the animals. The mouse here may be a male or a female. So, English language prefers the easy way out: treat it as of the neuter gender.

13. When objects without life are personified they are considered of
   (i)   The masculine gender if the object is remarkable for strength and violence. Ex. Sun, Summer, Winter, Time, Death etc.
   (ii) The feminine gender if the object is remarkable for beauty, gentleness and gracefulness. Ex: Earth, Moon, Spring, Nature, Mercy etc.
         For example:
         (a) The Sun came from behind the clouds and with **her** brilliance tore the veil of darkness. (Incorrect)
         (b) The Sun came from behind the clouds and with **his** brilliance tore the veil of darkness. (Correct)
   Convention does not see brilliance as a womanly quality, but a manly one.
         (a) Nature offers **his** lap to him that **seeks** it. (Incorrect)
         (b) Nature offers **her** lap to him that **seeks** it. (Correct)
   The offering of a lap is usually the mother's role. Hence, Nature here should be treated as a feminine noun.
   Tell which sentence is correct.
         (a) The earth goes round the sun in 365 days. Can you **calculate her speed**?
         (b) The earth goes round the sun in 365 days. Can you **calculate its speed**?
   Sentence b is correct. The error being made here is that personification is being brought where it does not exist. In the above statement the earth is being treated as a body (a thing), not a person. The scientist here is not concerned with the womanly qualities of the planet. So, neuter gender should be applied.

Following are rules regarding apostrophe :

14. Rules regarding apostrophe S ('s):
   (a) Singular noun: 's is added after the word.
   (b) Singular noun: Only an apostrophe is added when there are too many hissing sounds. *For example*: Moses' laws, for goodness' sake, For justice' sake.
   (c) Plural nouns ending in s like boys, cows: only (') is added after the word
   (d) Plural nouns not ending in s like men, children: ('s) is added after the word.
   (e) 'S is added primarily after the living things and personified objects. *For example*: Governor's bodyguard, horse's head, Nature's law, Fortune's favourite.
   (f) 'S is not used with inanimate or non-living things. *For example*: leg of the table, cover of the book.
   (g) But in nouns that denote time, distance or weight, ('s) is used. *For example*: a stone's throw, in a year's time, the earth's surface.

(h)   Some other common phrases where ('s) is used are to his heart's content, at his wit's end, out of harm's way.

(i)   When a noun consists of several words, the possessive sign is attached only to the last word.

For example:

(a)   The Queen's **of England** reaction is important in the Diana episode. (Incorrect)

(b)   The Queen **of England's** reaction is important in the Diana episode. (Correct)

Do not be mistaken that since it is the Queen's reaction, the ('s) should come after queen. You might think that putting it after England would make the reaction England's and not the Queen's. This is short-sightedness. Do not see Queen and England in isolation, Queen of England is one whole unit and the apostrophe should come at its end.

(j)   When two nouns are in apposition, the possessive sign is put to the latter only.

For example :

(a)   I am going to Stephen **Hawking's the scientist's country**. (Incorrect)

(b)   I am going to Stephen **Hawking the scientist's country**. (Correct)

(k)   When two or more nouns show joint possession, the possessive sign is put to the latter only.

For example:

(a)   Amitabh and Ajitabh are Bachchanji's sons. So Bachchanji **is Amitabh's and Ajitabh's father**. (Incoreect)

(b)   Amitabh and Ajitabh are Bachchanji's sons. So Bachchanji **is Amitabh and Ajitabh's father**. (Correct)

(I)   When two or more nouns show separate possession, the possessive sign is put with both.

For example.

(a)   The audience listened to Javed and Vajpayee's poems. (Incorrect)

(b)   The audience listened to Javed's and Vajpayee's poems. (Correct)

PRONOUN

A pronoun is a word used instead of a noun.

Rules regarding personal pronouns :

1.   Tell which sentence is correct-

(a)   The presents are for you and **me**.

(b)   The presents are for you and **I**.

Sentence a is correct. Pronoun has to agree with the case. Here it is the **objective case**. So, 'me' should be used instead of 'I'. *For example* : My uncle asked my brother and me to dinner.

2. Tell which sentence is correct
    (a)   He loves you more than **I**.
    (b)   He loves you more than **me.**
    Sentence a is correct 'Than' is a conjunction joining clauses. And the case of the pronoun to be used may be found by writing the clauses in full. So, in sentence a.) two clauses joined by 'than' are 'He loves you more' and 'I love you'. Being a subjective case, 'I' should be used.
    For example:
    (a)   He is taller than **I** (am).
    (b)   He loves you more than (he loves) **me**.

3. When a pronoun refers to more than one noun or pronouns of different persons, it must be of the first person plural in preference to the second and of the second person plural in preference to the third.
    For example :
    (a)   You and I, husband and wife, have to look after **your** home. (Incorrect)
    (b)   You and I, husband and wife, have to look after **our** home. (Correct)
    Now, common sense tells us that if we are a couple, wife and husband, the feeling of togetherness is expressed by our home, not your home. And so does grammar.
    Rule: 123. I stands for first person, 2 for second person and 3 for third person. The order of precedence is: 1 before 2 and 2 before 3. In the given example, we have 2 and 1. So I will apply; that is, first person. The number, of course, will be plural.
    Let us take another *example*.
    (a)   You and Hari have done **their duty**. (Incorrect)
    (b)   You and Hari have done **your** duty. (Correct)
    Applying 123 rule. You = 2 and Hari =3. So, 2. Second person plural gives 'your'.
    Similarly ,when all the three persons are taken into account, it has to be I; that is, first person plural.
    (a)   You, he and I have not forgotten your roots. (Incorrect)
    (b)   You, he and I have not forgotten **our roots**. (Correct)

4. **Each, either and neither** are always singular and are followed by the verb in the singular.
    For example :
    (a)   Neither of the accusations **is** true.
    (b)   Each boy took **his** turn.
    (c)   Each of the ladies performs **her** duty well.

5. (A) Please consider the following sentences.
        (a)   This is the boy. **He** works hard. (**He** subjective case)
        (b)   This is the boy. **His** exercise is done well. (**His** is possessive case)
        (c)   This is the boy. All praise **him**. (**Him** is objective case)

6.   An apostrophe is never used in 'its', 'yours' and 'theirs'.
7.   The complement of the verb **be**, when it is expressed by a pronoun, should be in the nominative form.
        For example.
        (a)   It was **he** (not **him**),
        (b)   It is **I** (not **me**) that gave the prizes away.
        (c)   It might have been **he** (not **him**).
8.   The case of a pronoun following **than** or **as** is determined by mentally supplying the verb.
        For example :
        (a)   He is taller than **I** (**am**).
        (b)   I like you better than **he** (**likes you**).
        (c)   They gave him as much as (**they gave**) **me**.
9.   A pronoun must agree with its Antecedent in **person, number and gender**.
        For example:
        (a)   All passengers must show **their** (**not his**) tickets.
        (b)   I am not one of those who believe everything **they** (**not I**) hear

Rules regarding demonstrative pronouns :

10.   **That** is used-
        A.   **After adjectives in the superlative degree**.
                For example-
                (a)   This is the best **that** we can do.
                (b)   He is the best speaker **that** we ever heard.
        B.   After the words **all, same, any, none, nothing, only**.
                For example:
                (a)   Man is the only animal **that** can talk.
                (b)   He is the same man **that** he has been.
        C.   After **two antecedents**, one denoting a person and the other denoting an animal or a thing.
                For example : The man and his pet **that** met with an accident yesterday died today.
11.   **What** and **That** refer to persons as well as things.

Rules regarding Relative pronouns :

12.   On combining each of the above pairs into one sentence
                (a)   This is the boy **who** works hard (Who in place of He)
                (b)   This is the boy **whose** exercise is done well. (**whose** in place of His)
                (c)   This is the boy **whom** all praise. (**Whom** in place of Him)
        The above sentences show when to use who, whose and whom. Who is the subjective case, Whose the possessive case and Whom the objective case.
13.   Who is used for persons only. It may refer to a singular or plural noun.
        For example :
        (a)   He **who** hesitates is lost.
        (b)   Blessed is he **who** has found his work.

14. Whose can be used for persons as well as things without life also.
    For example :
    (a) This is the hotel **whose** owner is a criminal.
    (b) This is the person **whose** will power is extraordinary.
15. Which is used for inanimate things and animals. 'Which' is used for both singular and plural nouns.
    For example :
    (a) I have found the book **which** I had lost last week.
    (b) The horse, **which** won the race yesterday, is my favourite.
16. When 'which' is used for selection, it may refer to a person as well as things.
    For example :
    (a) Which of the packets is yours?
    (b) Which of the boys has not done his homework?
17. **Who, Which, Whom, That, Whose** should be placed as near to the antecedent as possible.
    For example :
    (a) I with my family reside in Delhi, which consists of my wife and parents.
         This sentence is wrong as **which** relates to 'my' family'. So 'which' should be placed as near to family' as possible. So, the correct sentence is
    (b) I with my family which, consists of my wife and parents, reside in Delhi.
18. **Who** is used In the **nominative** cases and **whom** in the **objective** cases.
    For example :
    (a) There is Mr. Dutt, **who** (not **whom**) they say is the best painter in the town.
    (b) The Student, whom (not who) you thought so highly of, has failed to win the first prize.
19. When the **subject** of a verb is a **relative pronoun**, the verb should agree in number and person with the antecedent of the **relative**.
    For example :
    (a) This is **one** of the most interesting **novels that have** (not **has**) appeared this year. (Here, antecedent of **relative pronoun that** is **novels** and not **one**)
    (b) This is the only **one** of his **poems that is** (not **are**) worth reading. (Here the antecedent of **that** is **one** and not **poems**. Kindly note the difference between sentence **a and b**)

Other Useful Rules :

20. None is used in the singular or plural as the sense may require.
    For example:
    (a) Each boy was accompanied by an adult but there were none, with the orphan (Incorrect)
    (b) Each boy was accompanied by an adult but there **was** none with the orphan. (Correct)

    (c)   I am used to many guests everyday but there **was** none today. (Incorrect)

    (d)   I am used to many guests everyday but there **were** none today. (Correct)

21.   When 'one' is used as **pronoun**, its possessive form 'one's' should follow instead of his, her etc.

    For example : One must put **one's best** efforts if one wishes to succeed.

22.   With **let** objective case of the pronoun is used.

    For example : let **you** and **me** do it.

23.   If a pronoun has two antecedents, it should agree with the **nearer one**.

    For example :

    (a)   I hold in high esteem everything and **everybody who** reminds me of my failures.

    (b)   I hold in high esteem everybody and **everything, which** reminds me of my failures.

24.   In referring to **anybody, everybody, anyone, each** etc., the pronoun of the masculine or the feminine gender is used according to the context.

    For example.

    (a)   I shall be glad to help **everyone** of my **boys** in **his** studies.

    (b)   I shall be glad to help **everyone** of my **girls** in **her** studies.

    (c)   I shall be glad to help everyone of my **students** in **his** studies.

    But when gender is not determined, the pronoun of the **masculine gender** is used as in sentence c.

25.   (A)   The pronoun **one** should be used throughout, if used at all.

        For example:

        (a)   **One** must use **one's** best efforts if one wishes to succeed.

        (b)   **One** should be careful about what one says.

    (B)   **Plural** is commonly used with **none**.

        For example.

        (a)   **None** of his poems are well known.

        (b)   **None** of these words are now current.

26.   **Anyone** should be used when **more than two** persons or things are spoken of.

    For example : She was taller than **anyone** of her five sisters.

GERUND

A gerund is a verb form that functions as a noun. Gerunds always end in "ing," although not every verb ending in "ing" is a gerund. The verb is a gerund if it is acting as a noun.

I am running - regular verb

Running is good for you - gerund

Gerund as subject:

♦   Travelling is good for new experiences. (Travelling is the gerund.)

    Gerund as direct object:

♦   They do not like my singing. (The gerund is singing.)
     Gerund as subject complement:
♦   My cat's favorite activity is sleeping. (The gerund is sleeping.)
♦   My cat's favorite food is salmon. (The gerund has been removed.)
     Gerund as object of preposition:
♦   The police arrested him for speeding. (The gerund is speeding.)

A gerund phrase is a group of words consisting of a gerund and the modifier(s) and/or (pro)noun(s) or noun phrase(s) that function as the direct object(s), indirect object(s), or complement(s) of the action or state expressed in the gerund.

Points to remember:
1.   A gerund is a verbal ending in -ing that is used as a noun.
2.   A gerund phrase consists of a gerund plus modifier(s), object(s), and/ or complement(s).
3.   Gerunds and gerund phrases virtually never require punctuation.
     Participle

A participle is a word formed from a verb which can be used as an adjective. The two types of participles are the present participle (ending ing) and the past participle (usually ending -ed, -d, -t, -en, or -n).

Here are some participles being used as adjectives:

The Verb	The Past Participle	The Present Participle
To rise	the risen sun	the rising sun
To boil	the boiled water	the boiling water
To break	the broken news	the breaking news
To cook	the cooked	the cooking ham ham

PARTICIPLE PHRASES

It is really common to see participles in participle phrases. A participle phrase also acts like an adjective. In the examples below, the participle phrases are shaded and the participles are in bold:
♦   The man carrying the bricks is my father.
     (The participle phrase carrying the bricks describes the the man.)
♦   She showed us a plate of scones crammed with cream.
(The participle phrase crammed with cream describes the scones.)
Stunned by the blow, Peter quickly gathered his senses and searched frantically for the pepper spray.
(The participle phrase Stunned by the blow describes Mike.)
A participial phrase is a group of words consisting of a participle and the modifier(s) and/or (pro)noun(s) or noun phrase(s) that function as the direct object(s), indirect object(s), or complement(s) of the action or state expressed in the participle, such as:
Removing his coat, Jack rushed to the river.
Punctuation: When a participial phrase begins a sentence, a comma should be placed after the phrase.

- Arriving at the store, he found that it was closed.
- Washing and polishing the car, Jack developed sore muscles.
  If the participle or participial phrase comes in the middle of a sentence, it should be set off with commas only if the information is not essential to the meaning of the sentence.
- Peter, watching an old movie, drifted in and out of sleep.
- The church, destroyed by a fire, was never rebuilt.

Points to remember

- A participle is a verbal ending in -ing (present) or -ed, -en, -d, -t, -n, or -ne (past) that functions as an adjective, modifying a noun or pronoun.
- A participial phrase consists of a participle plus modifier(s), object(s), and/or complement(s).
- Participles and participial phrases must be placed as close to the nouns or pronouns they modify as possible, and those nouns or pronouns must be clearly stated.
- A participial phrase is set off with commas when it:
  (a) comes at the beginning of a sentence
  (b) interrupts a sentence as a nonessential element
  (c) comes at the end of a sentence and is separated from the word it modifies.

INFINITIVES

An infinitive is a verbal consisting of the word to plus a verb (in its simplest "stem" form) and functioning as a noun, adjective, or adverb. The term verbal indicates that an infinitive, like the other two kinds of verbals, is based on a verb and therefore expresses action or a state of being. However, the infinitive may function as a subject, direct object, subject complement, adjective, or adverb in a sentence. Although an infinitive is easy to locate because of the to + verb form, deciding what function it has in a sentence can sometimes be confusing.

- To wait seemed foolish when decisive action was required. (subject)
- Everyone wanted to go. (direct object)
- His ambition is to fly. (subject complement)
- He lacked the strength to resist. (adjective)
- We must study to learn. (adverb)

Be sure not to confuse an infinitive-a verbal consisting of to plus a verb-with a prepositional phrase beginning with to, which consists of to plus a noun or pronoun and any modifiers.

- Infinitives: to fly, to draw, to become, to enter, to stand, to catch, to belong
- Prepositional Phrases: to him, to the committee, to my house, to the mountains, to us, to this address

An Infinitive Phrase is a group of words consisting of an infinitive and the modifier(s) and/or (pro)noun(s) or noun phrase(s) that function as the actor(s), direct object(s), indirect object(s), or complement(s) of the action or state expressed in the infinitive, such as:

We intended to leave early.

The infinitive phrase functions as the direct object of the verb intended.

to leave (infinitive)

early (adverb)

I have a paper to write before class.

The infinitive phrase functions as an adjective modifying paper.

to write (infinitive)

before class (prepositional phrase as adverb)

Phil agreed to give me a ride.

The infinitive phrase functions as the direct object of the verb agreed.

to give (infinitive)

me (indirect object of action expressed in infinitive)

a ride (direct object of action expressed in infinitive)

They asked me to bring some food.

The infinitive phrase functions as the direct object of the verb asked.

me (actor or "subject" of infinitive phrase)

to bring (infinitive)

some food (direct object of action expressed in infinitive)

Everyone wanted Carol to be the captain of the team.

The infinitive phrase functions as the direct object of the verb wanted.

Carol (actor or "subject" of infinitive phrase) to be (infinitive)

the captain (subject complement for Carol, via state of being expressed in infinitive)

of the team (prepositional phrase as adjective)

ARTICLES

1. **A** or **an** does not refer to a particular person or thing. It leaves indefinite the person or thing spoken of.

   For example : I saw a doctor. (means I saw any doctor)

2. **An** is used before a word beginning with vowel sound (please note a word beginning with vowel sound and not necessarily a vowel itself).

   For example : an ass, an enemy, an inkstand, an orange, an umbrella, an hour.

3. **An** is placed before an abbreviation if the first letter of an abbreviation is F, H. L, M, N, R, S or X.

   For example :

   (a) An MBA was required for the post.

   (b) An SAO is an officer of high rank

4. A is used before a word beginning with a consonant sound.

   For example : a boy, a woman a horse, a one-rupee note, a university, a European (both university and European begin with a consonant sound of 'yu')

5. **A** and **an** are used with words 'few' and 'little' if they refer to a small number or a small amount. Words 'few' and 'little' without the articles means almost none.

   For example:
   (a) We have little time to spare. (means almost no time)
   (b) We have a little time to spare. (means some time)
   (c) Few persons were present at the meeting. (means almost no one was present)
   (d) A few persons were present at the meeting. (means some were present)

6. **A** is used in the following senses :
   A) In its original numerical sense of one.
   For example:
   (a) Not a word was said.
   (b) A word to the wise is sufficient.
   (B) In the vague sense of a **certain time.**
   (C) In the sense of any, to single out an individual as the representative of a class.
   For example : A pupil should obey his teacher.
   (D) To make a common noun of a proper noun.
   For example : A Daniel came to judgement. (A Daniel = A very wise man)

7. **The** points out a particular person or thing or someone or something already referred to.
   For example :
   (a) I saw the doctor. (means I saw some particular doctor)
   (b) The book you want is out of print.

8. **The** is used with names of gulfs, rivers, seas, oceans, groups of islands and mountain ranges.
   For example :
   The Persian Gulf, The Red Sea, The Indian Ocean, The British Isles, The Alps.

9. **The** is used before the name of certain books.
   For example : The Vedas, The Puranas, The Ramayana.
   But we never say 'The Valmiki's Ramayana'. The is not used when the name of a book is mentioned along with the author's name. So, 'Valmiki's Ramayana' is correct.

10. **The** is used before the names of things unique of their kind.
    For example : the sun, the sky, the ocean, the sea.

11. **The** is used before a plural common noun if it refers to a particular group among the class and not the whole class.
    For example : Drive away the cows from the field.

12. **The** is used before a proper noun only when it is qualified by an adjective.
    For example : The great Rani of Jhansi, the immortal Kalidas.

13. **The** is used before superlatives.
    For example :
    (a) Sachin was the best batsman in the world.
    (b) The best person should win.

14. **The** noun if emphasis is laid on the use of such a noun. Here, noun can be proper or abstract noun
    (a) the time for doing it.
    (b) occasion to help the distressed.
15. **The** is used with ordinals.
    For example :
    (a) He was the first student to finish his homework.
    (b) The second chapter of the book is very interesting.
16. **The** is used before an adjective when the noun is understood.
    For example :
    (a) The poor are always with us. (Here poor means poor people which is understood.)
    (b) The weak and the strong. (Here weak means weak people and strong means strong people.)
17. No article is used before a common noun when it refers to all the members of the class.
    For example :
    (a) Man is mortal.
    (b) Fish has high protein content.
    (c) What kind of flower is it?
18. The is used before a common noun to give it the meaning of an abstract noun.
    For example : The devil in him begins its misdeeds now and then.
19. No article is used before the names of materials such as gold, stone, wine, iron, wheat, wood, cloth.
    For example :
    (a) Gold is a precious metal.
    (b) Wheat grows in Uttar Pardesh, Haryana and Madhya Pardesh.
    (c) Iron is a useful metal.
    Note: But it is correct to say
    For example : An iron is a useful gadget.
    Because here we are not taking about material iron, but the object which is used to make clothes smooth.
20. No article is used before proper nouns.
    For example :
    (a) Delhi is the capital of India.
    (b) Newton was a great philosopher.
        But consider the following examples where an article is used before a proper noun.
    (a) This man is a second Newton.
    (b) Bombay is the Manchester of India.
    Here Newton and Manchester are not used as proper nouns but as common nouns. The first sentence means that this man is as great as Newton and the second sentence means that Bombay is a great manufacturing city like Manchester.

21. No articles are used before a common noun used in its widest sense.
     For example :
     (a) The science has developed much in the past hundred years.
          (Incorrect)
     (b) Science has developed much in the past hundred years. (Correct).
22. No article is used before the noun following 'Kind of':
     For example :
     (a) What kind of a hobby is this? (Incorrect)
     (b) What kind of hobby is this? (Correct)
23. No article is used before abstract nouns.
     For example :
     (a) Wisdom is the gift of heaven.
     (b) Honesty is the best policy.
          But consider the following examples where an article is used before
          an abstract noun.
     (a) The wisdom of Solomon is famous.
     (b) I cannot forget the kindness with which he treated me.
          Here the article is used before the abstract noun as the abstract
          noun has been qualified by an adjective or adjectival clause.
24. No article is used before languages, subject of arts and science.
     For example :
     (a) We are studying English.
     (b) Geometry is the toughest subject I have ever studied.
25. No article is used before words such as school, college, church, bed,
     table, hospital, market, prison.
     For example :
     (a) I went to school till last year.
     (b) I have never been to hospital.
          But an article is used before these words when reference is made to
          a definite place.
26. No article is used before the name of relations like father, mother, aunt,
     uncle.
     For example : Mother would like to see you.
     But if someone else's mother is being talked about then **the** should be
     used.
     For example : The mother would like to see you.
27. Article should not be used before positions that are held at one time by
     one person only.
     For example :
     (a) S D Sharma was elected the president of the country. (Incorrect)
     (b) S D Sharma was elected president of the country. (Correct)
28. Please consider this sentence
     (a) I have a black and white cat.
     Here I mean that I have one cat that is partly black and partly white.
     Now, consider this sentence

For example : I have a black and a white cat.

Here I mean that I have two cats one is black and the other white. Hence the rule is that when two or more adjectives qualify the same noun, the article is used before the first adjective only. But when they qualify different nouns, the article is used before each adjective separately.

Consider one more *example*.

(a)   The President and Chairman is absent.

(b)   The President and the Chairman are present.

Sentence a means that only one person is acting as president as well as chairman. Sentence b means that two different persons are acting as the President and the Chairman and both the persons are present.

TENSES

1.   Tense is the form taken by a verb to indicate time and **continuance** or **completeness** of action. The continuance or completeness of action is denoted by four subcategories.

   (a)   Simple Tense: It is need for habitual or routine actions in the Present Tense, action which is over in the Past Tense & action to happen in the Future Tense.

   The action is mentioned simply. Nothing is said about whether the action is complete.

   (b)   Continuous Tense : The action is incomplete or continuous or going on.

   (c)   Perfect Tense: The action is complete, finished or perfect with respect to a certain point of time.

   (d)   Perfect Continuous Tense: The action is going on continuously over a long period of time and is yet to be finished.

2.   The different tenses and the verb forms used in each tense are given below :

Singular with meaning	*Plural with meaning*
Name of Tenses	*Verb form used in Tenses*
Present simple / indefinite	Verb + s/es
Present continuous / Progressive	Is/am/are + verb + ing
Present perfect	Has / have + third form of verb
Present perfect continuous	Has/have + been + verb + ing
Past simple / indefinite	Second form of verb
Past continuous / Progressive	Was/were + verb + ing
Past perfect	Had + third form of verb
Past perfect continuous	Had been + verb + ing
Future simple / indefinite	Shall / will + verb
Future continuous / Progressive	Shall / will + be + verb + ing
Future perfect	Shall/will + Have + past participle
Future perfect continuous	Shall/will + have been + verb + ing

PREPOSITION

1. **In** is used with the names or countries and large towns; at is used when speaking of small towns and villages. *For example* :
    (a)   I live in Delhi.
    (b)   I live at Rohini in Delhi.
2. **In** and **at** are used in speaking of things at rest; **to** and **into** are used in speaking of things in motion. *For example* :
    (a)   He is in bed.
    (b)   He is at the top of the class.
    (c)   He ran to school.
    (d)   He jumped into the river.
    (e)   The snake crawled into its hole.
3. **On** is often used in speaking of things at rest; and **upon** for the things in motion. *For example*:
    (a)   He sat on a chair.
    (b)   The cat sprang upon the table.
4. **Till** is used of time and **to** is used for place.
    For example :
    (a)   He slept till eight o'clock.
    (b)   He walked to the end of the street.
5. **With** often denotes the instrument and **by** the agent. *For example* :
    (a)   He killed two birds with one shot.
    (b)   He was stabbed by a lunatic with a dagger.
6. **Since** is used before a noun or phrase denoting some point of time and is preceded by a verb in the perfect tense.
    For example :
    (a)   I have eaten nothing since yesterday.
    (b)   He has been ill since Monday last.
    From is also used before a noun or phrase denoting some point of time but is used with non-perfect tense.
    For example :
    (a)   I commenced work from 1st January.
    (b)   He will join school from tomorrow.
    For is used with a period of time. *For example* :
    (a)   He has been ill for five days.
    (b)   He lived in Bombay for five years.
7. Use of **in** before a period of time means at the end of period, but use of **within** before a period of time means before the end of period.
    For example :
    (a)   I shall return in an hour. (means I shall return at the end of an hour).
    (b)   I shall return within an hour. (means I shall return before the end of an hour).

8. **Scarcely** should be followed by 'when' and not by 'but'.
   For example : Scarcely had he gone, when **(not** than) a policeman knocked at the door.

9. The phrase 'seldom or ever' is wrong 'Seldom or never' is right.
   For example : Such goods are made for export, and are **seldom or never** used in this country.

10. Examine the following sentence:
    (a) This is as good, if not better than that.　　(Incorrect)
    (b) This is as good as, if not better than, that.　(Correct)
    (c) This is as good as that, if not better.　　(Correct)

11. **Beside** means at the side of while **besides** means in addition to. *For example* :
    (a) Beside the ungathered rice he lay.
    (b) Besides being fined, he was sentenced to a term of imprisonment.

12. **Above** and **below** merely denote position while **over** and **under** also carry a sense of covering or movement.
    (a) The bird flew above the lake.　　　　(Incorrect)
    (b) The bird flew over the lake.　　　　　(Correct)
    Here over is used as besides denoting upward position, movement is also involved.

13. **During** is used when reference is made to the time within which something happens. **For** is used when we are talking about how long something lasts.
    (a) There are few incidents of irregularity **for** the emergency years.
    　　　　　　　　　　　　　　　　　　(Incorrect)
    (b) There are few incidents of irregularity **during** the emergency years.
    　　　　　　　　　　　　　　　　　　(Correct)

14. **Compare** is followed by **to** when it shows that two things are alike. It is followed by **with** when we look at the ways in which two things are like and unlike each other.
    For example :
    (a) Sanath Jayasuria's bowling may be compared to the sales of a useful book, they score right from the beginning.
    　　　　　　　　　　　　　　　　　　(Incorrect)
    (b) Sanath Jayasuria's batting may be compared with the sales of a useful book; they score right from the beginning.
    　　　　　　　　　　　　　　　　　　(Correct)
    (c) If we compare Delhi University with the regional ones, we find the former to be much more efficient.
    　　　　　　　　　　　　　　　　　　(Incorrect)
    (d) If we compare Delhi University to the regional ones, we find the former to be much more efficient.
    　　　　　　　　　　　　　　　　　　(Correct)

CONJUNCTIONS

1. **Since** as conjunction means:
   (A) From and after the time when.
       For example :
       (a) Many things have happened since I left the school.
       (b) I have never seen him since that unfortunate event happened.
   (B) Seeing that,
       For example :
       (a) Since you wish it, it shall be done.
       (b) Since that is the case, I shall excuse you.

2. **Or** is used
   (A) To introduce an alternative.
       For example :
       (a) You must work or starve.
       (b) You may take this book or that one.
       (c) **He** may study law or medicine or engineering or he may enter into trade.
   (B) To introduce an alternative name or synonym.
       For example : The violin or fiddle has become the leading instrument of the modern orchesta.
   (C) To mean otherwise.
       For example : We must hasten or night will overtake us.

3. **If** is used to mean:
   (A) On the condition or supposition that.
       For example :
       (a) If he is here, I shall see him.
       (b) If that is so, I am content.
   (B) Admitting that.
       For example : If I am blunt, I am at least honest.
   (C) Whether.
       For example : I asked him if he would help me.
   (D) Whenever.
       For example : If I feel any doubt I enquire.

4. **That** is used:
   (A) To express a reason or cause.
       For example :
       (a) Not that I loved Caesar less but that I loved Rome more.
       (b) He was annoyed that he was contradicted.
   (B) To express a purpose and is equivalent to **in order that**.
       For example : He kept quiet that the dispute might cease.
   (C) To express a consequence, result or effect.
       For example : He bled so profusely that he died.

5.   **Lest** is used to express a negative purpose and is equivalent to 'in order that… not', 'for fear that'.
     For example :
     (a)   He lied lest he should be killed.
     (b)   I was alarmed lest we should be wrecked.

6.   **While** is used to mean:
     (A)   During that time, as long as.
           For example : while there is life there is hope.
     (B)   At the same time that.
           For example : While he found fault, he also praised.

7.   **Only** means except that, but, were it not that.
     For example :
     (a)   A very pretty woman, only she squints a little.
     (b)   The day is pleasant, only rather cold.

8.   The conjunctions **after, before, as soon as, until** are not followed by clause in the future tense. Present simple or present perfect tense is used to express a future event.
     For example :
     (a)   I will phone you after I arrive here.
     (b)   I will phone you after I have arrived here.

9.   **As if** used in the sense of as it would be is generally followed by a subject + were + complement.
     For example :
     (a)   He loves you as if you were his own child.
     (b)   Sometimes she weeps and sometimes she laughs as if she were mad.

10. The clause that begins with **as if** should be put into the past simple tense, if the preceding clause expresses a past action. But if it expresses a past action it should be followed by the past perfect tense.
     For example :
     (a)   He behaves as if he were a lord.
     (b)   He behaved as if he had been a lord.

11. While **as long as** is used to express time in sense of how long, **until** is used to express time in sense of before.
     For example :
     (a)   Until you work hard you will improve.   (Incorrect)
     (b)   As long as you work hard you will improve. (Correct)
     (c)   He learnt little as long as he was 15 years old. (Incorrect)
     (d)   He learnt little until he was 15 years old.   (Correct)

12. **No sooner** should be followed by (verb + subject) and than should begin another clause.
     For example :
     (a)   No sooner had I reached the station than the train left.
     (b)   No sooner did the bell ring than all the students rushed in.

13. When **as well as** is used, finite verb should agree in number and person with the first subject.

    For example : He as well as us is innocent.

14. **As well as** should never be used in place of **and** if the first subject is preceded by the word 'both'.

    For example :

    (a) Both Rani as well as Kajol came.   (Incorrect)

    (b) Both Rani and Kajol came.   (Correct)

15. **Because** is generally used when the reason is the most important part of a sentence.

    For example : Some people like him because he is honest and hard working.

    Since is used when the reason is already known or is less important than the chief statement.

    For example : Since you refuse to cooperate, I shall have to take legal steps.

    For is used when reason given is an afterthought.

    For example : The servant must have opened the box, for no one else had the key. For never comes at the beginning of the sentence and for is always preceded by a comma.

16. **Scarcely** should be followed by when and not by than,

    (a) Scarcely had he arrived than he had to leave again.
         (Incorrect)

    (b) Scarcely had he arrived when he had to leave again.
         (Correct)

17. Conjunctions such as either... or, neither... nor, not only... but also, both... and, whether, or etc. always join two words or phrases belonging to the same parts of speech.

    For example :

    (a) Either he will ask me or you.   (Incorrect)

    (b) He will ask either me or you.   (Correct)

    (c) Neither he reads nor writes English
         (Incorrect)

    (d) He neither reads nor writes English.
         (Correct)

    (e) Either you shall have to go home or stay here.
         (Incorrect)

    (f) You shall have either to go home or stay here.
         (Correct)

18. Conjunctions like neither...nor, either..or, should be followed by the same part of speech.

    For example :

    (a) He neither agreed to my proposal nor to his. (Incorrect)

    (b) He agreed neither to my proposal nor to his. (Correct)

19. Conjunction is not used before an interrogative adverb or interrogative pronoun in the indirect narration.
     For example :
     (a) He asked me that where I stayed.   (Incorrect)
     (b) He asked me where I stayed.   (Correct)

20. **Although** goes with yet or a comma in the other clause.
     For example :
     (a) Although Manohar is hardworking but he does not get a job.
          (Incorrect)
     (b) Although Manohar is hard working, yet he does not get a job.
          (Correct)

21. **Nothing else** should be followed by but not by than,
     For example :
     (a) Mr. Bureaucrat! This is nothing else than red-tapism.
                                                    (Incorrect)
     (b) Mr. Bureaucrat! This is nothing else but red-tapism.
               (Correct)

22. The correlative conjunctions **indeed... but** are used to emphasise the contrast between the first and the second parts of the statement.
     For example :
     (a) I am indeed happy with my school but it produces famous men.
          (Incorrect)
     (b) I am indeed happy with my school but it does not produce famous men.   (Correct)
     (c) I am indeed happy with my school that it produces famous men.
          (Correct)

23. In a **"not only ... but also..."** sentence, the verb should agree with the noun or pronoun mentioned second, that is; the one after 'but also', because this is the part being emphasised.
     For example :
     (a) Not only the students but also the teacher were responsible for what happened in the class.
          (Incorrect)
     (b) Not only the students but also the teacher was responsible for what happened in the class.
          (Correct)

24. **Such ... as** is used to denote a category whereas **such ...that** emphasises the degree of something by mentioning its consequence.
     For example :
     (a) Each member of the alliance agrees to take such action that it deems necessary.   (Incorrect)
     (b) Each member of the alliance agrees to take such action as it deems necessary.   (Correct)

Here "it seems necessary" is not a consequence of "such action". The sentence wants to imply that the action belongs to the category "as it deems necessary". In other words, what kind of action? Such action as it deems necessary.

(a) She looked at him in such distress as he had to look away. (Incorrect)

(b) She looked at him in such distress that he had to look away. (Correct)

Here, "he had to look away" is a consequence of "she looked at him in such distress." In other words, the degree of the distress of looking at him was such that (not as) he had to look away.

MODALS

The verbs like can, could, may, might, would, shall, should and ought are called modal verbs or modals. They are used with ordinary verbs to express possibility, permission, certainly, etc.

(1) **Can** usually expresses ability or capacity
I can swim across the river
Can you lift this table?

(2) **Can** is also used to express permission
You can go now.

(3) **May** is a more formal modal used to express permission:
You may come in.
May I leave the room now?

(4) **May** is also used to suggest possibility in an affirmative sentence.
He may be at home.
It may rain tomorrow.

(5) **Can** is used to suggest possibility in negative/interrogative sentence.
Can this be true?
It cannot be so.

(6) **May** when used in a negative sentence suggests an improbability whereas **can** suggests impossibility.
He may not come today.
She cannot sing.

(7) **Could** and **might** are used as past forms of 'can' and 'may'.
I could swim across the river when I was young.
I thought he might be at home.

(8) **Might** suggests less possibility or probability than may.
I might go to Bangalore next week suggests the probability of going is less than a sentence with 'may' will suggest.

(9) **Could** is used as a polite form of seeking permission or making a request.
Could you pass me the plate ?
Could I please talk to Mr. Grover?

(10) **Shall** is used with first person and will in all the persons to express future.
      I shall need the money tomorrow.
      When will you come next?
(11) **Shall** is used with the second and third person to express command, promise or threat.
      You shall never come near my child.
      You shall be punished for this.
      We shall go for a picnic this Sunday.
(12) Will You? indicates an invitation or request.
      Will you dine with us tonight?
      Will you lend me your car for a week?
(13) **Should** and **would** are used as past forms of shall and will.
      I expected that I would get a first class.
      She would sit for hours listening to the radio.
(14) **Should** is used to express duty or obligation.
      We should obey the laws.
      You should keep your premise.
(15) **Should** is used to express a supposition
      If it should rain, they will not come.
(16) **Should** can also be used to express probability.
      He should be in the library.
(17) **Must** is used to express necessity.
      You must improve your spelling.
(18) **Must** is also need to express obligation, and is a stronger word than should.
      We must follow the law.
(19) **Must** is also used to express logical certainty.
      Living alone in such a big city must be difficult.
(20) **Ought** is used to express moral obligation and is stronger than both should and must.
      We ought to love our parents.
(21) **Ought** is also used to express probability sometime when the probability is very strong.
      The book ought to be very useful.

Vocabulary

This is very important area of the vocabulary section. This section tests widely and exhaustively one's knowledge of the language and word power, but goes beyond that to test your ability to remember words with similar meanings or opposite meanings. Or, alternately, to discover the similarity or proximity between the meaning of the given word with one of those in the options.

These exercises can get confusing sometimes because more than one option may appear as the right answer or none of them may look like the right answer. For such questions a student may consider the following strategies:

STRATEGY 1

If you do not know the meaning of the given word, think of a context in which you might have used it, that may help you to figure out the meaning, for example, in the question below find the word nearest in meaning to

MAGNIFY

(a) Forgive (b) diminish (c) swell (d) extract

Now if you do not know what magnify means think of a magnifying glass and what it does. It expands or makes a thing look bigger. So the right answer will be (c).

STRATEGY 2

If you cannot find a correct antonym in the given option think of the antonyms you know of and subsequently check if there is any word in the given options which is synonymous to the antonyms in your mind. For example

INDUSTRIOUS

(a) stupid   (b) harsh (c) indolent (d) complex

If you don't know any of the words given as options think of antonyms you could think of, like lazy, idle. Now think of synonyms of lazy and you will know indolent is a synonym of lazy. So it will be the antonym to industrious. Formula → SYNONYM of ANTONYM is another ANTONYM.

STRATEGY 3

Look at the part of speech of the given word. A word may exist in various parts of speech. For example precipitate exists as a verb which means send rapidly into a certain state and also as a noun, precipitate, which means a substance de posited from a solution.

POLISH

(a) ruthlessness (b) honesty (c) indolence (d) gaucheness

Now is this the verb polish or noun polish? Since all options are nouns, this cannot be the verb polish related to shoes but noun polish which means culture and sophistication and the antonym to this would be gaucheness.

CONTEXTUAL MEANING

Contextual meaning or Contextual usage is another important word-based question. Contextual usage basically involves identifying the synonym/antonym of a word when it is used in a particular context so that the context provides you a clue to the meaning, even if the word is unfamiliar to you.

Example 1

MORIBUND : By the fourth century AD, the Roman Civilization was already moribund.

(1)	extinct	(2)	forgotten
(3)	flourishing	(4)	stagnant

In the context of the given sentence the meaning of the word will be stagnant, hence [4].

There may be sentences where most or even all of the options are synonymous to the highlighted word, but only one of them fits the particular context. This means that you have to be aware of the very subtle nuances of the words, making contextual usage more of a challenge to your command over words.

More Examples

GELID : It is hard to believe that any life could ever arise in the gelid environment of Titan.

(1)	Frigid	(2)	Suffocation
(3)	gelatinous	(4)	hostile

Gelid means icy cold or frozen. In the context also we can see that gelid can refer to a cold environment where no life can arise.

The answer is [1].

Strategies for contextual usage :

The following steps and strategies will be useful while attempting contextual usage questions:

(1)   Read the highlighted word first; if it is familiar to you try to think of a synonym for it before going on to read the sentence or the option.

(2)   If it is not a familiar word, simply read the sentence and try to understand its meaning from the context. Think of a word that could suitably take its place.

(3)   Read the options if one of them is the word you thought of in step 1 or 2, or its close synonym, then choose that as an answer not before at least glancing at the other options and trying to see if one of them might be more suitable.

(4)   If none of the options is similar to the word you thought of in step 1 or 2, then read all the options and see if any of them suit the context of the sentence.

(5)   If you cannot understand the word from the context of the sentence or if you have trouble understanding the sentence itself, then look at the options. Sometimes the options can give you a clue, if you know where to look. For example, if all the options, except one, have a negative / positive connotation then the exception is likely to be the answer. Also sometimes the words in the options are much more familiar ones than the question word, so using them in the sentence instead of the question word should help you eliminate the wrong options.

ONE WORD - A SMALL COLLECTION

Abdicate	-	Renounce a throne or high office
Acoustics	-	Science of the production, transmission, reception and effects of sound
Adolescence	-	The period of life from puberty to maturity
Actuary	-	One who calculates insurance and annuity premium etc
Amnesty	-	General pardon
Ad hoc	-	Created or done for a particular purpose as necessary.
Agoraphobia	-	Fear of open spaces, public places
Altruist	-	One who is habitually kind to others, selfless concern for the well-being or others.
Apiary	-	A place where bees are kept
Astrology	-	The study of the movements and relative positions of celestial bodies interpreted as having an influence human affairs and the natural world.
Astronomy	-	Scientific study of heavenly bodies
Barometer	-	An instrument for measuring the air pressure
Bibliography	-	A list of the books of a specific author or publisher or on a specific subject.
Blue Blood	-	The quality of being a noble person by birth
Blueprint	-	The word originated in the engineering industry where it means the final stage of paper design. So it may mean the final plan or layout. Example: The blueprint of the Five-Year Plan is ready.
Bonsai	-	The art of growing a plant in a pot that is prevented from reaching its natural size
Calligraphy	-	The art of decorative writing by hand
Catch-22	-	A situation from which one is prevented from escaping by something that is part of the situation itself
Cerebral	-	Connected with the brain
Celibacy	-	One who does not indulge in carnal pleasure
Cloak-and-Dagger	-	Involving or characterised by mystery, intrigue or espinoage, e.g., a cloak-and-dagger operation.
Colloquial	-	Suitable for ordinary, informal, or familiar conversation
Combustible	-	(or Inflammable) That can catch fire and burn easily
Consortium	-	A combination of several companies, banks, etc. for a common purpose

Contemporary	-	A person living at the same time as another
Counterfeit	-	Made exactly like something real in order to deceive
Déja vu	-	The feeling of remembering something that in fact one is experiencing for the first time
Dividend	-	The money which is divided among shareholders
Dormitory	-	A large room containing a number of beds
Elastic	-	Able to spring back into shape after being stretched
Enigmatic	-	That which is mysterious and very hard to understand
Entomology	-	The scientific study of insects
Evolution	-	Gradual development from simpler forms
Expressionism	-	A style of painting which expresses feelings rather than describing objects and experiences
Faeces	-	The solid waste material passed from the bowels
Good Samaritan	-	One who helps others in trouble, without thinking of oneself
Hinterland	-	The inner part of a country
Ideology	-	A set of ideas on which a political or economic system is based
Implacable	-	Impossible to satisfy, change, or make less angry
Ingest	-	To take into the stomach
Intestate	-	Not having made a will
Juxtapose	-	To place side by side or close together
Libertarian	-	One who believes that people should have freedom of expression
Limerick	-	A humorous short poem with five lines
Mascot	-	Chosen as a symbol or thought to bring good luck
Massacre	-	The unnecessary and indiscriminate killing of human beings
Monarchy	-	Rule by a king or queen
Necromancy	-	The practice which claims to learn about the future by talking with the dead
Nihilism	-	The belief that nothing has meaning or value
Oligarchy	-	A collective government formed by a few persons
Ontology	-	The branch of philosophy concerned with the nature of existence
Petrology	-	The scientific study of rocks
Prodigal	-	One who is wasteful or extravagant, especially in the use of money or property
Protagonist	-	First actor in a play. It means one who takes the leading part in a drama, novel or any other sphere
Skyscraper	-	A very tall modern city building
Somnambulism	-	The habit of sleep walking
Taxonomy	-	The system of putting plants and animals into various classes
Tunnel Vision	-	A condition in which one can see only straight ahead
Vicissitude	-	A change, especially a complete change, of condition or circumstances, as of fortune

Wasteland	-	Empty, unproductive, usually barren land
Xenophobia	-	Fear of strange or foreign people, customs, etc.
Zeitgeist	-	The intellectual and moral tendencies that characterize any age or epoch

IDIOMS & PHRASES

* *Beat back* (to compel to retire) : The firemen were *beaten back* by angry flames and the building was reduced to ashes.
* *Boil down to* (to amount to) : His entire argument *boiled down* to this that he would not join the movement unless he saw some monetary gain in it.
* *Cast aside* (to reject, to throw aside) : Men will *cast aside* truth and honesty for immediate gains.
* *Cry down* (to deprecate) : Some of the Western powers did their best to *cry down* India's success in the war.
* *To cut off with a shilling* (to give someone a mere trifle in the will) : The father was so angry with the son over his marriage that *he cut him off with a shilling.*
* *Egg on* (to urge on) : Who *egged* you on to fight a professional boxer and get your nose knocked off?
* *Gloss over* (explain away) : Even if you are an important person your faults cannot be *glossed over*.
* *To laugh in one's sleeves* (to be secretly amused) : While I was solemnly reading my research paper to the audience, my friends were *laughing in their sleeves* for they knew what it was worth.
* *Play off* (to set one party against another for one's own advantage) : It best serves the interests of the super powers to *play off* one poor nation against another.
* *Pull one through* (to recover, to help one recover) : Armed with the latest medicines, the doctor *will pull him through*.
* *Cost a slur upon* (by word or act to cast a slight reproach on someone) : Many a man casts a *slur* on his own good name with some mean act.
* *To catch a Tartar* (to encounter a strong adversary) : When Hitler marched in to Russia he little knew that he would *catch a Tartar* in the tough people of that country.
* *To come off with flying colours* (to come out of a conflict with brilliant success) : The 1971 election outcome was uncertain but finally the congress *came off with flying colours.*
* *To come off second best* (to be defeated in every contest) : Be it an election or a tambola, I have always come off the second best
* *To cut the Gordian knot* (to remove a difficulty by bold or unusual measures) : The Parliament threw out the Bill for Abolition of Privy Purses. The Government cut the Gordian knot by abolishing the privy purses through an ordinance.
* *To fall to one's lot* (to become one's fate): It fell to the lot of Mujib and. his colleagues to reconstruct the shattered economy of their nation.
* *To get into hot water* (to get into difficulty): The businessman *got into*

hot water with the Income-tax authorities for concealing his income from ancestral property.

- *To give someone the slip* (to dodge someone who is looking for you): The police had nearly got the dacoits when the *latter gave* them the *slip* in the Chambal ravines.
- *To go on a fool's errand* (to go on an expedition which leads to a foolish end): Many people earlier believed that going to the moon was like *going on a fool's errand*
- *To go to the wall* (to get the worst in a competition): In the struggle of life, the weakest *goes to the wall.*
- *To go to rack and ruin, to go to the dogs* (to be ruined): If a big war comes, our economy will *go to the dogs.*
- *To have one's hands full* (to be very busy): Pakistan could hardly expect active help from the U.S.A. *as her hands were already full with Vietnam,* Laos and West Asia problems.
- *To have a bone to pick with one* (to have a difference with a person which has not yet been fully expressed). The extreme leftists *have a bone to pick* with the police and if ever they come to power there may be unpleasantness between the two.
- *To have the whip hand of* (to have mastery over): After the split in the party Mrs. *Gandhi* has *the whip hand of* the Congress.
- *To have too many irons in the fire (to have so much work in* hand that some part of it is left undone or is done very badly): Let the Government not go in for nationalisation so fast. If they *have too many irons in the fire* they are bound to fare badly.
- *To have the tree or right ring* (To be genuine): Nixon's pronouncements on world peace do not *have the right ring.*
- *To have two strings to one's bow (*to have an alternative means of achieving one's purpose): A wife always has *two strings to her bow* if coaxing fails to achieve the desired end; tears succeed.
- *To have an axe to grind* (have personal interests to serve): Bigger nations supply arms to the smaller ones primarily because they (the bigger nations) *have their own axe to grind*
- *To keep the wolf from the door* (to keep away extreme poverty and hunger): Lakhs in India have to struggle everyday to *keep the wolf from the door.*
- *To make short work of (to* bring to sudden end): The locusts *made short work* of the ripe standing corn.
- *To make amends for* (to compensate for damage): By his kindness today he has made *amends pr* his past insolence.
- *To make common cause with* (to unite, to co-operate with): During the last elections the princes *made a common cause with* the rightist parties. Both went down.
- *To make a virtue of necessity* (to do a very disagreeable thing as though from duty but really because you must do it): When a minister knows that he is going to be booted out of the cabinet he *makes a virtue of necessity* and resigns on health grounds.

- *To make much ado about nothing* (make a great fuss about a trifle): Demonstrations and protests over the change in the timing of news bulletins over AIR was *making much ado about nothing*
- *To make a cat's paw or a tool of someone (to use someone as a means of attaining your* object): The super-powers have *made a cat's paw* of the smaller nations of Asia in their game of power politics.
- *To play into the hands of someone* (to act as to be of advantage to another) By raising the slogan 'Indira Hatao' the opposition *played into her hands* and Mrs. Gandhi won the elections hands down (easily).
- *To play second fiddle'* (to take a subordinate part) : With Mrs. Gandhi as the undisputed leader of the Congress and the nation, everyone else is content to *play second fiddle to her.*
- *To put the cart before the horse* (to begin at the wrong end to do a thing): Preparing the blue print of a project without the provision of funds is like *putting the cart before the horse.*
- *To put one's shoulder to the wheel* (to make great efforts ourselves): No amount of foreign aid will pull us out of the economic morass; we have to *put our own shoulders to the wheel.*
- *To set store by* (to value highly): India, *surely sets much store by* the Indo Soviet Treaty of Friendship.
- *To set the Thames on fire* (to do something extraordinary): He is a steady worker but never likely *to set the Thames on fire.*
- *To set one's house* in *order* (to arrange one's affairs): Let Pakistan *set her own house in order* before talking of the welfare of the Kashmiris.
- *To take into one's head* (to occur to someone): The Manager *look it into his head* that by shutting off the electricity for a few hours daily he could save on refrigeration costs.
- *To take the bull by the horns* (to grapple with a problem courageously instead of avoiding it): There is no short cut to prosperity. We have *to take the bull by the horns* and make people work like slaves.
- *To take a leap in the dark* (to do a hazardous thing without any idea of what it may result in): You *took a leap in the dark* in going into partnership with that man.
- *To throw cold water upon* (to discourage something): The doctor *threw cold water upon* my plans for a world tour by declaring that I could never stand the strain of it.
- *To throw up the sponge* (to give up a contest): Faced with stiff competition from big companies, many a small company will *throw up the sponge.*
- *To turn over a new leaf (to* change one's course of action completely): After a long career of crime the convict suddenly *turned over a new leaf* and became a model citizen.
- *To turn tail* (to retreat ignominiously): The enemy *turned tail* in the face of heavy onslaughts on its key positions.
- *To turn the tables* (to reverse someone's success or superiority): Pakistan started war with a blitz on our positions but the superior tactics of our Armed Forces soon *turned the tables* on them.

- *To cook or doctor an account* (to tamper with or falsify the account): From the balance sheet presented to the shareholders, the company seemed to be flourishing, but it afterwards turned out that the Secretary had *cooked the accounts.*
- *To bear* the *brunt* of (to endure the main force or shock of): The infantry has to *bear the brunt of a* battle.
- *To beard the lion in his den* (to oppose someone, in his stronghold): The Indian Army broke through strong Pakistani fortifications, and in the Shakargarh area *bearded the lion in his own den.*

EXERCISE

DIRECTIONS (Qs. 1-26) : In the following questions out of the four alternatives, choose the one which best expresses the meaning of the given word.

1. Luxuriant
   - (a) Luxury loving
   - (b) Lovely
   - (c) Rich
   - (d) Abundant
2. Cantankerous
   - (a) Cancerous
   - (b) Ferocious
   - (c) Quarrelsome
   - (d) Fissiparous
3. Onus
   - (a) Sadness
   - (b) Happiness
   - (c) Responsibility
   - (d) Criticism
4. Derision
   - (a) Humiliation
   - (b) Embarrassment
   - (c) Ridicule
   - (d) Condemnation
5. Trite
   - (a) Commonplace
   - (b) Clever
   - (c) Brief
   - (d) Impudent
6. Genial
   - (a) Cordial
   - (b) Unselfish
   - (c) Careful
   - (d) Specific
7. Accrue
   - (a) Accumulate
   - (b) Accommodate
   - (c) Grow
   - (d) Suffice
8. Barren
   - (a) Good
   - (b) Wholesome
   - (c) Unproductive
   - (d) Profitable
9. Infamy
   - (a) Notoriety
   - (b) Glory
   - (c) Integrity
   - (d) Familiarity
10. Intrepid
    - (a) Hesitant
    - (b) Fearless
    - (c) Extrovert
    - (d) Rash
11. Prodigal
    - (a) Exclusive
    - (b) Productive
    - (c) Lavish
    - (d) Carefree

12. Perspicuous
    (a) Relevant
    (b) Precise
    (c) Brief
    (d) Clear
13. Annexure
    (a) Retirement
    (b) Commencement
    (c) Attachment
    (d) Development
14. Notion
    (a) Thought
    (b) Fact
    (c) Truth
    (d) Hypothesis
15. Vivacious
    (a) Poisonous
    (b) Energetic
    (c) Tricky
    (d) Slow
16. Apprise :
    (a) Praise
    (b) Inform
    (c) Conceal
    (d) Assess
17. Periodic :
    (a) Infrequent
    (b) Continuous
    (c) Occasional
    (d) Regular
18. Venal
    (a) Corrupt
    (b) Comprehensible
    (c) Legible
    (d) Forgivable
19. Wily
    (a) Angry
    (b) Wise
    (c) Stupid
    (d) Cunning
20. Advocate:
    (a) Predict
    (b) Pronounce
    (c) Support
    (d) Determine
21. Preamble :
    (a) Definition
    (b) Mediation
    (c) Conclusion
    (d) Introduction
22. Students are asked to **collate** for an important programme by the principal.
    (a) Assemble
    (b) Describe
    (c) Narrate
    (d) Prescribe
23. Analogy
    (a) Difference
    (b) Comparison
    (c) Addition
    (d) Deletion
24. Elastic
    (a) free   (b) liberal
    (c) flexible   (d) broad
25. Interference
    (a) honour
    (b) deference
    (c) obstruction
    (d) fearful
26. Pawn
    (a) Scrounge (b) Hire
    (c) Pledge   (d) Sponge

DIRECTIONS (Qs. 27-30) : Out of the four alternatives, choose the one which best expresses the meaning of the given word.

27. Vocation
    (a) virtue
    (b) holiday
    (c) break up
    (d) occupation

28. Gourmet
    (a) fussy
    (b) constant
    (c) gastronome
    (d) praise
29. Board
    (a) Frame
    (b) Lodging
    (c) Food
    (d) Furniture
30. Feeble
    (a) Playful
    (b) Pretty
    (c) Small
    (d) Weak

DIRECTIONS (Qs. 31-55) : Choose the word opposite in meaning to the given word.

31. Liberty
    (a) Serenity
    (b) Slavery
    (c) Serfdom
    (d) Subordination
32. Disorderly
    (a) Chaotic
    (b) Organized
    (c) Adjusted
    (d) Arranged
33. Elevation
    (a) Reduction
    (b) Humiliation
    (c) Depression
    (d) Debasement
34. Glossy
    (a) Dull   (b) Shining
    (c) Weary   (d) Tired
35. Appropriate
    (a) Dissimilar
    (b) Incomparable
    (c) Unsuitable
    (d) Disparate

36. Zenith
    (a) Climax   (b) Crisis
    (c) Acme   (d) Nadir
37. Influx
    (a) Reflex
    (b) Deflection
    (c) Effluent
    (d) Exodus
38. Orderly
    (a) Semitic
    (b) Colic
    (c) Democratic
    (d) Chaotic
39. Pathetic
    (a) Comic
    (b) Ridiculous
    (c) Dramatic
    (d) Trivial
40. Cordial
    (a) Fast
    (b) Heartfelt
    (c) Friendly
    (d) Hostile
41. Obtuse
    (a) Sharp-witted
    (b) Transparent
    (c) Timid
    (d) Blunt
42. Brutal
    (a) Adamant
    (b) Humane
    (c) Fearless
    (d) Criminal
43. Pompous
    (a) Uppish
    (b) Humble
    (c) Meek
    (d) Grandiose
44. Safe
    (a) Rash
    (b) Insecure
    (c) Beneficial
    (d) Harsh

45. Redundant
    (a) Repentant
    (b) Surplus
    (c) Singular
    (d) Required
46. Fair
    (a) Untrue   (b) Unjust
    (c) Coarse   (d) Harsh
47. Boisterous
    (a) Serenity
    (b) Calm
    (c) Cheerful
    (d) Courageous
48. Substantial
    (a) Flimsy   (b) Hefty
    (c) Actual   (d) Excess
49. Equilibrium
    (a) Work out
    (b) Disturb
    (c) Imbalance
    (d) Unevenness
50. Immortal
    (a) Eternal
    (b) Permanent
    (c) Deathly
    (d) Temporary
51. Focus
    (a) Disappear
    (b) Disperse
    (c) Link
    (d) Layer
52. Veteran
    (a) Activist
    (b) Enthusiast
    (c) Novice
    (d) Master
53. Superfluous
    (a) Essential
    (b) Excess
    (c) Unwanted
    (d) Necessary
54. Gloomy
    (a) Heavy   (b) Gay
    (c) Sad   (d) Forlorn
55. Start
    (a) Continue   (b) Break
    (c) Begin   (d) Resume

DIRECTIONS (Qs. 56–77) : In the following questions, out of the four alternatives, choose the one which can be substituted for the given words/ sentence.

56. Science of the races of mankind
    (a) Genealogy
    (b) Epistemology
    (c) Ethnology
    (d) Sociology
57. One who hides away on a ship to obtain a free passage
    (a) Compositor
    (b) Stoker
    (c) Stowaway
    (d) Shipwright
58. Clues available at a scene
    (a) circumstantial
    (b) derivative
    (c) inferential
    (d) suggestive
59. An unexpected piece of good fortune
    (a) windfall
    (b) philanthropy
    (c) benevolence
    (d) turnstile
60. An emolument over and above fixed income or salary
    (a) Honorarium
    (b) Sinecure
    (c) Perquisite
    (d) Prerogative
61. The animals of a particular region.
    (a) Flora   (b) Museum
    (c) Zoo   (d) Fauna
62. A post with little work but high salary
    (a) Director
    (b) Trustee
    (c) Sinecure
    (d) Ombudsman

63. Something that causes death
    (a) Dangerous
    (b) Fatal
    (c) Brutal
    (d) Horrible
64. A person who writes decoratively
    (a) Calligrapher
    (b) Collier
    (c) Choreographer
    (d) Cartographer
65. Pertaining to cattle
    (a) Canine   (b) Feline
    (c) Bovine   (d) Verminous
66. To look at someone in an angry or threatening way
    (a) Glower   (b) Gnaw
    (c) Gnash   (d) Grind
67. Release of a prisoner from jail on certain terms and condition
    (a) Parole
    (b) Parley
    (c) Pardon
    (d) Acquittal
68. One who hates women:
    (a) Misogynist
    (b) Misogamist
    (c) Ambivert
    (d) Misanthrope
69. A person who consumes human flesh :
    (a) Cannibal
    (b) Javage
    (c) Captor
    (d) Carnivore
70. A school boy who cuts classes frequently is a :
    (a) Defeatist
    (b) Sycophant
    (c) Truant
    (d) Martlinet
71. Stealing of ideas or writings of someone else.
    (a) autism
    (b) scepticism
    (c) mesmerism
    (d) plagiarism
72. A study of sounds is known as
    (a) semantics
    (b) sylistics
    (c) linguistics
    (d) phonetics
73. Words inscribed on a tomb
    (a) Epilogue   (b) Epitaph
    (c) Epitome   (d) Epistle
74. That which has a double meaning
    (a) doubtless
    (b) uncertain
    (c) controversial
    (d) ambiguous
75.. Murder of a king
    (a) homicide   (b) fratricide
    (c) regicide   (d) parricide
76. A place where birds are kept
    (a) Aviary   (b) House
    (c) Aquarium   (d) Apiary
77. Science regarding principles of classification.
    (a) taxidermy
    (b) taxonomy
    (c) toxicology
    (d) classicology

DIRECTIONS (Qs. 78-80) : In the following questions, four alternatives are given for the Idiom / Phrase underlined in the sentence. Choose the alternative which best expresses the meaning of the Idiom/Phrase.

78. The police <u>cordoned off</u> the area after the explosion.
    (a) The police checked everyone in the area
    (b) The police did not allow anyone to leave the area
    (c) The police filled the whole area
    (d) The police isolated the area

79. The manager hesitated to assign the job to the newcomer as he was <u>wet behind the ears</u>.
    (a) stupid and slow-witted
    (b) young and inexperienced
    (c) drenched-in the rain .
    (d) unpunctual and lethargic

80. Mrs. Roy <u>keeps an open house</u> on Saturday evening parties— you'll find all kinds of people there.
    (a) keeps the doors of the house open
    (b) keeps the gates open for a few persons
    (c) welcomes all members
    (d) welcomes a select group of people

DIRECTIONS (Qs. 81-83) : In the following questions, four alternatives are given for the idiom / phrase underlined in the sentence. Choose the alternative which best expresses the meaning of the idiom / phrase.

81. The man <u>changed colours</u> when I questioned him on the allocation of funds.
    (a) turned pale
    (b) got numbed
    (c) turned happy
    (d) get motivated

82. We cannot depend on him for this assignment as it needs careful handling and he is <u>like a bull in a china shop</u>.
    (a) a felicitous person
    (b) a clumsy person
    (c) a tactful person
    (d) a no-nonsense person

83. The mother always insists on keeping the house <u>spick and span</u>.

    (a) open   (b) locked
    (c) safe   (d) tidy

DIRECTIONS (Qs. 84-88) : In the following questions, four alternatives are given for the Idiom / Phrase. Choose the alternative which best expresses the meaning of the Idion / Phrase.

84. Hue and cry
    (a) lot of laughter
    (b) an uproar
    (c) a burst of anger
    (d) plenty of tears

85. To win laurels
    (a) to achieve success
    (b) to win the hearts of ladies
    (c) to win praise
    (d) to win a lottery

86. To pay heed
    (a) to submit
    (b) to listen
    (c) to care for
    (d) to understand

87. To eat the humble pie
    (a) feel huniliated
    (b) feel abandoned
    (c) feel rejected
    (d) feel glorified

88. A tall order
    (a) too difficult a task
    (b) a normal task
    (c) a simple task
    (d) an easy task

DIRECTIONS (Qs. 89-92): Four alternatives are given for the Idiom/ Phrase underlined in the sentence. Choose the alternative which best expresses the meaning of the Idiom\Phrase.

89. With great difficulty, he was able to carve out a niche for himself.
    (a) became a sculptor
    (b) did the best he could do
    (c) destroyed his career
    (d) developed a specific position for himself

90. You will succeed if you follow my advice to the letter.
    (a) about writing letters
    (b) written in the letter
    (c) in every detail
    (d) very thoughtfully

91. A critic's work is to read between the lines.
    (a) to comprehend the meaning
    (b) to appreciate the inner beauty
    (c) to understand the inner meaning
    (d) to read carefully

92. Where discipline is concerned I put my foot down.
    (a) take a firm stand
    (b) take a light stand
    (c) take a heavy stand
    (d) take a shaky stand

SOLUTIONS

1. **(d)** The word **Luxuriant (Adjective)** means : growing thickly and strongly; rich in something that is pleasant or beautiful; abundant.

2. **(c)** The word **Cantankerous (Adjective)** means : bad tempered and always complaining.
   Hence, the words **cantankerous** and quarrelsome are synonymous.

3. **(c)** The word Onus (Noun) means : the responsibility for something.

4. **(c)** The word **Derision (Noun)** means : rodicule; mockery; a strong feeling that somebody/something is ridiculous and not worth considering seriously.

5. **(a)** The word **Trite (Adjective)** means : dull and boring because it has been expressed so many times before; not original; banal; very ordinary and containing nothing that is interesting or important.
   Hence, the words **trite** and **commonplace** are synonymous.

6. **(a)** The word **Genial (Adjective)** means : friendly and cheerful; affable; cordial.

7. **(a)** The word **Accrue (Verb)** means : to increase over a period of time; to allow a sum of money or debts to grow over a period of time. Therefore grow in the correct mearest word.

8. **(c)** The word **Barren (Adjective)** means: not good enough for plants to grow on it; infertile unproductive.

9. (a) The word **Infamy (Noun)** means: the state of being well known for something bad or an evil act notoriety.

10. (b) The word **Intrepid (Adjective)** means : very brave not afraid of danger or difficulties fearless.

11. (c) The word **Prodigal (Adjective)** means : too willing to spend money or waste time, energy or materials extravagant lavish.

12. (b) The word **Perspicuous (Adjective)** means precise clear and accurate.

13. (c) The word **Annexure (Noun)** means: attachment; appendix

14. (a) The word **Notion (Noun)** means : belief; desire; intention; thought.

15. (b) The word **Vivacious (Adjective)** means : having a lively, attractive personality; energetic.

16. (b) Apprise means to inform someone.

17. (d) Periodic means happening regularly over a period of time.

18. (a) The word **Venal (Adjective)** means : corrupt; prepared to do dishonest or immoral thing in return for money.
         Look at the sentence : Venal leaders should be denied vote.

19. (d) 'Wily' means 'cunning' which also means skillful or clever.

20. (c) Advocate means to argue for or support a cause.

21. (d) Preamble is a statement made at the beginning of something.

22. (a) Collate refers to, arranging in the correct order. Option (a) assemble is the correct synonym.

23. (b) Analogy denotes comparison.

24. (c) Elastic means able to encompass much variety and change; flexible and adaptable.

25. (c) Interference means act of interfering or obstructing.

26. (c) Pawn as a noun means something given as security for loan; a pleage or gaurantee. Therefore, 'Pledge' is the synonym of 'Pawn'.

27. (d) 'Vocation' means the work in which a person is employed or occupation. Therefore, occupation is the synonym of vocation.

28. (c) 'Gourmet' means a connoisseur of good food. Whereas Gastronome means a lover of good food. Therefore, 'Gastronome' is the synonym of 'Gourmet'.

29. (c) Board means daily meals that you pay for when you are paying to stay at a hotel.

30. (d) 'Feeble' means lacking physical strength. Therefore, 'weak' is the correct synony m of 'Feeble.

31. (b) The word **Liberty (Noun)** means : freedom to live as you choose without too many restrictions from

government or authority.

The word **slavery (Noun)** means: state of being a slave: a system of legally owning another person and forcing to work for them.

32. (d) The word **Disorderly (Adjective)** means : showing lack of control untidy deranged. Its antonym should be arranged.

33. (c) The word **Elevation (Noun)** means to increase in the level of something.

The word **Depression (Noun)** means : the state of feeling very sad and without hope; part of a surface; that is lower than the parts around it.

34. (a) The word **Glossy (Adjective)** means shining, smooth and shiny.

Its antonym should be dull.

35. (c) The word **Appropriate (Adjective)** means : suitable acceptable or correct for the particular circumstances.

Its antonym should be **unsuitable.**

36. (d) The word **Zenith (Noun)** means : the highest point; peak; the time when something is strongest and most successful.

The word **Nadir (Noun)** means : the worst moment of a particular situation.

37. (d) The word **Influx (Noun)** means : the fact of a lot of people, money or things arriving somewhere.

The word **Exodus (Noun)** means : a situation in which many people leave a place at the same time.

38. (d) The word **Orderly (Adjective)** means : arranged or organised in a neat, careful and logical way; tidy; behaving well.

The word **Chaotic (Adjective)** means : in a state of complete confusion and lack of order.

39. (a) The meaning of Pathetic (adj.) : Sad, affecting. The meaning of comic (noun) : funny. "Comic" is opposite to given word.

40. (d) The word **Cordial (Adjective)** means : pleasant and friendly. The word **Hostile (Adjective)** means : very unfriendly or aggressive.

41. (a) Obtuse means stupid or slow to understand

42. (b) humane means gentle, benevolent, civilised; brutal is cruel and violent.

43. (b) The opposite of 'pompous' is 'humble'.

44. (b) Safe means free from harm. Its opposite is insecure.

45. (c) Redundant means excessive. Its opposite is singular.

46. (b) Fair means impartial. Its opposite is unjust.

47. (b) Boisterous means noisy and mischievous. Its opposite is calm.

48. (a) Flimsy means insubstantial and easily damaged.

49. (c) Equilibrium means balance. Its opposite is imbalance.

50. (d) Immortal means death-defying or endless. Its opposite is temporary.

51. (b) Focus means the main or central point. Its opposite is disperse that means spread across.

52. (c) Veteran means experienced. Whereas, Novice means a person just learning something.

53. (d) Superfluous means unnecessary. Its opposite is necessary.

54. (b) Gloomy means sad and dark. Whereas it's opposite is gay which means happy.

55. (b) Start means to begin. Whereas it's opposite is break.

56. (c) The study of different people.

57. (c) A stowaway is a person who secretly boards a ship to travel free.

58. (a) Circumstantial is a description of full details or a particular scene.

59. (a) Windfall refers to get a large amount unexpectedly.

60. (a)   61. (d)

62. (c) Sinecure is a position with no work but with financial benefit.

63. (b) Fatal

64. (a)   65. (c)

66. (a) An angry look

67. (a) Parole

68. (a) A person who dislikes women.

69. (a)

70. (c) Truant refers to a pupil who stays away from school without leave or explanation.

71. (d)   72. (d)   73. (b)

74. (d) Ambiguous means having more than one possible meaning.

75. (c) regicide means the act of killing a king.

76. (a) Aviary is a building where birds are kept.

77. (b)   78. (d)   79. (b)

80. (c)

81. (a) turned pale means colourless

82. (b) a clumsy person means plump

83. (d) tidy means clean

84. (b)   85. (c)   86. (b)

87. (a)   88. (a)

89. (d) In the sentence, 'to carve out a niche' means 'to develop a specific position for him'. The word 'niche' means 'a specialized area or sector'.

90. (c) The alternative meaning of the phrase 'to the letter' is 'in every detail'.

91. (c) The meaning of the idiom 'to read between the lines' is 'to understand the inner meaning'. So, the critic's work is to understand the inner meanings.

92. (a) The meaning of the idiom 'put my foot down' is 'to take a firm stand'. So, as the meaning of the sentence implies that where discipline matters, one should take a firm stand.

Fill in the Blanks

FILL IN THE BLANKS OR SENTENCE COMPLETION

STRATEGY 1

> **BEFORE YOU LOOK AT THE CHOICES, READ THE SENTENCE AND THINK OF A WORD THAT MAKES SENSE**

Your problem is to find the word that best completes the sentence in both thought and style. Before you look at the answer choices, see if you can come up with a word that makes logical sense in the context. Then look at all five choices. If the word you thought of is one of your five choices, select that as your answer. If the word you thought of is not one of your five choices, look for a synonym of that word. Select the synonym as your answer.

This technique is helpful because it enables you to get a sense of the sentence as a whole without being distracted by any misleading answers among the answer choices. You are free to concentrate on spotting key words or phrases in the body of the sentence and to call on your own "writer's intuition" in arriving at a stylistically apt choice of word.

See how the process works in a typical model question.

1. Because experience had convinced her that he was both self-seeking and avaricious, she rejected the likelihood that his donation had been.................

   (a) redundant   (b) frivolous

   (c) inexpensive   (d) ephemeral

   (d) altruistic

This sentence presents a simple case of cause and effect. The key phrase here is self-seeking and avaricious. The woman has found the man to be selfish and greedy. Therefore, she refuses to believe he can do something.............. What words immediately come to mind? Selfless, generous, charitable? The missing word is, of course, altruistic. The woman expects selfishness (self-seeking) and greediness (avaricious), not altruism (magnanimity). The correct answer is Choice E.

Practice of Funda 1 extensively develops your intuitive sense of just the exactly right word. However, do not rely on Funda 1 alone. On the test, always follow up Funda 1 with Funda 2.

STRATEGY 2

> **BEFORE YOU LOOK AT THE CHOICES, READ THE SENTENCE AND THINK OF A WORD THAT MAKES SENSE**

Never decide on an answer before you have read all the choices. You are looking for the word that best fits the meaning of the sentence as a whole. In order to be sure you have not been hasty in making your decision, substitute all the answer choices for the missing word. Do not spend a lot of time doing so, but do try them all. That way you can satisfy yourself that you have come up with the best answer.

See how this Funda helps you deal with another question.

1.   The evil of class and race hatred must be eliminated while it is still in an ....state; otherwise it may grow to dangerous proportions.

   (a)   Amorphous   (b)   overt
   (c)   uncultivated   (d)   embryonic
   (e)   independent

On the basis of a loose sense of this sentence's meaning, you might be tempted to select Choice A. After all, this sentence basically tells you that you should wipe out hatred before it gets too dangerous. Clearly, if hatred is vague or amorphous, it is less formidable than if it is well defined. However, this reading of the sentence is inadequate: it fails to take into account the sentence's key phrase.

The key phrase here is 'grow to dangerous proportions'. The writer fears that class and race hatred may grow large enough to endanger society. He wants us to wipe out this hatred before it is fully-grown. Examine each answer choice, eliminating those answers that carry no suggestion that something lacks its full growth. Does overt suggest that something isn't fully-grown? No, it suggests that something is obvious or evident. Does uncultivated suggest that something isn't fully grown? No, it suggests that something is unrefined or growing without proper care or training. Does independent suggest that something isn't fully-grown? No, it suggests that something is free and unconstrained. Only one word suggests a lack of full growth: embryonic (at a rudimentary, early stage of development). The correct answer is Choice D.

STRATEGY 3

> **IN DOUBLE-BLANK SENTENCES, GO THROUGH THE ANSWERS, TESTING THE FIRST WORD I**
> **N EACH CHOICE (AND ELIMINATING THOSE THAT DON'T FIT)**

In a sentence completion question with two blanks, read through the entire sentence to get a sense of it as a whole. Then insert the first word of each answer pair in the sentence's first blank. Ask yourself whether this particular word makes sense in this blank. If the initial word of an answer pair makes no sense in the sentence, you can eliminate that answer pair.

(Note: Occasionally this Funda will not work. In some questions, for example, the first words of all five answer pairs may be near-synonyms. However, the Funda frequently pays off, as it does in the following example.)

1.   Critics of the movie version of The Colour Purple .... its saccharine, overoptimistic mood at odds with the novel's more ....tone.

    (a)   applauded, sombre   (b)   condemned, hopeful

    (c)   acclaimed, positive   (d)   denounced, sanguine

    (e)   decried, acerbic

For a quick, general sense of the opening clause, break it up. What does it say? Critics...........the movie's sugary sweet mood.

How would critics react to something sugary sweet and over-hopeful? They would disapprove. Your first missing word must be a synonym for disapprove.

Now eliminate the misfits. Choices A and C fail to meet the test: applauded and acclaimed signify approval, not disapproval. Choice B, condemned, Choice D, denounced and Choice E, decried, however, all disapprobation; they require a second look.

To decide among Choices B, D, and E, consider the second blank. The movie's sugary, overly hopeful mood is at odds with the novel's tone: the two moods disagree. Therefore, the novel's tone is not hopeful or sugary sweet. It is instead on the bitter or sour side; in a word, acerbic, the correct answer is clearly Choice E.

Remember that, in double-blank sentences, the right answer must correctly fill both blanks. A wrong answer choice often includes one correct and one incorrect answer. ALWAYS test both words.

EXERCISE

DIRECTIONS (Qs. 1-35) : Fill the blank with correct alternatives.

1. The new government took ___________ last year.
   - (a) out
   - (b) after
   - (c) over
   - (d) upon

2. Mohan's career has taken some ___________ twists and turns.
   - (a) incentive
   - (b) interesting
   - (c) interactive
   - (d) intuitive

3. The bus ___________ fifty passengers fell ___________ the river.
   - (a) with; into
   - (b) for; upon
   - (c) over; on
   - (d) of; at

4. It is raining ___________ . Do not go out.
   - (a) heavily
   - (b) fast
   - (c) soundly
   - (d) strongly

5. She tries to adjust ___________ her relations.
   - (a) for
   - (b) at
   - (c) so
   - (d) with

6. She was remarkably ___________ in singing and dancing.
   - (a) accomplished
   - (b) conducive
   - (c) fluctuating
   - (d) cooperative

7. Sheila gained an advantage ___________ me.
   - (a) upon
   - (b) from
   - (c) on
   - (d) over

8. It is cool today, ___________?
   - (a) aren't it
   - (b) didn't it
   - (c) wasn't it
   - (d) isn't it

9. The book ultimately reached the person ___________ it belonged.
   - (a) who
   - (b) where
   - (c) to whom
   - (d) to who

10. Besides being reputed, he is famous for his ___________ .
    - (a) humanities
    - (b) hostility
    - (c) humility
    - (d) humiliation

11. There was a queue of people in the rain, patiently waiting to get ___________ the coach.
    - (a) at
    - (b) on
    - (c) onto
    - (d) in

12. I ___________ a terriable dream last night.
    - (a) had
    - (b) got
    - (c) saw
    - (d) have

13. Mr. Ahamed went ___________ a very tough time, when he incurred a loss in his business.
    - (a) about
    - (b) off
    - (c) through
    - (d) over

14. The lawyer advised the convict not to ___________ anything.
    - (a) hold up
    - (b) hold over
    - (c) hold back
    - (d) hold in

15. Hospital services across the capital _________ for three hours due to the strike.
    - (a) were disrupted
    - (b) had been disrupted
    - (c) are disrupted
    - (d) have disrupted
16. The School Annaual Sports Day is postponed and it would now _______________ on the 14th of next month.
    - (a) to be held
    - (b) been held
    - (c) being held
    - (d) be held
17. The coach leaves at 5.20, so get to the station __________ that.
    - (a) before   (b) after
    - (c) until   (d) from
18. When the morning _______the murder was discovered.
    - (a) came
    - (b) happened
    - (c) arrived
    - (d) occurred
19. The smell of the Sea called _____________ memories of her childhood.
    - (a) on   (b) black
    - (c) up   (d) for
20. He has the full facts ___ but is deliberately hiding them.
    - (a) under his sleeves
    - (b) upon his sleeves
    - (c) up his sleeve
    - (d) in his sleeves
21. The appearance of the city ________ day by day.
    - (a) could change
    - (b) changed
    - (c) had changed
    - (d) is changing
22. The police fired on the mob when they _________ .
    - (a) turned noisy
    - (b) turned violent
    - (c) became abusive
    - (d) fizzled out
23. There were so many ________ points in his speech that the audience ________ to get the message.
    - (a) superficial - listened
    - (b) relevant   - hastened
    - (c) interesting - tried
    - (d) irrelevant - failed
24. The little boy ran ________ fast that he was ________ for breath.
    - (a) so - gasping
    - (b) too - fighting
    - (c) so - inhaling
    - (d) very - struggling
25. He was so ________ at his job that he was asked to give a ________ to the visitors.
    - (a) adept - demonstration
    - (b) able - disclosure
    - (c) agile - demolition
    - (d) accurate - display
26. She was so ________ that she was ________ by all.
    - (a) proud : respected
    - (b) excellent : warned
    - (c) talented : praised
    - (d) stupid : admired
27. The ________ of the 'chief' was ________ upon him.
    - (a) title, bestowed
    - (b) name, dismissed
    - (c) title, imposed
    - (d) appointment, thrown

28. All orders must __________ the rules
    (a) conform to
    (b) conforms to
    (c) conforming with
    (d) conforms with
29. She failed to __________ to her name.
    (a) line up   (b) shine up
    (c) keep up   (d) rise up
30. As the doctor __________ into the room, the nurse handed him the temperature chart of the patient.
    (a) came
    (b) was coming
    (c) comes
    (d) is coming
31. The economic __________ has affected our sales tremendously.
    (a) showdown
    (b) slowdown
    (c) crackdown
    (d) touchdown
32. This house __________ ten rooms
    (a) consisted with
    (b) consist of
    (c) consists of
    (d) consists by
33. Have you even _____ the wolf cry ?
    (a) heard   (b) heard of
    (c) hear out   (d) hear
34. Afreen ________ that the weather was very pleasant that day ?
    (a) suggested
    (b) argued
    (c) announced
    (d) remarked
35. Mrs. Hall was prepared to excuse the scientist's strange habits and ________ temper.
    (a) irritate
    (b) irate
    (c) irritable
    (d) irritation

SOLUTIONS

1. (c) Take over, here it means came into force or effect
2. (b) interesting, exciting or fortunate
3. (a) with; into, here it means consisting of and plunged
4. (a) heavily or massively
5. (d) with is the rigtht preposition
6. (a) accomplished, proficient or skilful
7. (d) over
8. (d) It is cool today, isn't it? is the right tag question
9. (c) The book ultimately reached the person to whom it belonged.
10. (c) Besides being reputed, he is famous for his humility.
11. (c) There was a queue of people in the rain, patiently waiting to get onto the coach. Onto has the word to in it, which

reminds us that its meaning includes the sense of movement towards something. The preposition on does not have this sense of movement, and it tells you only about location.

12. (a) I had a terrible dream last night. Had is used because the action was completed before another action in the past.

13. (c) Mr. Ahamad went through a very tough time, when he incurred a loss in his business.

14. (c) The lawyer advised the convict not to hold back anything.

15. (a) Hospital services across the capital were disrupted for three hours due to the strike.

16. (d) The school Annual Sports Day is postponed and it would now be held on the 14th of next month. The sentence is in passive form of past participle.

17. (a) The coach leaves at 5:20, so get to the station before that.

18. (a) Arrive means to reach a destination by movement or progress; happen denotes an event coming to pass (in time, so that it is real and actual at some time); occur also means (of an event) coming to pass (in time, so that it is real and actual at some time); come means happen or arrive, example: Dawn comes early in June.

19. (c) The phrase call up here denotes having and bringing to mind a memory of something; bringing back knowledge from memory.

20. (c) Up (one's) sleeve means hidden but ready to be used: He still has a few tricks up his sleeve.

21. (d) The phrase day by day means gradually and progressively; "his health is weakening day by day."

22. (b) The police could only fire the mob when it turned violent.

23. (b) 24. (a) 25. (a)

26. (c) 27. (a)

28. (a) The phrase means to reach the necessary stated standard

29. (c) 'Keep up' means move or progress at the same rate.

30. (a) correct use of tense

31. (b) 'Slowdown' means a decline in economic activity.

32. (c) Consists of comprises of

33. (a) Have you heard is correct use.

34. (d) Here 'remarked' refers to giving your opinion about something or stating a fact.

35. (c) Since 'irritable' means showing a tendency to be easily annoyed.

<table>
<tr><td>CHAPTER
4</td><td></td></tr>
</table>

Parajumbles

SENTENCE OR WORD REARRANGEMENT

In this type of questions, basically, you are given a paragraph or sentence - but the sentences (in case of paragraph) or words (in case of sentence) are not in the right order. It's up to you to untie this knot and rearrange the sentences or words so that they logically make sense.

Sentences or words rearrangement questions are included in BANK exams as they

- Help students relate events in a logical manner
- Sequence sentences based on English usage skills

HOW TO TACKLE THESE TYPES OF QUESTIONS?

To tackle these types of questions, you have to know three things-

- Theme of the paragraph that might be created on un-jumbling the sentences
- Initiating sentence, which starts the paragraph
- Links have to be found between two sentences. Once a link of this type is created, it becomes easy to eliminate irrelevant choices.

HOW TO SAVE TIME WHILE SOLVING THESE QUESTIONS?

It is very important to read selectively and search for transition words or other keywords.

The best way is to establish a link between any two (or more) statements. Once a link is found, you get to know which statements will come together. Then, look in the options. Select the option with those statements together.

EXAMPLE 1.

    A. 1971 war changed the political geography of the subcontinent
    B. Despite the significance of the event there has been no serious book about the conflict
    C. Surrender at Dacca aims to fill this gap
    D. It also profoundly altered the geo-strategic situation in South-East Asia

    (a) ACBD   (b) CADB
    (c) BADC   (d) ADBC

Explanation : We can see that sentence A is most likely the starting sentence. Now that we know A is the starting sentence we can eliminate choice (b) and (c) as they start with C and B respectively.

This narrows down our possibilities to option (a) and option (d).

Now we can see in option (a), C follows sentence A but the gap spoken of in sentence C has no correlation with political geography of the subcontinent spoken of in sentence A , so we can rule out Option (a).

Therefore answer has to be option (d), as we can also see it elaborates on the change mentioned in sentence A.

EXERCISE

DIRECTIONS (Qs. 1-25) : In the following questions, the 1st and the last sentences of the passage are numbered 1 and 6. The rest of the passage is split into four parts and named P, Q, R and S. These four parts are not given in their proper order. Read the sentence and find out which of the four combinations is correct. Then find the correct answer.

1. 1. Education in India had a glorious beginning.
    P. But after the British rule, it faced many changes.
    Q. It went on for centuries with the same glory.
    R. English as the medium of instruction had a very great response.
    S. One of the changes was the introduction of English as the medium of instruction.
    6. As the Britishers left we had a complexity of opinions regarding English
    (a) PQRS   (b) QPSR
    (c) PQSR   (d) SRPQ

2. 1. It is easy to criticize the people at the helm, for the slow progress in every field.

P. We are well aware that the intellectuals are leaving our country for better employment opportunities.
Q. Then question remains unanswered because our country cannot show opportunities to the intellectuals.
R. Then, what about their obligation to the Motherland?
S. First, we should ask ourselves as to what is happening to the young intellectuals in India.
6. This situation of 'Brain-Drain' leads to a variety of problems.
    (a) PSQR   (b) RPSQ
    (c) PSRQ   (d) SPRQ

3. 1. It is the responsibility of parents to teach the young moral values in life.
    P. Many children take advantage of their parents busy schedule.
    Q. This result in children's ignorane of social values.
    R. The reason behind it is that parents are quite busy nowadays.

S. Nowadays parents spend very meagre time with children.

6. As such, the society is going away from the value system.

(a) SRPQ   (b) PQRS
(c) SQRP   (d) SPQR

4. 1. The man who does his duty without any selfish desire for fruit may be called a sanyasi as well as yogi.

P. The man who has achieved much evenness of temper will be serene, because his mere thoughts are changed with the strength of action.

Q. He would practise yoga. i.e., evenness of temper, and cannot but perform action.

R. The root of the matter is that one should not allow his mind to fit from object to desire to another and from that to a third.

S. But he who abstains from action altogether is only an idler.

6. A yogi is one who is not at teached to his objects of sense or to action and whose mind has ceased to roam restlessly.

(a) SRQP   (b) RQPS
(c) QRSP   (d) PRSQ

5. 1. This was an important day for Alattook.

P. It was a cold day, but Alatook would be warm.

Q. For the first time he was going to hunt seals alone.

R. First he put on his fur-lined jacket.

S. Then he put on mittens and boots of deerskin to protect his hands and feet from the cold.

6. Finally he picked up the gun he had cleaned so carefully the day before.

(a) PQRS   (b) QPRS
(c) PRSQ   (d) QRPS

6. 1. The most vulnerable section of the society are the students.

P. Revolutionary and new fledged ideas have a great appeal to them.

Q. Agitations may be non-violent methods of protest.

R. They cannot resist the charm of persuasion.

S. They are to be taught that without discipline they cannot get proper education.

6. However if these become violent, the antisocial elements get encouraged and they put all proper working out of gear.

(a) PRSQ   (b) RSQP
(c) SRPQ   (d) RPQS

7. 1. Venice is a strange city.

P. There are about 400 odd bridges connecting the islands of Venice.

Q. There are no motor cars, no horses and no buses there.

R. These small islands are close to one another.

S. It is not one island but a hundred islands.

6. This is because Venice has no streets.

(a) SRPQ   (b) PSRQ
(c) RQPS   (d) QSRP

8. 1. One of the most terrible battles of the American Civil War was fought in July 1863, at Gettysburg.

P. The chief speech on that occasion was given by Edward Everett, a celebrated orator.

Q. Lincoln was asked to make a few remarks.

R. In November of that year a portion of the battlefield was dedicated as a final resting place for men of both armies who died there.

S. Everett's speech lasted 2 hours. Lincoln's for 2 minutes; it was over almost before the crowd realized that it had begun.

6. But the Gettysburg speech is now one of the world's immortal pieces of literature.

(a) SQRP   (b) RPQS
(c) PQRS   (d) QPSR

9. 1. The teacher training agency in England hopes to make teaching one of the top three professions.

P. They have also demanded that the campaign should be matched by improved pay scales, work load and morale so as to avoid recruitment problems with an aim to raise the image of the teaching profession.

Q. A series of advertisements are now being screened showing famous people speaking about teachers they remember and admire.

R. An amount of $100 million has been set aside to combat the shortage of applicants for teacher training.

S. Teacher Unions have welcomed this campaign.

6. It is high time for the Indian Government also to think on similar lines and take steps to lift up the sinking morale of the teaching profession.

(a) QRPS   (b) RPSQ
(c) RQSP   (d) QPSR

10. 1. Some say that failure is like toxic waste.

P. I see failure more as a fertilizer.

Q. Thinking about it pollutes and undermines the attitudes needed for success.

R. The seeds of success must be planted afresh.

S. It can be used to enrich the soil of your mind.

6. Turning failure into a fertilizer is accomplished by using your errors as steps in learning.

(a) SRQP   (b) PQSR
(c) SPQR   (d) QPSR

11. 1. There are a lot of ways to communicate : speaking, singing, clapping, hooting.

P. Even animals communicate with one another.

Q. Only humans can express their thoughts and feelings in words because of our superior brain.

R. Both humans and animals also communicate through body language.

S. But their ways differ from the humans.

6. Sometimes we don't use words but make gestures (like traffic signs) or simple movements of the hand in order to communicate.

(a) PRSQ   (b) QPRS
(c) PQRS   (d) PSQR

12. 1. Fires in the Steppes or bushes scared humans earlier.

P. Gradually, they learnt to appreciate the power of fire.

Q. It gave them light and warmth and kept away wild animals.

R. About 700,000 years ago, humans started fire accidentally by lightning.

S. They could harden the tips of wooden spears and cook meat in it.

6. Soon they learnt to produce fire by striking flintstone and pyrite with each other or by rubbing lumbers.

(a) QSPR   (b) PQSR
(c) PQRS   (d) QRSP

13. 1. When the Impressionists
P. they made them look like
Q. everyday and often putting
R people you would see
S. painted pictures of people
6. more emphasis on the scene.

(a) RQPS   (b) SRQP
(c) PRQS   (d) SPRQ

14. 1. Sherlock Holmes is the
P. who is in a state of grace
Q. is raised to the status
R. because in him scientific curiosity
S. exceptional individual
6. of a heroic passion.

(a) PRQS   (b) SRQP
(c) SPRQ   (d) RPSQ

15. 1. The goals of our present system
P. schooling is to prepare
Q. students for the examination system
R. which will take them to the
S. of primary and secondary
6. best technical institutions in the country

(a) SPQR   (b) QPRS
(c) PRQS   (d) PSQR

16. 1. Egotism is the; most common fault of mankind.
P. However, with time it becomes an exaggerated form of self display.

Q. It is the product of a perfectly natural desire to display oneself.

R. This is necessary as it impairs the personality and frustrates all efforts at self improvement.

S. Beyond any shadow of doubt, it is a defect that ought to be constantly hunted down, and scotched.

6. One should always be on guard not to give into egotism.

(a) RSPQ   (b) PSRQ
(c) PQRS   (d) QPSR

17. 1. The watchman
P. and found two thieves
Q. woke up when
R. with black masks
S. he heard the dog barking
6. trying to get in

(a) QSRP   (b) PQRS
(c) QSPR   (d) SPQR

18. 1. The student
P. touched the
Q. arrived and
R. their teacher
S. feet of
6. with reverence

(a) RQSP   (b) QPSR
(c) QPRS   (d) QRSP

19. 1. This summer was the most
P. to believe that next
Q. and we have reason
R. scorching in living memory
S. year and the year after
6. will be hotter still

(a) SRPQ   (b) SPQR
(c) QSPR   (d) RQPS

20. 1. Falcons have sharp angular wings
P. to dive sharply
Q. and allow them
R. to chase their prey

S.   that give them the speed
6.   to capture their victims
(a)   QPRS   (b)   PRSQ
(c)   SRQP   (d)   SQPR

21. 1.   Everyone
P.   the case calmly
Q.   acknowledges
R.   who knows you
S.   when he considers
6.   that you have been wronged.
(a)   PSQR   (b)   QRSP
(c)   SRPQ   (d)   RQSP

22. 1.   It is those good works
P.   that lead to peak performance
Q.   which we do with passion
R.   our understanding of our
       purpose
S.   and which come to reflect
6.   in this life.
(a)   PRQS   (b)   QPSR
(c)   QSRP   (d)   SRQP

23. 1.   I am a self confessed
       technophobe.
P.   I believe that computer is
       responsible for the dying
       of the art of conversation.
Q.   I have come to hate
       technology and the way it
       dominates every aspect of
       life.

R.   For many, it has become
       the most important object
       both in home and at the
       workplace.
S.   One of the worst offenders
       is the computer.
6.   Small wonder then, that I
       have managed to keep this
       ubiquitous machine out of
       my home.
(a)   PQRS   (b)   QSRP
(c)   RPSQ   (d)   SRPQ

24. 1.   Moisturisers for the face
P.   as oily ones may block
Q.   in greater concentration on
       the face
R.   the oil glands found
S.   should be chosen carefully.
6.   and cause pimple/acne to
       break out.
(a)   SRPQ   (b)   SQPR
(c)   SPRQ   (d)   SPQR

25. 1.   These
P.   about the heavenly
Q.   experiments by the
       scientists
R.   with amazing knowledge
S.   will supply us
6.   bodies.
(a)   PSQR   (b)   PSRQ
(c)   QSRP   (d)   RQPS

SOLUTIONS

1.   (b)   2. (d)   3. (a)   4. (a)
5.   (b)   6. (a)   7. (a)   8. (b)
9.   (c)   10. (d)   11. (d)   12. (b)
13.   (d)   14. (c)   15. (a)   16. (d)
17.   (c)   The correct combination is
             QSPR.
18.   (b)   The correct combination is
             QPSR.
19.   (d)   The correct combination is
             RQPS.
20.   (c)   The correct combination is
             SRQP.
21.   (d)   The correct combination is
             RQSP.
22.   (b)   The correct combination is
             QPSR.
23.   (b)   The correct combination is
             QSRP.
24.   (c)   The correct combination is
             SPRQ.
25.   (c)

Voices and Speeches

ACTIVE & PASSIVE VOICE

Passive voice is used when the focus is on the action; not on who or what is performing the action. In passive voice, the object of a verb appears to perform an action so that the effect of that action appears to fall on the subject. In active voice, the subject of a verb performs an action. The effect of the action may or may not fall on an object, that is, the verb may or may not have an object.

Examples : The maid opened the door. The girl laughs, in the first sentence, 'opened' is the verb or the action; the 'maid' is the subject or the 'doer' who performs that action; and the 'door' is the object on whom the effect of that action is directed. In the second sentence, 'laughs' is the verb or the action; and the 'girl' is the subject or the doer of that action. There is no object because the effect of the girl's laughing cannot be directed at another object.

Example : His car was stolen. Here, the focus is on the fact that his car was stolen. It is not known, however, who did it. Example: A mistake has been made. In this case, the focus is on the fact that a mistake has been made, but nobody is blamed.

When interchanging active sentences in passive voice, note the following:

*   the object of the active sentence becomes the subject of the passive sentence
*   the finite form of the verb is changed (to be + past participle)
*   the subject of the active sentence becomes the object of the passive sentence (or is dropped)

RULES OF CHANGING ACTIVE VOICE

	ACTIVE VOICE	PASSIVE VOICE
Present Simple	He delivers the letters.	The letters are delivered by him.
Past Simple	He delivered the letters.	The letters were delivered by him.
Future Simple	He will deliver the letters.	The letters will be delivered by him.
Present Continuous	He is delivering the letters.	The letters are being delivered by him.
Past Continuous	He was delivering the letters.	The letters were being delivered by him.

Going to	He is going to deliver the letters.	The letters are going to be delivered by him.
Present Perfect	He has delivered the letters.	The letters have been delivered by him.
Past Perfect	He had delivered the letters.	The letters had been delivered by him.
Infinitive	He has to deliver the letters.	The letters have to be delivered by him.
Modals	He must deliver the letters.	The letters must be delivered by him.

USES OF PASSIVE

1. When the agent (=the person who does the action) is unknown, unimportant or obvious from the context.

   Tom was shot. (Who shot Tom is not known)

   This museum was built in 1774. (Unimportant agent)

   She was arrested. (Obviously by the police)

2. To make more polite or formal statements

   The room hasn't been cleaned. (more polite) You haven't cleaned the room. (less polite)

3. When the action is more important than the agent

   Around 12 people have been killed in the flood.

4. To put emphasis on the agent.

   The new mall will be inaugurated by the mayor.

DIRECT AND INDIRECT SPEECH

Conveying the exact words of the speaker in his own actual words without any change to another person is called 'the Direct Speech'. Sam said, "I am going to the market now". Reporting of what a speaker said in our own words to another person without quoting his exact words is called 'Indirect Speech'. Sam said that he was going to the market then.

Rules of changing Direct into Indirect Speech

Changes in Tenses : The past perfect and past perfect continuous tenses do not change.

	Direct Speech	**Indirect Speech**
Simple Present Changes To Simple Past	"I always drink tea", he said	He said that he always drank tea.
Present Continuous Changes To Past Continuous	"I am reading a book", she said.	She said that she was reading a book.
Present Perfect Changes To Past Perfect	She said, "He has finished his work"	She said that he had finished his work.
Present Perfect Continuous Changes To Past Perfect Continuous	"I have been to England", he told me.	He told me that he had been to England.
Simple Past Changes To Past Perfect	"Bill arrived on Saturday", he said.	He said that Bill had arrived on Saturday.
Past Perfect Changes To Past Perfect (No Change In Tense)	"I had just come back from work," he said.	He said that he had just come back from work.
Past Continuous Changes To Past Perfect Continuous	"We were living in Hong Kong", they told us.	They told us that they had been living in Hong Kong.
Future Changes To Present Conditional	"I will be in Italy on Saturday", she said	She said that she would be in Italy on Saturday.
Future Continuous Changes To Conditional Continuous	He said, "I'll be visiting mother next Monday."	He said that he would be visiting mother next Monday.

When it is uncertain if the statement is true or when we are reporting objectively, the past tense is often used.

Indirect Speech Conversion	**Direct Speech Condition**
Present Tenses in the Direct Speech are changed into Past Tense.	If the reporting or principal verb is in the Past Tense.
Do Not Change Tense of reported Speech in Indirect Speech sentence	If in direct speech you find say/says or will say.
	Direct speech the words within the quotation marks talk of a universal truth or habitual action.
	The reporting verb is in a present tense.

Words expressing nearness in time or places are generally changed into words expressing distance.

	Direct Speech	Indirect Speech
Change of place and time	Here	There
	Today	that day
	this morning	that morning
	Yesterday	the day before
	Tomorrow	the next day
	next week	the following week
	next month	the following month

	Direct Speech	Indirect Speech
Change of place and time	Now	Then
	Ago	Before
	Thus	So
	Last Night	the night before
	This	That
	These	Those
	Hither	Thither
	Hence	Thence
	Come	Go

Changes in Pronouns

The pronouns of the Direct Speech are changed where necessary, according to their relations with the reporter and his hearer, rather than with the original speaker.

	Direct Speech	Indirect Speech
The first person of the reported speech changes according to the subject of reporting speech.	He says, "I am in fifth class."	He says that he is in fifth class.
The second person of reported speech changes according to the object of reporting speech.	He says to them, "You have completed your job."	He tells them that they have completed their job.
The third person of the reported speech doesn't change.	She says, "She is in ninth class."	She says that she is in ninth class.

Changes in Modals

	Direct Speech	**Indirect Speech**
CAN changes into COULD	He said, "I can touch the ceiling".	He said that he could touch the ceiling.
MAY changes into MIGHT	He said, "I may buy a house"	He said that he might buy a house.
MUST changes into HAD TO	He said, "I must resign from the job"	He said that he had to resign from the job.
These Modals Do Not Change: Would, could, might, should, ought to.		
Would	She said, "she would apply for a visa"	She said that she would apply for a visa.
Could	He said, "I could climb the ladder."	He said that he could climb the ladder.
Might	Tom said, "I might help him".	Tom said that he might help him.
Should	She said, "I should go to the pub."	She said that she should go to the pub.
Ought to	She said to me, "you ought to wait for her."	She said to me that I ought to wait for her.

Changes in Imperative Sentences

Imperative sentences consist any of these four: Order, request, advice and suggestion.

Mood in Direct Speech	**Reporting verb in indirect verb**
Order	ordered
Request	requested / entreated
Advice	advised / urged
Never	told, advised or forbade (No need of "not" after "forbade")
Direction	directed
Suggestion	suggested to
Warning	warn
(If a person is addressed directly)	called

Changes in Exclamatory Sentences

Exclamatory sentences express emotions. Interjections such as Hurrah, wow, alas, oh, ah are used to express emotions.

Rules of conversion of Exclamatory Direct Speech into Indirect Speech

1.   Exclamatory sentence changes into assertive sentence.
2.   Interjections are removed.
3.   Exclamation mark changes into full stop.
4.   Wh- words like 'what' and 'how' are removed and before the adjective of reported speech we put 'very.'

Mood in Direct Speech	Reporting verb in indirect verb
sorrow	Exclaimed with sorrow/ grief/ exclaimed sorrowfully or cried out
happiness	exclaimed with joy/ delight/ exclaimed joyfully
surprise	exclaimed with surprise/ wonder/ astonishment
appreciation	applauded

Rules of conversion of Interrogative Direct Speech

Changes	Direct Speech	Indirect Speech Condition
Reporting Verb	said/ said to	Asked, enquired or demanded.
Joining Clause	If sentence begins with auxiliary verb	joining clause should be if or whether.
	If sentence begins with "wh-" questions	no conjunction is used as "question-word" itself act as joining clause.
Punctuation	Question Mark	Full Stop
Helping Verbs	sentences is expressing positive feeling	do/does is removed from sentence.
	if 'No' is used in interrogative sentences	do/does is changed into did.
	Did or has/have	Had

EXERCISE

DIRECTIONS (Qs. 1-25) : In the following questions, a sentence has een given in Active Voice/Passive Voice, Out of the four alternatives suggested, select the one which best expresses the same sentence in Passive/Active Voice.

1. They have made a film based on this novel.
   - (a) A film was based on this novel and made.
   - (b) A film have been made based on this novel
   - (c) A film, based on this novel, has been made
   - (d) A film has been based and made on this novel.

2. The people couldn't move me to the hospital and the doctor operated on me at home.
   - (a) I couldn't be moved to the hospital and was operated on at home by the doctor.
   - (b) I couldn't be moved to the hospital and I had to be operated on at home.
   - (c) I couldn't be moved to the hospital and I was operated at home by the doctor.
   - (d) I couldn't be moved to the hospital by the people and operated on at home.

3. Why did he deprive you of the membership?
   - (a) Why you were deprived of the membership?
   - (b) Why weere you depreived of his membership by him?
   - (c) Why was he deprived of his membership?
   - (d) Why were you deprived of your membership by him?

4. The news has been bought to us by him.
   - (a) He brought us the news
   - (b) He has brought us the news
   - (c) He was brought the news to us
   - (d) We brought the news to him.

5. Not a word was spoken by the criminal inself-defence.
   - (a) The criminal spoke not a word inself-defence.
   - (b) The criminal in self-defence spoke no word
   - (c) The criminal did not speak a word inself-defence
   - (d) The criminal spoke in self-defence not a word.

6. The agent had disclosed the secret before it was evening.
   - (a) The secret was disclosed by the agent before it was evening
   - (b) The secret had disclosed by the agent before it had been evening
   - (c) The secret had been disclosed by the agent before it was evening
   - (d) The secret was disclosed by the agent before it had been evening.

7. Surely the lost child must have been found by now.
   - (a) Surely must have found the lost child by now.
   - (b) Surely someone must have found the lost child by now
   - (c) Surely now must have found the lost child
   - (d) Now must have found the lost child surely.

8. We serve hot meals till 10.30 guests can order, coffee and sandwiches upto 11.30.

   (a) Hot meals are serving till 10.30: coffee and sandwiches are ordering by guests till 11.30.

   (b) Hot meals are being served till 10.30 : coffee and sandwiches are being ordered till 11.30.

   (c) Hot meals are served till 10.30, coffee and sandwiches may be ordered till 11.30.

   (d) Hot meals will be served till 10.30, coffee and sandwiches will be ordered upto 11.30.

9. Lie face-down; stretch your arms in front.

   (a) You are face down, arms are to be outstretched

   (b) You should be lying face down, with arms outstretched.

   (c) You should be lying face down; let arms stretch out.

   (d) Let face be down; let arms be stretched out.

10. The Greeks expected to win the international trophy.

   (a) It was expected that the Greeks would win the international trophy.

   (b) The international trophy was expected to be won by the Greeks.

   (c) It was expected that the Greeks will win the international trophy.

   (d) It was expected by the Greeks that they would win the international trophy.

11. She will bring cakes.

   (a) Cakes will be brought by her

   (b) Cakes are to be bought by her

   (c) Cakes are to be brought by her

   (d) Cakes will be bought by her

12. Promises should be kept.

   (a) You should have kept your promises.

   (b) One must keep one's promises.

   (c) You had to keep promises.

   (d) Promises should have been kept.

13. Give the order.

   (a) An order was given by someone.

   (b) Order was given.

   (c) Order given.

   (d) Let the order be given.

14. My neighbour described his history to me.

   (a) His history had been described by my neighbour to me.

   (b) His history was described to me by my neighbour .

   (c) Description of his history to me was done by my neighbour.

   (d) My neighbour's history was described to me by himself.

15. Many cities had been destroyed by the invaders in those days.

   (a) The invaders destroy many cities in these days.

   (b) Many cities were destroyes in those days by invaders

   (c) Many invaders destroyed cities in those days.

   (d) In those days the invaders had destroyed many cities.

16. Can she write an interesting story ?
    (a) Can an interesting story be written by her
    (b) Could an interesting story be written by her?
    (c) Can an interesting story be written for her ?
    (d) Can an interesting story be written to her?

17. The poet. Blake, wrote many poems for children.
    (a) Many are the poems written by children for the poet Blake.
    (b) Children wrote many poems by the poet Blake.
    (c) Many poems were written for children by the poet. Blake.
    (d) Many poems were written by children for the poet. Blake.

18. Each person exhibited various facial expressions.
    (a) Various facial expressions were being exhibited by each person.
    (b) Various facial expressions have been used by each person.
    (c) Various facial expressions exhibited by each person.
    (d) Various facial expressions were exhibited by each person.

19. The girls ate a mango yesterday.
    (a) A mango is being eaten by the girls yesterday.
    (b) A mango has been eaten by the girls yesterday.
    (c) A mango is eaten by the girls yesterday.
    (d) A mango was eaten by the girls yesterday.

20. Your manners irritate me..
    (a) I am being irritated by your manners.
    (b) I am irritated by your manners.
    (c) I am irritated by my manners.
    (d) Manners are irritating me.

21. The boys laughed at the old man.
    (a) The old man was being laughed at by the boys.
    (b) The old man was laughed at by the boys.
    (c) The old man was laughed by the boys.
    (d) The old man was being laughed by the boys.

22. Ideas are generated by Group discussions.
    (a) Group discussions have generated ideas.
    (b) Group discussions generates ideas.
    (c) Group discussions generated idea.
    (d) Group discussions generate ideas.

23. Who is singing such a sweet song?
    (a) By whom is such a sweet song sung ?
    (b) By whom is such a sweet song being sung ?
    (c) By whom is such a sweet song sang ?
    (d) By whom has such a sweet song sung ?

24. Please give me your pen and take your seat.
    (a) You are warned to give me your pen and take your seat.
    (b) You are ordered to give me your pen and take your seat.
    (c) Let your pen given me and take your seat.
    (d) You are requested to give me your pen and take your seat.

25. The prisoner is known to have assaulted the warden earlier too.

   (a) It is known that the warden has been assaulted by the prisoner earlier too.

   (b) It is known that the warden has assaulted the prisoner earlier too.

   (c) It is known that the prisoner has assaulted the warden earlier too.

   (d) The warden was assaulted by the prisoner earlier too.

DIRECTIONS (Qs. 26-45) : In the following questions, a sentence has been given in Direct / Indirect form. But of the four alternatives suggested, select the one which best expresses the same sentence in Indirect / Direct

---

26. I said to my friend. "Can you pick me up after work?"

   (a) I asked my friend if he can pick me up after work. '

   (b) I asked my friend if he could pick me up after work.

   (c) I told my friend to pick me up after work.

   (d) I told my friend if I could pick him up after work.

27. Suman said to me. "Did you enjoy the Olympic Games in London ?"

   (a) Suman asked me if I had enjoyed the Olympic Games in London.

   (b) Suman asked me did I enjoy the Olympic Games in London.

   (c) Suman asked me if I enjoyed the Olympic Games in London.

   (d) Suman asked me if I was enjoyed the Olympic Games in London.

28. My friend told me. "This is not a good book to read."

   (a) My friend told me that that will not be a good book to read.

   (b) My friend told me that this was not a good book to read.

   (c) My friend told me that that was not a good book to read.

   (d) My friend told me that that is not a good book to read.

29. Dhanya complained, "I am losing weight steadily."

   (a) Dhanya complains that she was losing weight steadily.

   (b) Dhanya complained that she was losing weight steadily.

   (c) Dhanya complains that she is losing weight steadily.

   (d) Dhanya complained that she is losing weight steadily.

30. My mother said "You have been sleeping for twelve hours."

   (a) My mother said that I had been sleeping for twelve hours.

   (b) My mother said that she had been sleeping for twelve hours.

   (c) My mother said that I have been sleeping for twelve hours.

   (d) My mother said that I was sleeping for twelve hours.

31. Rajan said to Urvashi. "I'm going to Kashmir tomorrow."

   (a) Rajan said Urvashi I am going to Kashmir tomorrow.

   (b)   Rajan said to Urvashi that he was going to Kashmir tomorrow.

   (c)   Rajan told to Urvashi he was going to Kashmir the next day.

   (d)   Rajan told Urvashi that he was going to Kashmir the next day.

32. She said to me. "Have you finished your work ?

   (a)   She asked me if she had finished my work.

   (b)   She asked me if she had finished her work.

   (c)   She asked me if I had finished my work.

   (d)   She asked me if I have finished my work.

33. "Turn around." he told her.

   (a)   He asked to her to turn around.

   (b)   He asked turn around.

   (c)   He told her turn around.

   (d)   He asked her to turn around.

34. He said. "I have been studying in this college for two years."

   (a)   He said for two years he studied in that college.

   (b)   He said that he had been studying in that college for two years.

   (c)   He said he studied in that college for two years.

   (d)   He said he had studied in that college for two years.

35. Mary said to Simon. "Sharon and Peter are getting engaged next month."

   (a)   Mary told Simon that Sharon and Peter were getting engaged next month.

   (b)   Mary told Simon that Sharon and Peter are getting engaged next month.

   (c)   Mary told Simon that Sharon and Peter will be getting engaged next month.

   (d)   Mary told Simon that Sharon and Peter was getting engaged next month.

36. He said, "I will return tomorrow."

   (a)   He said that he will return tomorrow.

   (b)   He said that he would return tomorrow.

   (c)   He said that he would return the next day.

   (d)   He said that I would return the next day.

37. "What a wonderful time we had there!" she exclaimed.

   (a)   She exclaimed that she had quite a wonderful time there.

   (b)   She exclaimed that she had quite a wonderful time there.

   (c)   She exclaimed that they had quite a wonderful time there.

   (d)   She exclaimed that they have quite a wonderful time there.

38. The teacher said to the students, " You should obey your parents. You should be of help to them."

   (a)   The teacher advised the students to obey their parents and added that they should be of help to them.

   (b)   The teacher commanded the student to obey their parents and further added that they should be of help to them.

   (c)   The teacher requested the student to obey their parents and added they should be of help of them.

   (d)   The teacher advised the students that they shoulds obey their parents and should be of help to them.

39.   My mother said, "Please go to the shop."

   (a)   My mother told me to please go to the shop.

   (b)   My mother requested me to go to the shop.

   (c)   My mother requested me going to the shop.

   (d)   My mother asked me to be going to the shop.

40.   The reporter said,"We have been following the matter closely for a month."

   (a)   The reporter said that they had been following the matter closely for a month.

   (b)   The reporter said that we had been following the matter closely for a month.

   (c)   The reporter said that they have been following the matter closely for a month.

   (d)   The reporter said that they has been following the matter closely for a month.

41.   "What are you doing here?" she asked me.

   (a)   She asked what I was doing here.

   (b)   She wants to know what I am doing here.

   (c)   She wants to know what I was doing here.

   (d)   She wanted to know what I was doing there.

42.   The lawyer said to his client, "We will win the case."

   (a)   The lawyer told to his client that they would win the case.

   (b)   The lawyer said that the client would win the case.

   (c)   The lawyer told the client that they should win the case.

   (d)   The lawyer told the client that they would win the case.

43.   The watchman warned the boys not to go deep into the case.

   (a)   The watchman said to the boys,"You are not going deep into the sea."

   (b)   The watchman said,"Boys, don't go deep into the sea.

   (c)   The watchman said, "Boys didn't go deep into the sea.

   (d)   The watchman said to the boys, "Why do you go deep into the sea.

44.   The shopkeeper told me to be kind enough to pay for the tape-recorder in cash.

   (a)   The shopkeeper said to me, "Will you pay for the tape-recorder kindly in cash."

   (b)   The shopkeeper said, "Be kind enough to pay for the tape-recorder in cash."

   (c)   The shopkeeper exclaimed to me, "Be kind enough to pay for the tape-recorder in cash!"

    (d) The shopkeeper ordered me, "PLease be kind enough to pay for the tape recorder in cash.

45. She asked her brother if he could give her some money them.

    (a) She said to her brother, "Could I give you some money now?"

    (b) She said to her brother, "Can you give me some money then?"

    (c) She said to her brother, "Can you give me some money now?"

    (d) She asked her brother, "Give me some money now."

SOLUTIONS

1. (c) A film, based on this novel, has been made

2. (a) I couldn't be moved to the hospital and was operated on at home by the doctor.

3. (d) Why were you deprived of your membership by him?

4. (b)

5. (c) The criminal did not speak a word in self-defence.

6. (c) The secret had been disclosed by the agent before it was evening.

7. (b) Surely some one must have found the lost child by now.

8. (c) Hot meals are served till 10.30: coffee and sandwiches may be ordered till 11.30.

9. (d) Let face be down : let arms be stretched out.

10. (d) It was expected by the Greeks that they would win the international trophy.

11.	(a)	12.	(b)	13.	(d)
14.	(b)	15.	(d)	16.	(a)
17.	(c)	18.	(d)	19.	(d)
20.	(b)	21.	(b)	22.	(b)
23.	(b)	24.	(a)	25.	(a)
26.	(a)	27.	(c)	28.	(c)
29.	(b)	30.	(a)	31.	(d)
32.	(c)	33.	(d)	34.	(b)
35.	(a)	36.	(c)	37.	(a)
38.	(d)	39.	(b)	40.	(b)
41.	(d)	42.	(c)	43.	(b)
44.	(b)	45.	(c)		

DIRECTIONS (Qs. 1-5): In the following questions, some of the sentences have errors and some have none. Find out which part of a sentence has an error. The number of that part is your answer. Your answer is (d) i.e., No error.

1. He is a university professor (a)/ but of his three sons (b)/ neither has any merit. (c)/ No error (d)

2. After knowing truth, (a)/ they took the right decision (b)/ in the matter. (c)/ No error (d)

3. It is time you (a)/ decide on your next (b)/ course of action. (c)/ No error (d)

4. He who has suffered most (a)/ for the cause, (b)/ let him speak. (c)/ No error (d)

5. A cup of coffee (a)/ is an excellent complement (b)/ to smoked salmon. (c)/ No error (d)

DIRECTIONS (Qs. 6-25) : Some of the sentences have errors and some have none. Find out which part of a sentence has an error. The number of that part is your answer. If there is no error, your answer is (d).

6. Judge in him (a)/ prevailed upon the father (b)/ and he sentenced his son to death. (c)/ No error (d).

7. Nine tenths (a)/ of the pillar (b)/ have rotted away. (c)/ No error (d).

8. One major reason (a)/ for the popularity of television is (b)/ that most people like to stay at home. (c)/ No error (d).

9. Our efforts are (a)/ aimed to bring about (b)/ a reconciliation. (c)/ No error (d).

10. Three conditions (a)/ critical for growing (b)/ plants are soil, temperature, chemical balance or amount of moisture (c)/ No error (d).

11. Instead of being (a)/ helpful he was (b)/ being hindrance. (c) / No error (d)

12. Where (a)/ have I (b)/ to deposit fees ? (c)/ No error (d)

13. By the time she had finished her work (a)/ I had nearly given up (b)/ all hope of arriving at the party in time. (c)/ No error (d)

14. Some categorically suspected (a) / having seen the (b)/ guard and thief together. (c) No error (d)

15. He was (a)/ not in a position to state (b)/ the speed the ship travelled. (c)/ No error (d)

16. When one hears of the incident (a)/ about the plane crash (b)/ he feels very sorry. (c)/ No error (d)

17. I went there (a)/ with a view to survey (b)/ the entire procedure. (c)/ No error (d)

18. It had laid (a)/ in the closet (b)/ for a week before we found it. (c)/ No error (d)

19. He was present (a)/ in the court (b)/ to give witness. (c)/ No error (d)

20. He laughed (a)/ her (b)/ as she fell off the tree. (c) / No error (d)

21. Hasan plays (a) / both – cricket and billiards (b) /at the national level. (c) / No error. (d)

22. My father gave me (a) / a pair of binocular (b) / on my birthday. (c) / No error. (d)
23. Kalidas is (a) / a Shakespeare (b) /of India. (c) / No error. (d)
24. The teacher as well as his students, (a) / all left (b) / for the trip. (c) / No error. (d)
25. More you (a) / think of it, (b) / the worse it becomes.(c) / No error. (d)

DIRECTIONS (Qs. 26-35) : In questions, a part of the sentence is underlined. Below are given alternatives to the underliend part at (a), (b) and (c) which may improve the sentence. Choose the correct alternative. In case no improvement is needed, your answer is (d).

26. Sordid and sensational books tend to <u>vitiate</u> the public taste.
   (a) divide
   (b) distract
   (c) distort
   (d) No improvement
27. <u>By studyding</u> AIDS has engaged many researchers in the last decade.
   (a) Important study
   (b) Now that the study
   (c) The study of
   (d) No improvement
28. His Master's thesis <u>was highly estimated</u> and is now being prepared for publication.
   (a) was highly discussed
   (b) was highly commended
   (c) is highly appraised
   (d) No improvement
29. No sooner had she realized her blunder <u>than she began to take</u> corrective measures.
   (a) then she began to take
   (b) than she began taking
   (c) when she began to take
   (d) No improvement

30. A good scholar <u>must be precise and possess originality.</u>
   (a) must be precise and original
   (b) must be possess precision and original
   (c) must be precision and possess originality
   (d) No improvement
31. His life is hanging **with** a thread.
   (a) from   (b) by
   (c) to
   (d) No improvement
32. After twenty years of exile, the prisoner was **in** the end of his tether.
   (a) on   (b) though
   (c) at
   (d) No improvement
33. Grandfather is often so tired that he drops in his armchair.
   (a) slides away
   (b) falls out
   (c) slips in
   (d) No improvement
34. The court was forced to respect the profundity of the learned judge's knowledge.
   (a) probity   (b) proximity
   (c) prodigality
   (d) No improvement
35. He has lost his nearly all many pets.
   (a) all his nearly many pets
   (b) his many pets nearly all of them
   (c) nearly all his many pets
   (d) No improvement

DIRECTIONS (Qs. 36-50) : In question, a sentence/ part of the sentence is underlined. Below are given alternatives to the underlined sentence/part of the sentence at (a), (b) and (c) which may improve the sentence. Choose the correct alternative. In case no improvement is needed your answer is (d).

36. If he <u>had</u> time he will call you
    (a) would have
    (b) would have had
    (c) has
    (d) No improvement
37. The workers are <u>hell bent at getting</u> what is due to them.
    (a) hell bent on getting
    (b) hell bent for getting
    (c) hell bent upon getting
    (d) No improvement
38. We are <u>looking forward to see</u> you tomorrow:
    (a) looking forward towards seeing
    (b) looking forward for seeing
    (c) looking forward to seeing
    (d) No improvement
39. they could not tell me <u>why did he not eat</u> his lunch.
    (a) why not had he eaten
    (b) why he did not eat
    (c) why had he not eaten
    (d) No improvement
40. He <u>who will bid the highest</u> will get the product.
    (a) who bids the highest
    (b) who the highest bids
    (c) who would bid the highest
    (d) No improvement
41. John <u>had told</u> me that he hasn't done it yet.
    (a) told
    (b) tells
    (c) was telling
    (d) No improvement
42. The clients <u>are waiting</u> outside since morning and will continue to wait until you meet them.
    (a) have waited
    (b) have been waiting
    (c) were waiting
    (d) No improvement
43. He may have grown taller <u>when i last saw him</u>
    (a) from when I last saw him
    (b) since I last saw him
    (c) before I last saw him
    (d) No improvement
44. While crossing the highway, a five year old child was knocked <u>out</u> by a passing car.
    (a) away   (b) up
    (c) down
    (d) No improvement
45. During his long discourse, he did not <u>touch</u> that point.
    (a) touch upon
    (b) touch in
    (c) touch of
    (d) No improvement
46. The climate of Karnataka <u>is cooler than</u> Tamil Nadu.
    (a) is cooler to
    (b) is cooler than of
    (c) is cooler than that of
    (d) No improvement
47. The Tsunami victims <u>suffered of</u> cholera.
    (a) suffered from
    (b) suffered under
    (c) suffered in
    (d) No improvement
48. <u>I gave to</u> Sana the keys.
    (a) I gave
    (b) I gave to the
    (c) I gave the
    (d) No improvement
49. <u>If he smokes less he might get rid of his cough.</u>
    (a) If he smoked less he would get rid of his cough.
    (b) If he had smoked less he might get rid of his cough.
    (c) If he smokes less he might have got rid of his cough.
    (d) No improvement.
50. <u>He compensated the loss to me.</u>
    (a) He compensated the loss for me.
    (b) He compensated me to the loss
    (c) He compensated me for the loss.
    (d) No improvement.

SOLUTIONS

1. (c) Neither is used for two things. For more than two things, none should be used.
2. (a) After knowing the truth will be correct usage.
3. (b) It is time/It is high time is followed by the clause in simple past that shows present time. Hence, decided on your next should be used.
4. (c) Replace let him speak by should be allowed to speak.
5. (d)
6. (a) Sometimes Common Nouns are used as Abstract Nouns as they express qualities. In this situation, we use 'the' before them. Hence. The Judge in him should be used.
7. (b) The structure of some sentences is :
Indefinite number + of + Noun
Indefinite quantity + of + Noun
In these sentences, the subject is one that comes after 'of'. Here, the word pillar is singular, hence, has rotted away should be used.
8. (c) Here, replace that most people like to stay at home by most of the people like to stay at home.
9. (b) The word aim takes preposition 'at'.

Hence, at bringing about should be used.
10. (c) Chemical balance and amount of moisture.
11. (c) Here, a hindrance .... should be used.
Look at the sentences :
To be honest, she was more of a hindrance than a help.
The high price is a major hindrance to potent buyers.
12. (b) Here, I have .... should be used.
13. (a) Here, By the time she finished her work (Simple Past) .... should be used.
14. (a) Here, Some were surprised/ Some categorically denied .... should be used.
15. (c) Here, the speed the ship sailed/travelled at .... should be used.
16. (b) Here, indefinite article i.e. about a plane crash should be used. No particular incident is evident here.
17. (b) With a View to should be followed by gerund i.e. suveying.
18. (a) Here, time period is given. Hence. Past Perfect Continuous i.e. It had been lying ....should be used.
19. (c) Here, to provide evidence/ as a witness .... should be used.

20. (b) Here, it is a preposition related error. Hence, at her should be used here.
21. (d)
22. (b) Delete 'pair of' before binocular because the word 'binocular' itself suggests a pair.
23. (b) 'a' should be replaced with 'the'. Here Kalidas is not Shakespeare but he is compared with Shakespeare.
24. (b) Delete 'all' before 'left'. Here the usage of 'all' is superfluous as 'the teacher as well as his students' itself signifies everyone.
25. (a) Add 'the' before 'more'. Here the sentence consists of two clauses- Principal and Subordinate, where the Principal clause should be given more stress by adding 'the' before 'more'.
26. (b) distract the public taste
27. (c) the study of AIDS
28. (b) was highly commended
29. (d)
30. (a) precise and original
31. (b) Hang by a thread/hair means : to be in great danger.
32. (c) Be at the end of your tether means : to feel that you cannot deal with a difficult situation any more because you are too tired, worried etc.
33. (d) drop into position in a chair
34. (d)
35. (c) nearly all his many pets

36. (a) would have correct
37. (c) fully committed to achieving a goal
38. (c) looking forward for seeing
39. (b) why he did not eat
40. (a) who bids the highest
10. (b) tells
42. (b) have been waiting
43. (b) since I last saw him
44. (c) knock down
45. (a) touch upon
46. (c) Here we compare the climate of Karnataka with the climate of Tamil Nadu and not with the Tamil Nadu itself; hence we use 'than that of'.
47. (a) If someone suffers from an unpleasant or difficult experience or situation, then we use 'suffer from.' Ex: Shiela is suffering from ill health. Lately factories are suffering from a desperate shortage of labours.
48. (a) The correct arrangement of sentence is - I gave Sana the keys.
49. (a) When you are using if to talk about something that is unlikely to happen or is impossible, use the past tense in the if-clause, not present. Ex: If someone gave me (NOT gives or would give me) the money, I'd buy a car tomorrow.
50. (c) 'He compensated me for the loss,' is the correct answer.

Reading Comprehension

Comprehension is the process of making meaning from a written text. Typically, a candidate might have difficulty understanding due to limited vocabulary and/or a lack of familiarity with the subject matter. Both these constraints may be remedied by reading more widely and making friends with a good dictionary.

How to Improve Reading Comprehension

Reading is all about information. It's not about the number of words you read, but the amount of value you extract from them. The key to improve reading comprehension isn't moving your eyes across a page more quickly. It's about creating a mental framework that helps you process words and ideas.

With a bit of practice, anyone can read faster and more productively. The steps outlined below will help you to extract the maximum amount of information in the least amount of time.

Before reading the text, ask yourself what you already know about its topic. Try to recall as much information as you can. Think of related ideas you've learned in the past. Make brief notes about your thoughts or discuss what you remember with others. Reading comprehension requires motivation, mental frameworks for holding ideas, concentration and good study techniques. Here are some suggestions.

Improve Your Reading Comprehension by Researching the Topic

Background information may appear on book covers and inner flaps of book jackets. Many books include an introductory section and a mini-biography about the author. Book publisher's websites may also include background information. Think about the information you read. Ask:

- What kind of text is this?

- What new information did I learn, and what do I expect to learn?

- Is this text informative or entertaining, fact or fiction?

- What interests me about this book?

Develop a Broad Background

Broaden your background knowledge by reading newspapers, magazines and books. Become interested in world events.

Improve Your Understanding

As you read, what questions come to mind? Read on to find the answers.

You can think about the questions and answers or jot them down on paper. Research indicates that writing notes by hand can increase comprehension and recall among students who are not learning disabled in writing. For those who have LDs in writing mechanics, pair the writing with discussion to improve understanding and recall.

Know the Structure of Paragraphs

Good writers construct paragraphs that have a beginning, middle and end. Often, the first sentence will give an overview that helps provide a framework for adding details. Also, look for transitional words, phrases or paragraphs that change the topic.

Identify the Type of Reasoning

Does the author use cause and effect reasoning, hypothesis, model building, induction or deduction, systems thinking?

Anticipate and Predict

Really smart readers try to anticipate the author and predict future ideas and questions. If you're right, this reinforces your understanding. If you're wrong, you make adjustments quicker.

Look for the Method of Organization

Is the material organized chronologically, serially, logically, functionally, spatially or hierarchicaley.

Create Motivation and Interest

Preview material, ask questions, discuss ideas with classmates. The stronger your interest, the greater your comprehension.

Pay Attention to Supporting Cues

Study pictures, graphs and headings. Read the first and last paragraph in a chapter, or the first sentence in each section.

Highlight, Summarise and Review

Just reading a book once is not enough. To develop a deeper understanding, you have to highlight, summarize and review important ideas.

Build a Good Vocabulary

For most educated people, this is a lifetime project. The best way to improve your vocabulary is to use a dictionary regularly. You might carry around a pocket dictionary and use it to look up new words. Or, you can keep a list of words to look up at the end of the day. Concentrate on roots, prefixes and endings.

As you read, make a list of unfamiliar vocabulary words. Look up the meanings of the words in the dictionary, and jot definitions down by hand. Writing definitions by hand will help you remember the definition much more than by typing or by reading alone.

Monitor Effectiveness

Good readers monitor their attention; concentration and effectiveness. They quickly recognise if they've missed an idea and backup to reread it.

Test Yourself to Determine How Well You've Learned the material.

After your reading session, quiz yourself on the main points. What was the main idea? Who are the characters in the story? What information did you learn? Jot down your thoughts in your own words to help you remember them and give you deeper insight into the topic. If expressive writing is difficult for you, jot shorter notes and discuss the reading with a friend or parent.

EXERCISE

DIRECTIONS (Qs. 1-50) : In the following passages, you have one brief passage with 5 questions following the passage. Read the passage carefully and choose the best answer to each question out of the four alternatives.

PASSAGE -1

Every profession of trade, every art and every science has its technical vocabulary, the function of which is partly to designate things or processes which have no names in ordinary English and partly to secure greater exactness in nomenclature. Such special dialects or jargons are necessary in technical discussion of any kind. Being universally understood by the devotees of the particular science or art, they have the precision of a amthematical formula. Besides, they save time, for it is much more economical to name a process than to describe it. Thousands of these technical terms are very properly include din every large dictionary, yet, as a whole, they are rather on teh outskirts of the English language than actually within its borders.

Different occupations, however, differ widely in the character of their special vocabularies. In trades and handicrafts and other vocations like farming and fishing that have occupied great numbers of men from remote times, the technical vocabuulary is very old. An average man now uses these in his own vocabularly. The special dialects of law, medicine, divinity and philosophy have become familiar to cultivated persons.

1. Special words used in technical discussion
    (a) may become part of common speech
    (b) never last long
    (c) should resemble mathematical formula
    (d) should be confined to scientific fields

2. The writer of this article is
    (a) a scientist
    (b) a politician
    (c) a linguist
    (d) a businessman

3.   This passage is primarily concerned with
     (a)   various occupations and professions
     (b)   technical terminology
     (c)   scientific undertakings
     (d)   a new language
4.   It is true that
     (a)   various professions and occupations often interchange words
     (b)   there is always a non-technical word that may be substituted for the technical word
     (c)   the average man often uses in his own vocabulary what was once technical language not emant for him
     (d)   everyone is interested in scientific findings
5.   In recent years, there has been a marked increase in the numebr of technical terms in the nomenclature of
     (a)   Farming
     (b)   Fishing
     (c)   Sports
     (d)   Government

PASSAGE-2

In May 1966, The World Health Organisation was authorised to initiate a global campaign to eradicate small pox. The goal was to eradicate the disease in one decade. Because similar projects for malaria and yellow fever had failed, few believed that smallpox could actually be eradicated, but eleven years after the initial organisation of the campaign, no cases were reported in the field.

The strategy was not only to provide mass vaccinations, but also to isoate patients with active small-pox in order to contain the spread of the disease and to break the chain of human transmission. Rewards for reporting small-pox assisted in motivating the public to aid health workers. One by one, each small-pox victim was sought out, removed from contact with others and treated. At the same time, the entire, village where the victim had lived was vaccinated.

Today small pox is no longer a threat to humanity. Routine vaccinations have been stopped worldwide.

6.   Which of the following is the best title for the passage ?
     (a)   The World Health Organisation
     (b)   The Eradication of Small-pox
     (c)   Small-pox Vaccinations
     (d)   Infectious Diseases
7.   What was the goal of the campaign against small-pox?
     (a)   To decrease the spread of small-pox worldwide.
     (b)   To eliminate small-pox worldwide in ten years.
     (c)   To provide mass vaccinations against small-pox worldwide.
     (d)   To initiate worldwide projects for small-pox, malaria and yellow fever at the same time.
8.   According to the paragraph what was the strategy used to eliminate the spread of small-pox?
     (a)   Vaccination of the entire village
     (b)   Treatment of individual victims.
     (c)   Isolation of victims and mass vaccinations
     (d)   Extensive reporting of out breaks
9.   Which statement doesn't refer to small-pox?
     (a)   Previous projects had failed.
     (b)   People are no longer vaccinated for it.
     (c)   The World Health Organisation mounted a worldwide campaign to eradicate the disease.
     (d)   It was a serious threat.

10. It can be inferred that
    (a) no new cases of small-pox have been reported this year.
    (b) malaria and yellow fever have been eliminated.
    (c) small-pox victims no longer die when they contract the disease
    (d) small-pox is not transmitted from one person to another.

PASSAGE-3

Two years later, in November 1895, he signed his final will. He left the bulk of his fortune, amounting to about £1,75,000 to a trust fund administered by Swedish and Norwegian trustees. The annual interest shall be awarded as prizes to those persons who during the previous year have rendered the greatest services to mankind. The interest shall be divided into five equal parts– now amounting to about £8,000 each– one of which shall be awarded to the person who has made the most important discovery or invention in the realm of physics, one to the person who has made the most important chemical discovery or improvement, one to the person who has made the most important physiological or medical discovery, one to the person who has produced the most outstanding work of literature, idealistic in character, and one to the person who has done the best work for the brotherhood of nations, the abolition or reduction of standing armies, as well as for the formation or popularization of peace congress.

11. The said prize is awarded
    (a) once in 5 years
    (b) every year
    (c) once in 4 years
    (d) once in 2 years

12. Which is the prize that is referred to in the passage?
    (a) Nobel Prize
    (b) Magsaysay Award
    (c) Pulitzer Prize
    (d) Booker Prize

13. The number of prizes in the field of science are
    (a) Four   (b) One
    (c) Three   (d) Five

14. Total annual prize money amounts to
    (a) £8,000   (b) £1,750,000
    (c) £350,000   (d) £40,000

15. Prize is awarded for outstanding work in
    (a) Chemistry
    (b) Literature
    (c) Physics
    (d) All the above

PASSAGE-4

If an opinion contrary to your own makes you angry, that is a sign that you are subconsciously aware of having no good reason for thinking, as you do. If someone maintains that two and two are five, or that Iceland is on the Equator, you feel pity rather than anger, unless you know so little of arithmetic or geography that his opinion shakes your own contrary conviction.

16. If someone else's opinion makes us angry, it means that
    (a) we are subconsciously aware of having no good reason for becoming angry
    (b) there may be good reasons for his opinion but we are not consciously aware of them
    (c) our own opinion is not based on good reason and we know this subconsciously
    (d) we are not consciously aware of any reason for our own opinion

17. "Your own contrary conviction" refers to
    (a) the fact that you feel pity rather than anger
    (b) the opinion that two and two are four and that Iceland is a long way from the Equator
    (c) the opinion that two and two are five and that Iceland is on the Equator
    (d) the fact that you know so little about arithmetic or geography

18. Conviction means
    (a) persuasion
    (b) disbelief
    (c) strong belief
    (d) ignorance

19. The writer says if someone maintains that two and two are five you feel pity because you
    (a) have sympathy
    (b) don't agree with him
    (c) want to help the person
    (d) feel sorry for his ignorance

20. The second sentence in the passage
    (a) builds up the argument of the first sentence by restating it from the opposite point of view
    (b) makes the main point which has only been introduced by the first sentence
    (c) simply adds, a further point to the argument already stated in the first sentence
    (d) illustrates the point made in the first sentence

PASSAGE-5

"People very often complain that poverty is a great evil and that it is not possible to be happy unless one has a lot of money. Actually, this is not necessarily true. Even a poor man, living in a small hut with none of the comforts and luxuries of life, may be quite contented with his lot and achieve a measure of happiness. On the other hand, a very rich man, living in a palace and enjoying everything that money can buy, may still be miserable, if, for example, he does not enjoy good health or his only son has taken to evil ways. Apart from this, he may have a lot of business worries which keep him on tenterhooks most of the time. There is a limit to what money can buy and there are many things which are necessary for a man's happiness and which money cannot procure.

Real happiness is a matter of the right attitude and the capacity of being contented with whatever you have is the most important ingredient of this attitude".

21. The phrase "on tenterhooks" means:
    (a) in a state of thoughfulness
    (b) in a state of anxiety
    (c) in a state of sadness
    (d) in a state of forgetfulness

22. It is true that:
    (a) money alone can give happiness
    (b) money always gives happiness
    (c) money seldom gives happiness
    (d) money alone cannot give happiness

23. A rich man's life may become miserable if he:
    (a) has evil son, bad health and business worries
    (b) does not enjoy good health
    (c) has business worries
    (d) has business worries and his only son has taken to evil ways

24. Which of the following is the most appropriate title to the passage?
    (a) Poverty, a great evil
    (b) The key of happiness
    (c) Contentment, the key of happiness
    (d) Money and contentment
25. Which of the following statement is true?
    (a) Only a poor but contented man can be happy
    (b) A poor but contented man can never be happy
    (c) A poor but contented man can be happy
    (d) A poor but contented man is always happy

PASSAGE- 6

The problem of water pollution by pesticides can be understood only in context, as part of the whole to which it belongs - the pollution of the total environment of mankind. The pollution entering our waterways comes from many sources, radioactive wastes from reactors, laboratories and hospitals; fallout from nuclear explosions; domestic wastes from cities and towns; chemical wastes from factories. To these is a added a new kid of fallout - the chemical sprays applied to crop lands and gardens, forests and fields. Many of the chemical agents in this alarming melange initiate and augment the harmful effects of radiation, and within the groups of chemicals themselves there are sinister and little - understood interactions, transformations and summations of effect.

Ever since the chemists began to manufacture substances that nature never invented, the problem of water purification have become complex and the danger to users of water has increased. As we have seen, the production of these synthetic chemicals in large volume began in the 1940's. It has now reached such proportion that an appalling deluge of chemical pollution is daily poured into the nation's waterways. When inextricably mixed with domestic and other wastes discharged into the same water, these chemicals sometimes defy detection by the methods in ordinary use by purification plants. Most of them are so complex that they cannot be identified. In rivers, a really incredible variety of pollutants combine to produce deposits that sanitary engineers can only despairingly refer to as "gunk".

26. All the following words mean 'chemicals' except:
    (a) sands
    (b) substances
    (c) pesticides
    (d) deposits
27. The main argument of paragraph 1 is:
    (a) that there are sinister interaction in the use of chemicals
    (b) that there are numerous reasons for contamination of water supplies
    (c) that there are many dangers from nuclear fallout
    (d) that pesticides are dangerous
28. The word 'gunk' in the last line refers:
    (a) to the waste products deposited by sanitary engineers
    (b) to the debris found in rivers
    (c) to unidentifiable chemicals found in water
    (d) to the domestic water supplies

29. Water pollution can only be understood:
    (a) in relation to world contamination
    (b) by the whole human race
    (c) in context
    (d) in relation to the number of pesticides that exist

30. Water contamination has become serious:
    (a) since water pollution was difficult to assess
    (b) since nature has taken a hand in pollution
    (c) since chemists began to use new substances
    (d) since businessmen authorised the use of chemicals.

PASSAGE-7

"Nobody knows my name" is the title of one of James Baldwin's celebrated books. Who knows the name of the old man sitting amidst ruins pondering over his hubble-bubble? We do not. It does not matter. He is there like the North Pole, the Everest and the Alps but with one difference. The North Pole, the Everest and the Alps will be there when he is not there any more. Can we really say this? "Dust thou act to dust returneth" was not spoken of the soul. We do not know whether the old man's soul will go marching on like John Brown's. While his body lies mouldering in the grave or becomes ash driven by the wind or is immersed in water, such speculation is hazardous. A soul's trip can take one to the treacherous shoals of metaphysics where there is no "yes" or "no". "Who am I?" asked Tagore of the rising sun in the first dawn of his life, he received no answer. "Who am I?" he asked the setting sun in the last twilight of his life. He received no answer.

We are no more on solid ground with dust which we can feel in our hands, scatter to the wind and wet with water to turn it into mud. For this much is sure, that in the end, when life's ceaseless labour grinds to a halt and man meets death, the brother of sleep, his body buried or burnt, becomes dust. In the form of dust he lives, inanimate yet in contact with the animate. He settles on files in endless government almirahs, on manuscripts written and not published on all shelves, on faces and hands. He becomes ubiquitous all pervasive, sometimes sneaking even into hermetically sealed chambers.

31. What is the difference between the old man and the North Pole, the Everest and the Alps?
    (a) he ponders over his hubble-bubble while they don't
    (b) they are known to all while he is known to none
    (c) they remain while he will soon become dust
    (d) they are not as old as he

32. What, according to the passage, happens to a person's soul after death?
    (a) the soul also dies with the body
    (b) the soul continues to live after the body is dead
    (c) the soul certainly becomes dust after death
    (d) it is dangerous to guess

33. Which of the following statement is true?
    (a) The rising sun told Tagore who he was
    (b) The rising sun did not tell Tagore who he was
    (c) The rising sun advised Tagore to ask no questions
    (d) The rising sun told Tagore that he would become dust

34. What happens to man after he becomes dust?
    (a) he disappears from the world for ever
    (b) he appears in the form of man again
    (c) he becomes all pervasive as dust
    (d) he often sneaks into hermetically sealed chambers

35. What figure of speech is used in the expression 'the brother of sleep'?
    (a) Simile
    (b) Metaphor
    (c) Oxymoron
    (d) Irony

PASSAGE-8

To write well you have to be able to write clearly and logically, and you cannot do this unless you can think clearly and logically. If you cannot do this yet you should train yourself to do it by taking particular problems and following them through, point by point, to a solution, without leaving anything out and without avoiding any difficulties that you meet.

At first you find clear, step-by-step thought very difficult. You may find that your mind is not able to concentrate. Several unconnected ideas may occur together. But practice will improve your ability to concentrate on a single idea and think about it clearly and logically. In order to increase your vocabulary and to improve your style, you should read widely and use a good dictionary to help you find the exact meanings and correct usages of words.

Always remember that regular and frequent practice is necessary if you want to learn to write well. It is no good waiting until you have an inspiration before you write. Even with the most famous writers, inspiration is rare. Someone said that writing is ninety-nine percent hard work and one percent inspiration, so the sooner you get into the habit of disciplining your-self to write, the better.

36. To write well, a person must train himself in
    (a) dealing with a difficult problem
    (b) not leaving anything out
    (c) thinking clearly and logically
    (d) following a step-by-step approach

37. Initially it is difficult to write because
    (a) a good dictionary is not used
    (b) ideas occur without any sequence
    (c) aids to correct writing are not known
    (d) exact usages of words are not known

38. According to the passage, writing style can be improved by
    (a) thinking logically
    (b) writing clearly
    (c) undergoing training
    (d) reading widely

39. Famous writers have achieved success by
     (a) using their linguistic resources properly
     (b) disciplining their skill
     (c) following only one idea
     (d) waiting for inspiration
40. All the following words mean 'exact' except
     (a) precise   (b) accurate
     (c) very   (d) erect

PASSAGE-9

Stuck with the development dilemma? Stay away from management courses. Seriously, one of the biggest complaints that organisations have about management courses is that they fail to impact the participants' on-the-job behaviour. Some management trainers stress the need for follow-up and reinforcement on the job. Some go so far as briefing the participants' managers on what behaviour they should be reinforcing back on the job. Other include a follow-up training day to review the progress of the participants. None of this is really going far enough.

The real problem is that course promoters view development as something which primarily, takes place in a classroom. A course is an event and events are, by definition limited in time. When you talk about follow-up after a course, it is seen as a nice idea, but not as an essential part of the participants' development programme. Any rational, empowered individual should be able to take what has been learnt in a course and transfer it to the work place - or so the argument goes. Another negative aspect of the course mindset is that, primarily, development is thought to be about skill-acquisition.

So, it is felt that the distinction between taking the course and behaving differently in the work place parallels the distinction between skill-acquisition and skill-application. But can such a sharp distinction be maintained? Skills are really acquired only in the context of applying them on the job, finding them effective and, therefore, reinforcing them.

The problem with courses is that they are events, while development is an on-going process which, involves, within a complex environment, continual interaction, regular feedback and adjustment. As we tend to equate development with a one-off event, it is difficult to get seriously motivated about the follow-up. Anyone paying for a course tends to look at follow-up as an unnecessary and rather costly frill.

41. What is the passage about?
     (a) personal management
     (b) development dilemma
     (c) management courses
     (d) course promotors' attitude
42. Which of the following statements is false?
     (a) Some management trainers stress the need for follow-up and reinforcement on the job
     (b) Some suggest a follow-up training day to review the progress of the participants
     (c) Some go to the extent of briefing the participants' managers on what behaviour they should be reinforcing back on the job
     (d) The real problem is that course promoters view development as something which does not take place during a course.
43. The writer's attitude, as reflected in the passage, is
     (a) critical
     (b) ironic
     (c) sympathetic
     (d) philosophical

44. The course promoters' attitude is
    (a) self-righteous
    (b) indifferent
    (c) easy-going
    (d) unprogressive
45. The word 'mindset' here means
    (a) a determined mind
    (b) a (fixed) attitude of mind
    (c) an open mind
    (d) mindful

PASSAGE-10

One may look at life, events, society, history, in another way. A way which might, at a stretch, be described as the Gandhian way, though it may be from times before Mahatma Gandhi came on the scene. The Gandhian reaction to all grim poverty, squalor and degradation of the human being would approximate to effort at self-change and self-improvement, to a regime of living regulated by discipline from within. To change society, the individual must first change himself. In this way of looking at life and society, words too begin to mean differently. Revolution, for instance, is a term frequently used, but not always in the sense it has been in the lexicon of the militant. So also with words like peace and struggle. Even society may mean differently, being some kind of organic entity for the militant, and more or less a sum of individuals for the Gandhian. There is yet another way, which might, for want of a better description, be called the mystic. The mystic's perspective measures these concerns that transcend political ambition and the dynamism of the reformer, whether he be militant or Gandhian. The mystic measures the terror of not knowing the remorseless march of time; he seeks to know what was before birth, what comes after death? The continuous presence of death, of the consciousness of death, sets his priorities and values: militants and Gandhians, kings and prophets, must leave all that they have built; all that they have unbuilt and depart when messengers of the buffalo-riding Yama come out of the shadows. Water will to water, dust to dust. Think of impermanence. Everything passes.

46. The Gandhian reaction of poverty is
    (a) a total war on poverty
    (b) self-discipline
    (c) self-abnegation
    (d) a regulated distribution of wealth
47. According to Gandianism, the individual who wants to change society
    (a) should destroy the existing society
    (b) must re-form society
    (c) must change himself
    (d) may change society without changing himself
48. Who, according to the passage, finds new meaning for words like revolutions, peace and struggle?
    (a) A Gandhian who believes in non-violent revolution
    (b) A militant
    (c) A mystic
    (d) A Gandhian who disciplines himself from within
49. The expression 'water will to water, dust to dust' means
    (a) water and dust can mix well
    (b) man will become water after death
    (c) man will one day die and become dust
    (d) man will become dust and water after death
50. What does society mean to a Gandhian?
    (a) a sum of individuals
    (b) an organic entity
    (c) a regime of living regulated by discipline from within
    (d) a disciplined social community

SOLUTIONS

1. (c)   2. (c)   3. (b)

4. (c) The average man often uses in his own vocabulary what was once technical language not meant for him

5. (d)

6. (b) The Eradication of Small-pox

7. (b) To eliminate smallpox world-wide in ten years.

8. (c) Isolation of victims and mass vaccinations

9. (a) Previous projects had failed.

10. (c) Small-pox victims no longer die when they contract the disease

11. (b)   12. (a)   13. (c)

14. (a)   15. (d)   16. (c)

17. (a)   18. (c)   19. (d)

20. (d)   21. (b)   22. (d)

23. (a)   24. (c)   25. (c)

26. (a)   27. (b)   28. (c)

29. (a)   30. (c)   31. (c)

32. (d)   33. (b)   34. (c)

35. (b)   36. (c)   37. (b)

38. (d)   39. (b)   40. (d)

41. (c) The passage is about the management courses

42. (d) Look at the sentence : The real problem is that course promoters view development as something which primarily, takes place in a class room.

43. (a) Critical

44. (d) Unprogressive

45. (b) a (fixed) attitude of mind

46. (b) self-discipline

47. (c) must change himself

48. (a) A gandhian who believes in non-violent revolution.

49. (c) Man will one day die and become dust

50. (c) a regime of living regulated by discipline from within

CHAPTER 1 — Analogy & Classification

ANALOGY

In questions based on analogy, a particular relationship is given and another similar relationship has to be identified from the alternatives provided.

For example :

1. Action Object Relationship

Illustration 1:

Shoot is to Gun as Eat is to ....

(a) Hunger (b) Thirst
(c) Dinner (d) Fruit

Sol. **(d)** The relationship between the given words is that 'shoot' is the action and 'Gun' is the specified object of action . Similarly 'eat' is the action and 'fruit' is the specified object.

2. Antonym Relationship

Illustration 2:

INTROVERT :EXTROVERT

(a) ANGLE : TANGENT (b) EXTREME : INTERIM
(c) AGAINST : FAVOUR (d) ACTION : LAW

Sol. **(c)** The related words are opposite in meaning .

3. Grammatical Relationship

Illustration 3:

Clever is to Beautiful as Sour is to.........

(a) Lemon (b) Cunning
(c) Loathing (d) Taste

Sol. **(b)** The related words are Adjectives.

4. Part Whole Relationship

Illustration 4:

MAN : MAMMAL

(a) HALL : SNOW (b) NATIVE : INHABITANT
(c) OFFSPRING : FAMILY (d) LIBERTY : URBANISM

Sol. **(c)** Man is a part of the whole species of mammal, so is an offspring of the whole family.

5.   Sequence Relationship

Illustration 5:

.........is to Dusk as Summer is to Monsoon.

(a) Evening   (b) Dawn

(c) Night   (d) Noon

Sol. **(a)**   Summer season is immediately followed by monsoon (rainy season) and evening is immediately followed by dusk.

6.   Volume Relationship

Illustration 6:

GALLONS : SWIMMING POOL

(a)   SPECTATORS : AUDITORIUM

(b)   CURRENCY : SHARES

(c)   DUST : MOUNTAIN

(d)   BOOKS : CATALOGUE

Sol. **(a)**   Gallons of water is needed to fill a swimming pool and large number of spectators can be admitted into an auditorium .

7. Relation Analogy

Illustration 7 :

Pigeon : Peace : : White flag : ?

(a) Enmity   (b) Victory

(c) Surrender   (d) War

Sol. **(c)**   Pigeon is a symbol of peace and white flag is a symbol of surrender.

8. Simple Analogy

Illustration 8 :

Cyclone is related to Anticyclone in the same way as Flood is related to .... ?...........

(a) Devastation   (b) Havoc

(c) River   (d) Drought

Sol. **(d)**   Both words are opposite to each other.

9. Choosing a Similar Word

Illustration 9 :

Potato : Carrot : Raddish

(a) Tomato   (b) Spinach

(c) Sesame   (d) Groundnut

Sol. **(d)** All grow underground.

10. Detecting Analogies

Illustration 10:

Mars : Mercury : Venus :
(a)   They have no opposite motion
(b)   They are evil planets
(c)   They are the planets nearest to the earth
(d)   They have no corresponding lucky stone.

Sol. **(c)**

11. Three Word Analogy

Illustration 11 :

Evaporation : Cloud : Rain
(a) Sneezing : Cough : Cold   (b) Accident : Injury : Pain
(c) Tanning : Leather : Purse   (d) Bud : Flower : Fragrance

Sol. **(b)**   First causes the second and second leads to the third.

12. Number Analogy

Illustration 12 :

583 : 293 : 488 : ?
(a)   777   (b)   945
(c)   1155   (d)   324

Sol. **(b)**   Sum of digits of the first number is 2 more than the sum of digits of
the second number.

13. Alphabet Analogy

Illustration 13 :

ACE : FHJ : : OQS : ?
(a)   PRT   (b)   RTU
(c)   TVX   (d)   UWY

Sol. **(c)**   Each letter of the first group is moved five steps forward to obtain
the corresponding letter of the second group.

CLASSIFICATION

Classification means 'to sort the items of a given group on the basis of a certain
common quality they possess and then spot the stranger or odd one out'.

ODD ONE OUT WORDS

In this type of classification, four words are given, out of which three are
almost same in matter or meaning and one word is different from the other
three. One has to find out the word which is different from the rest.

DIRECTIONS (Illustration 14) : Choose the word which is least like the other words in the group.

    (a) Copper   (b) Zinc

    (c) Brass   (d) Aluminium

Sol. (c) Here, all except Brass are metals, while Brass is an alloy. Hence, the answer is (c).

ODD ONE OUT LETTER COMPARISON

In this classification of letters, four groups of letters or a series of letters are given as options. One has to select the option as answer which does not share the commonness of the others.

DIRECTIONS (Illustration 15) : Choose the option which is least like the others in the group.

    (a) PTSQ   (b) UYXV

    (c) INMJ   (d) KONL

Sol. (c)

$$P \xrightarrow{+4} T \xrightarrow{-1} S \xrightarrow{-2} Q$$

$$U \xrightarrow{+4} Y \xrightarrow{-1} X \xrightarrow{-2} V$$

$$K \xrightarrow{+4} O \xrightarrow{-1} N \xrightarrow{-2} L$$

But,

$$I \xrightarrow{+5} N \xrightarrow{-1} M \xrightarrow{-3} J$$

GROUP OF NUMBERS

The group of numbers can be consecutive numbers in natural or reverse series, multiplication, subtraction and mathematical rules can also be used to frame the groups.

Illustration 16: Which of the following pair of numbers is different from the other three pairs ?

    (a) 14, 28   (b) 40, 80

    (c) 16, 32   (d) 15, 35

Sol. (d) In each pair the second number is double the first number. In option (d), the number 35 should have been 30, the very reason as to why it is the odd one out.

CHOOSING THE ODD NUMERAL

In this type of question, certain numbers are given, out of which all except one share some common property and hence are alike, while one is different and this number is to be chosen as the answer.

Illustration 17: Choose the one which is different from others in the group.

(a) 8	(b) 64
(c) 125	(d) 28

Sol. **(d).** All except 28 are perfect cubes of some number.

EXERCISE

DIRECTIONS (Qs. 1-30) : Out of the four choices given for each question, you have to select one that will maintain the relationship on the two sides of the sign : : the same if it is substituted for the question mark '?'

1.   12 : 30 : : 20:?
  (a) 25   (b) 32
  (c) 35   (d) 42

2.   3 : 10 : : 8, ?
  (a) 10   (b) 13
  (c) 14   (d) 17

3.   13 : 19 : : ? : 31
  (a) 21   (b) 23
  (c) 25   (d) 26

4.   48 : 122 : : 168 : ?
  (a) 284   (b) 286
  (c) 288   (d) 290

5.   TSR : FED :: WVU ?
  (a) CAB   (b) MLK
  (c) PQS   (d) GFH

6.   ACBD : EFGH : : OQPR –
  (a) STUV   (b) RSTU
  (c) UVWX   (d) QRST

7.   CEG : EGC : : LNP :
  (a) LPN   (b) UWY
  (c) NPL   (d) MOP

8.   E : V : : I : ....
  (a) Q   (b) R
  (c) S   (d) T

9.   ACE : FGH :: LNP ?
  (a) QRS   (b) PQR
  (c) QST   (d) MOQ

10.   211 : 333 :: 356 : ?
  (a) 358   (b) 359
  (c) 423   (d) 388

11.   Wine : Grapes :: Vodks : ?
  (a) Apple   (b) Potatoes
  (c) Oranges   (d) Flour

12.   Race : Fatigue : : Fast : ?
  (a) Food   (b) Hunger
  (c) Appetite   (d) Weakness

13.   9 : 80 : : 7 : ?
  (a) 48   (b) 50
  (c) 78   (d) 82

14.   Moon : Satellite : : Earth : ?
  (a) Sun
  (b) Planet
  (c) Solar system
  (d) Asteroid

15.   Ocean : Water : : Glacier : ?
  (a) Refrigerator
  (b) Ice
  (c) Mountain
  (d) Cave

16. Bank : River : : Coast : ?
    (a) Flood   (b) Waves
    (c) Sea   (d) Beach
17. Knife : Chopper : : ? : ?
    (a) Walking   :   Fitness
    (b) Swim   :   Float
    (c) Scissors   :   Cloth
    (d) Quilt   :   Blanket
18. Fury : Ire :: ? : ?
    (a) Amusement : Happiness
    (b) Joke   :   Laugh
    (c) Cry   :   Hurl
    (d) Convulsion : Spasm
19. Food : Hungry :: ? : ?
    (a) Thought   :   Politics
    (b) Water   :   River
    (c) Rest   :   Weary
    (d) Wine   :   Intoxication
20. Man : Walk :: Fish : ?
    (a) Swim   (b) Eat
    (c) Live   (d) Sleep
21. Medicine : Sickness :: Book : ?
    (a) Ignorance
    (b) Knowledge
    (c) Author
    (d) Teacher
22. Supervisor : Worker ::
    (a) Junior : Senior
    (b) Elder : Younger
    (c) Debtor : Creditor
    (d) Officer : Clerk
23. Thunder : Rain :: Night : ...
    (a) Day   (b) Dusk
    (c) Darkness   (d) Evening
24. NUMBER : UNBMER :: GHOST : ?
    (a) HOGST   (b) HOGTS
    (c) HGOST   (d) HGSOT
25. Court : Justice : : School : ?
    (a) Teacher   (b) Student
    (c) Ignorance (d) Education
26. 'JKLM' is related to 'XYZA' in the same way as 'NOPQ' is related to
    (a) RSTU   (b) YZAB
    (c) DEFG   (d) BCDE

27. 'Engineer' is related to 'Machine' in the same way as 'Doctor' is related to
    (a) Hospital   (b) Body
    (c) Disease   (d) Medicine
28. 'Chapter' is related to 'Book' in the same way as 'brick' is related to
    (a) heap   (b) building
    (c) clay   (d) mason
29. Marathon is to race as hibernation is to
    (a) Winter   (b) Sleep
    (c) Dream   (d) Bear
30. *Chef* is related to *Restaurant* in the same way as *Druggist* is related to .....?
    (a) Medicine   (b) Pharmacy
    (c) Store   (d) Chemist

DIRECTIONS (Qs. 31-50) : In each of the following questions, four terms have been given, out of which three are alike in some manner and one is different. Choose the odd one out.

---

31. (a) Venus   (b) Saturn
    (c) Earth   (d) Mercury
32. (a) Metre   (b) Furlong
    (c) Acre   (d) Mile
33. (a) Raniganj (b) Jharia
    (c) Baroda   (d) Bokaro
34. (a) Faraday   (b) Newton
    (c) Edison   (d) Beethoven
35. (a) RATES   (b) TREAT
    (c) GREAT   (d) HEARD
36. (a) YXWV   (b) TSRQ
    (c) HGFD   (d) MLKJ
37. (a) PUT   (b) END
    (c) OWL   (d) ARM
38. (a) STUA   (b) RQPA
    (c) MLKA   (d) HGFA
39. (a) BDYW   (b) CEXZ
    (c) DFYW   (d) EGXV
40. (a) UAZF   (b) SCXH
    (c) RDWJ   (d) KBPG

41.	(a) ABCD	(b) EGIK
	(c) ACDF	(d) CFIL
42.	(a) JUDGE	(b) SCANT
	(c) CROWD	(d) FLUSH
43.	(a) Rose	(b) Lotus
	(c) Marigold	(d) Lily
44.	(a) USTO	(b) OOT
	(c) TTOU	(d) SST
45.	(a) BCD	(b) NPR
	(c) KLM	(d) PQR

46.	(a) 248	(b) 326
	(c) 414	(d) 392
47.	(a) Mango	(b) Apple
	(c) Brinjal	(d) Grapes
48.	(a) JOT	(b) OUT
	(c) FED	(d) DIN
49.	(a) KP	(b) MN
	(c) HR	(d) GT
50.	(a) 9611	(b) 7324
	(c) 2690	(d) 1754

SOLUTIONS

1. **(d)** $12 = 3^2 + 3$,
$30 = 5^2 + 5$:
$20 = 4^2 + 4$:
$? = 6^2 + 6$

2. **(d)** $3 = 2^2 - 1$,
$10 = 3^2 + 1$
$8 = 3^2 - 1$,
$? = 4^2 + 1$

3. **(b)** 13 and 19 are primes with 17 left out in between.

4. **(d)** $48 = 7^2 - 1, 122 = 11^2 + 1$:
$168 = 13^2 - 1, ? = 17^2 + 1$

5. **(b)** The letters are consecutive and written in reverse order.

6. **(a)** A B C D   O P Q R
E F G H   S T U V

7. **(c)** CEG is formed by skipping the letters in between them, the second set EGC is formed by simply putting the first letter of CEG at last to form EGC, and so on.

8. **(b)** The 5th letter from A correspond to 5th from Z and therefore 9th letter 'I' from A would correspond 9th letter 'R' from Z.

9. **(a)** The three letters moved 5, 4, and 3 and steps forward respectively.

10. **(d)** $211 \Rightarrow 2+1+1 = 4 \left.\right]^{+5}$
$333 \Rightarrow 3+3+3 = 9 \left.\right]$

Similarly,

$356 \Rightarrow 3+5+6 = 14 \left.\right]^{+5}$
$388 \Rightarrow 3+8+8 = 19 \left.\right]$

11. **(b)** As Wine is made up by grapes, similarly Vodka is made up by rye or wheat or potatoes .

12. **(c)** Race causes fatigue and fast causes hunger.

13. **(a)** The logic is x : (x² – 1). So the missing number is $7^2 - 1$ i.e. 48.

14. **(b)** Moon is a satellite and Earth is a planet.

15. **(b)** First consists of the second.

16. **(c)** Bank is the land beside a river and coast is the land beside a sea.

17. **(d)** Both knife and chopper are used for the same purpose i.e. cutting. Similarly, both quilt and blanket are used for protection from cold.

18. **(d)** Second is more intense form of the first. Convulsion and spasm means any violent contraction of muscles.

19. **(c)** A hungry person requires food and a weary person requires rest.

20. **(a)** As a man covers some distance after walking, in the same way, a fish covers some distance after swimming. Hence the correct answer is (a).

21. **(a)** As medicine cures sickness, in the same way, books remove ignorance.

22. **(d)** As supervisor supervises the worker, in the same way, officer supervises the clerk.

23. **(c)** As 'Rain' is followed by 'Thunder', similarly 'Darkness' is followed by 'Night'.

24. **(d)** First two letters of the first term are in reverse order in the second term and so are the next two letters.

25. **(d)** First is the place where the second is imparted.

26. **(d)** Each letter of JKLM stands for each corresponding letter of XYZA, 14 places before.

27. **(c)** First tackles the second.

28. **(b)** As 'Chapter' is a part of a 'Book', in the same way, 'brick' is a part of a 'Building'.

29. **(d)** A marathon is a long race and hibernation is a lengthy period of sleep.

30. **(b)** Second is the working place of the first.

31. **(c)** All except Earth denote Roman or Greek Gods and Goddesses.

32. **(c)** All except Acre are units of measuring distance, while acre is a unit of area.

33. **(c)** All except Baroda are famous for coal fields.

34. **(d)** All except Beethoven were scientists, while Beethoven was a musician.

35. **(d)** E, A, T appears in some order in all other words.

36. **(c)** Letters not continuous.

37. **(a)** All other groups begin with a vowel.

38. **(a)** In all other groups, the first three letters are in a reverse alphabetical order.

39. **(b)** First and second letters are alternate: fourth and third letters are alternate.

40. **(c)** In other groups, there is a gap of one letter, two letters and three letters between successive pair of letters.

41. **(c)** This is the only group that does not follow any rule while the others follow some rule.

42. **(a)** In other pairs only one vowel is used

43. **(b)** All except Lotus grows on land while lotus grows in water.

44. **(a)** Except USTO, all others have at least one letter repeated.

45. **(b)** All other groups contain three consecutive letters of the alphabet.

46. **(d)** In all the rest numbers, the third digit is the product of first and second digit.

47. **(c)** Except 'Brinjal' all the rest are the names of fruits, while 'Brinjal' is the name of a vegetable.

48. **(b)** This is the only group containing two vowels.

49. **(c)** In all other groups, the first letter occupies the same position from A onward as the second letter occupies from Z backward e.g., K is the eleventh letter from the beginning and P is the eleventh letter from the end of the alphabet.

50. **(b)** In all other numbers, the sum of the digits is 17.

CHAPTER 2

Series & Inserting Character

SERIES

NUMBER SERIES

In this type of series, the set of given numbers in a series are related to one another in a particular pattern or manner. The relationship between the numbers may be

(i) Consecutive odd/even numbers,

(ii) Consecutive prime numbers,

(iii) Squares/cubes of some numbers with/without variation of addition or subtraction of some number,

(iv) Sum/product/difference of preceding number(s),

(v) Addition/subtraction/multiplication/division by some number, and

(vi) Many more combinations of the relationships given above.

Illustration 1 :

Find the missing term in the following sequence.

$$5, 11, 24, 51, 106, \ldots\ldots\ldots\ldots$$

Sol. Double the number and then add to it

1, 2, 3, 4 etc.

Thus the next term is $2 \times 106 + 5 = 217$.

Illustration 2:

Find the wrong term in the series $3, 8, 15, 24, 34, 48, 63$.

(a) 15	(b) 12
(c) 34	(d) 63

Sol. **(c)** $8-3=5; 15-8=7; 24-15=9$

$$34-24=10$$
$$48-34=14$$
$$63-48=15$$

Obviously difference should be 11 & 13 instead of 10 & 14.

Therefore, 34 is the wrong term.

ALPHABET SERIES

In this type of question, a series of single, pairs or groups of letters or combinations of letters and numbers is given. The terms of the series form a certain pattern as regards the position of the letters in the English alphabet.

Illustration 3 : In the following questions, various terms of a letter series are given with one term missing as shown. Choose the missing term out of the options.

AZ, GT, MN, ..., YB

(a) KF
(b) RX
(c) SH
(d) TS

Sol. **(c)** The logic is +6 and –6.

$$\begin{array}{c}
\quad -6 \quad\quad -6 \quad\quad -6 \quad\quad -6 \\
A\ Z \quad G\ T \quad M\ N \quad S\ H \quad Y\ B \\
\quad +6 \quad\quad +6 \quad\quad +6 \quad\quad +6
\end{array}$$

CONTINUOUS PATTERN SERIES

This type of question usually consists of a series of small letters which follow a certain pattern. However, some letters are missing from the series. These missing letters are then given in a proper sequence as one of the alternatives.

DIRECTIONS (Illustration 4) : In each of the following letters series, some of the letters are missing which are given in that order as one of the alternatives below it. Choose the correct alternative.

.... bcc .... ac .... aabb .... ab cc

    (a)   aabca   (b)   abaca   (c)   bacab   (d)   bcaca

Sol. **(c)** The series is b b c c a a / c c a a b b / a a b b c c.

The letter pairs move in a cyclic order.

ALPHA - NUMERIC SERIES

A series in which both alphabets and numbers are used is called Alpha numeric.

DIRECTIONS (Illustration 5) : In each of the following questions, a letter number series is given with one or more terms missing as shown by (?). Choose the missing term out of the given alternatives.

2A11, 4D13, 12G17, ?

    (a)   36I19   (b)   36J21   (c)   48J21   (d)   48J23

Sol. **(d)**   **1st number :** $2 \xrightarrow{\times 2} 4 \xrightarrow{\times 3} 12 \xrightarrow{\times 4} (48)$

       Middle letter : $A \xrightarrow{+3} D \xrightarrow{+3} G \xrightarrow{+3} (J)$

       3rd number : $11 \xrightarrow{+2} 13 \xrightarrow{+4} 17 \xrightarrow{+6} (23)$

INSERTING CHARACTER

In such type of questions, a figure, a set of figures, an arrangement or a matrix is given, each of which bears certain characteristics, be it numbers, letters or a group/ combination of letters/ numbers, following a certain pattern.

The candidate has to find a missing character in the figure out of the given options.

Let us develop the ability to identify missing character with the help of following examples.

Illustration 6 :

11	3	49
5	19	?
7	13	100

    (a)   96   (b)   120   (c)   144   (d)   100

Sol. **(c)** In a row the third term is the square of the average of the first two numbers.

$$\therefore \ ? = \left(\frac{5+19}{2}\right)^2 = 12^2 = 144.$$

EXERCISE

DIRECTIONS (Qs. 1-70): Find the missing term in the series.

1. EJO, TYD, INS, XCH, ?
    (a) NRW   (b) MRW
    (c) MSX   (d) NSX

2. J2Z, K4X, I7V, ?, H16R, M22P
    (a) I11T   (b) L11S
    (c) L12T   (d) L11T

3. B Y C X D W E ?
    (a) S   (c) T
    (b) U   (d) V

4. 3, 8, 35, 48, ?, 120
    (a) 64   (b) 72
    (c) 80   (d) 99

5. B D G K ? V
    (a) N   (b) P
    (c) Q   (d) M

6. B C D B D D B E D B F D
    B G ?
    (a) B D   (b) B F
    (c) H B   (d) D B

7. A D E H I L M P Q T U ?
    (a) X Y   (b) Y Z
    (c) U V   (d) V W

8. 3, 6, 18, 72, 360, ...
    (a) 1296   (b) 2160
    (c) 2254   (d) 4329

9. 5, 9, 21, 37, 81, ...
    (a) 153   (b) 150
    (c) 158   (d) 151

10. 1, 2, 10, 4, 3, 14, 9, 5, ...
    (a) 19   (b) 20
    (c) 17   (d) 18

11. Z, S, W, O, T, K, Q, G, ..., ...
    (a) N, C   (b) N, D
    (c) S, E   (d) O, D

12. E D C H G F K J I N ?
    (a) L M   (b) O P
    (c) M O   (d) M L

13. A L W B M X C N ?
    (a) V   (b) W
    (c) Y   (d) X

14. 0, 2, 2, 3, 3, 5, 8, 4, 10, ?
    (a) 6   (b) 7
    (c) 9   (d) 15

15. 2, 3, 10, 15, 26, 35, 50, 63, ?
    (a) 80   (b) 82
    (c) 83   (d) 84

16. 5, 14, 27, 44, 65, ?
    (a) 88   (b) 90
    (c) 109   (d) 130

17. 3, 5, 9, 17, 33, ?
    (a) 48   (b) 49
    (c) 63   (d) 65

18. 1, 2, 7, 7, 13, 12, ?
    (a) 19   (b) 18
    (c) 12   (d) 14

19. 5, 6, 10, 19, 35 ?
    (a) 50   (b) 55
    (c) 60   (d) 71

20. 4, 6, 6, 15, 8, 28, 10, ?
    (a) 36   (b) 39
    (c) 45   (d) 38

21. 1, 2, 9, ?, 65, 126
    (a) 28   (b) 82
    (c) 99   (d) 108

22. P 3 C   R 5 F   T 8 I   V 12 L ?
    (a) Y 17 O   (b) X 17 M
    (c) X 17 O   (d) X 16 O

23. CFL   EIK   GLJ   IOI   ?
    (a) KRH   (b) KRJ
    (c) JRH   (d) KOH

24. Z, L, X, J, V, H, T, F, ..., ...
    (a) R, D   (b) R, E
    (c) S, E   (d) Q, D

25. 2, 4, ?, 16, 32
    (a) 6   (b) 10
    (c) 8   (d) 12

26. 0, 7, 26, ?, 124, 215
    (a) 37   (b) 51
    (c) 63   (d) 88

27. 1, 8, 9, ?, 25, 216, 49
    (a) 60   (b) 64
    (c) 70   (d) 75

28. 2, 9, 28, ?, 126, 217
    (a) 36   (b) 42
    (c) 56   (d) 65

29. 2, 12, 36, 80, 150, ?
    (a) 194   (b) 210
    (c) 252   (d) 258

30. 25, 43, 44, 53, ?, 72
    (a) 55   (b) 63
    (c) 65   (d) 71

31. 24, 6, 18, 9, 36, 9, 24, ?,
    (a) 24   (b) 12
    (c) 8   (d) 6

32. 1, 1, 2, 3, 5, 8, 13, ?
    (a) 20   (b) 21
    (c) 28   (d) 36

33. 7, 13, 27, 53, ?, 213
    (a) 106   (b) 107
    (c) 105   (d) 108

34. 24, 46, 68, ?
    (a) 801   (b) 89
    (c) 88   (d) 810

35. 6, 7, 15, 46, 185 ?
    (a) 226   (b) 230
    (c) 271   (d) 926

36. 5, 8, 14, 26, ?, 98
    (a) 62   (b) 50
    (c) 40   (d) 35

37. 1, 3, 6, 10, 15, ?, 28
    (a) 20   (b) 21
    (c) 22   (d) 24

38. 14, 12, 21, ?, 28, 24, 35, 30
    (a) 16   (b) 18
    (c) 20   (d) 22

39. 1, 8, 81, 16, ?, 1296
    (a) 16   (b) 25
    (c) 64   (d) 125

40. 1, 1, 2, 6, 24, 120, ?
    (a) 1440   (b) 720
    (c) 480   (d) 240

41. 5, 9, 17, 33, 65, ?
    (a) 100   (b) 111
    (c) 129   (d) 145

42. 3, 4, 5, 5, 12, 13, 7, 24, 25, 9, 41 ?
    (a) 16   (b) 24
    (c) 35   (d) 40

43. 0, 1, 3, 7, 15, ?, 63
    (a) 18   (b) 21
    (c) 31   (d) 41

44. 1, 4, 27, 256, ?
    (a) 5   (b) 25
    (c) 3125   (d) 625

45. – a b a a a b a – a – a
    (a) a b a   (b) abb
    (c) aab   (d) b a b

46. 1, 1, 1, 2, 4, 8, 3 —, —
    (a) 6, 12   (b) 9, 18
    (c) 18, 27   (d) 9, 27

47. 2, 3, 10, 15, 26, —
    (a) 37   (b) 36
    (c) 35   (d) 48

48. 1, 1, 1, 2, 2, 4, 3, 8, 5, 16, 8 —
    (a) 24   (b) 32
    (c) 48   (d) 64

49. 24, 49, ?, 94, 15, 31, 59, 58
    (a) 51   (b) 63
    (c) 77   (d) 95

50. 4, 15, 16, ?, 36, 63, 64
    (a) 25   (b) 30
    (c) 32   (d) 35

51. 3, 6, 24, 30, 63, 72, ?, 132
    (a) 42   (b) 58
    (c) 90   (d) 120

52. 1, 1, 2, 4, 7, 11, 16, ?,
    (a) 20   (b) 21
    (c) 22   (d) 23

53. 8, 24, 16, ?, 7, 14, 6, 18, 12, 5, 5, 10
    (a) 14   (b) 10
    (c) 7   (d) 5

54. 8, 1, 64, 27, ?, 125
    (a) 216   (b) 196
    (c) 169   (d) 81

55. 5, 12, 7, 15, 8, 18, 10, ?
    (a) 28   (b) 21
    (c) 11   (d) 10

56. 78, 79, 81, ?, 92, 103, 119
    (a) 88   (b) 85
    (c) 84   (d) 83

57. b – a – bab – ab – a
    (a) a b a b   (b) b a b a
    (c) b a bb   (d) a bb a

58. a – baa – baa – ba
    (a) aab   (b) bab
    (c) bba   (d) bbb

59. a – bbc – aab – caaa – bca –
    (a) cabad   (b) bacba
    (c) bbaaa   (d) aabba

60. – baa – ba –aab –
    (a) baba   (b) bbaa
    (c) abbb   (d) bbab

61. abc – c – c –ba – – bca
    (a) abacb   (b) babac
    (c) baabc   (d) bacba

62. – b aa – bbb – ab –
    (a) a b a b   (b) a a b b
    (c) b a a b   (d) b b a b

63. ab – –a – dcacb – acd –
    (a) dcbdb   (b) cdbbd
    (c) dabdb   (d) cdbdb

64. 336, 210, 120, —, 24, 6, 0
    (a) 40   (b) 50
    (c) 60   (d) 70

65. 1, 1, 2, 4, 3, 27, 4 —, —
    (a) 5, 64   (b) 64, 81
    (c) 64, 5   (d) 16, 5

66. m n o n o p q o p q r s — — —
    — —
    (a) mnopq   (b) oqrst
    (c) pqrst   (d) qrstu

67. 3, 5, 9, 16, 22, 30, 41, ?
    (a) 49   (b) 50
    (c) 51   (d) 52

68. 2, 3, 6, 7, 10, ...
    (a) 11   (b) 13
    (c) 14   (d) 14

69. 8, 15, 24, 35, ...
    (a) 42
    (b) 52
    (c) 48
    (d) None of these

70. 1, 1, 4, 2, 9, 3, 16, 4, ...
    (a) 18   (b) 15
    (c) 25   (d) 32

DIRECTIONS (Qs. 71-88) : What should come in question mark?

71.

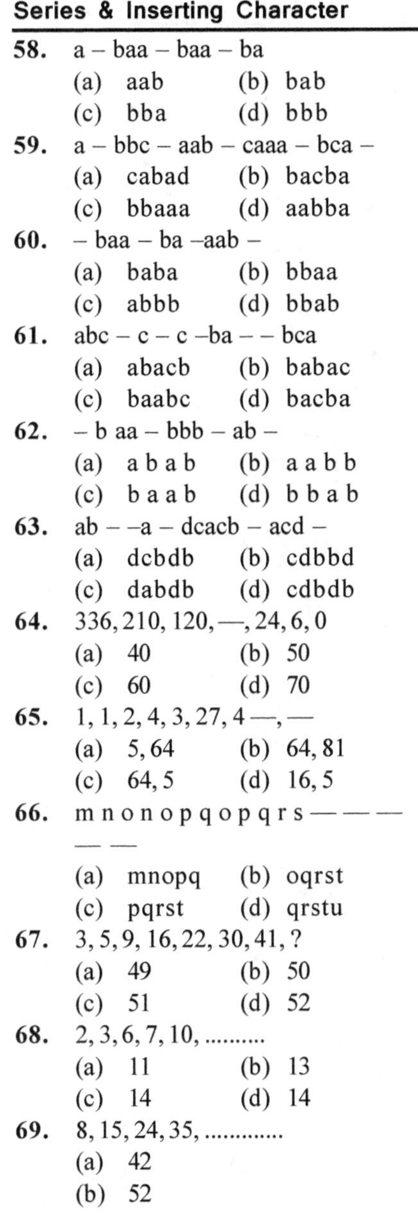

    (a) 19   (b) 23
    (c) 25   (d) 31

72.

    (a) 35   (b) 48
    (c) 72   (d) 120

73.

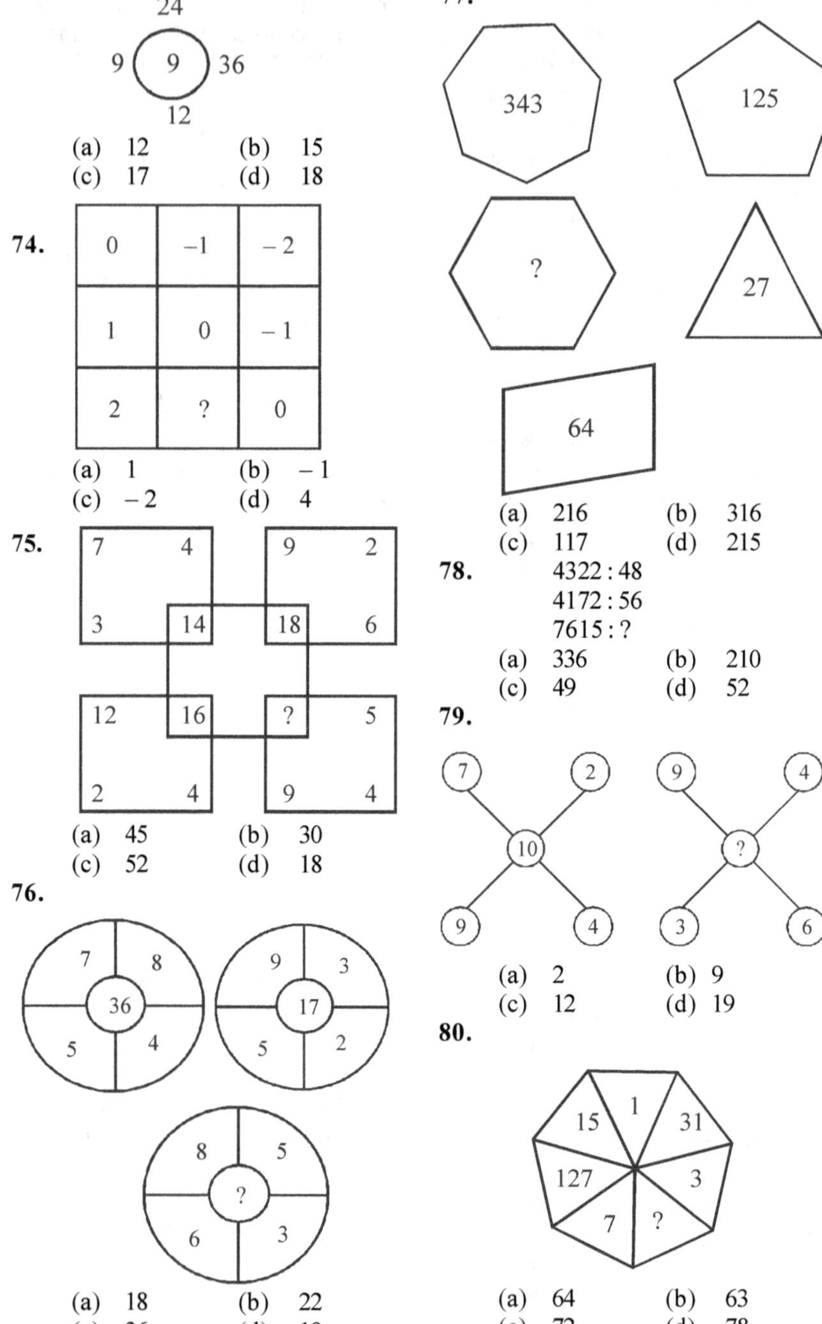

(a) 12 (b) 15
(c) 17 (d) 18

74.

(a) 1 (b) −1
(c) −2 (d) 4

75.

(a) 45 (b) 30
(c) 52 (d) 18

76.

(a) 18 (b) 22
(c) 36 (d) 19

77.

(a) 216 (b) 316
(c) 117 (d) 215

78.   4322 : 48
        4172 : 56
        7615 : ?

(a) 336 (b) 210
(c) 49 (d) 52

79.

(a) 2 (b) 9
(c) 12 (d) 19

80.

(a) 64 (b) 63
(c) 72 (d) 78

81.

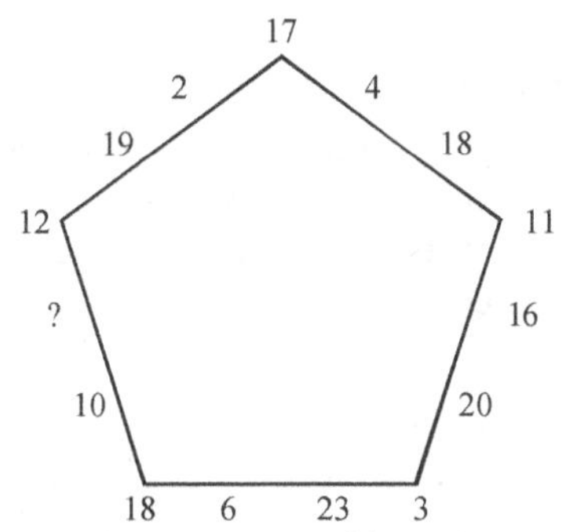

(a) 9   (b) 10
(c) 12   (d) 16

82.

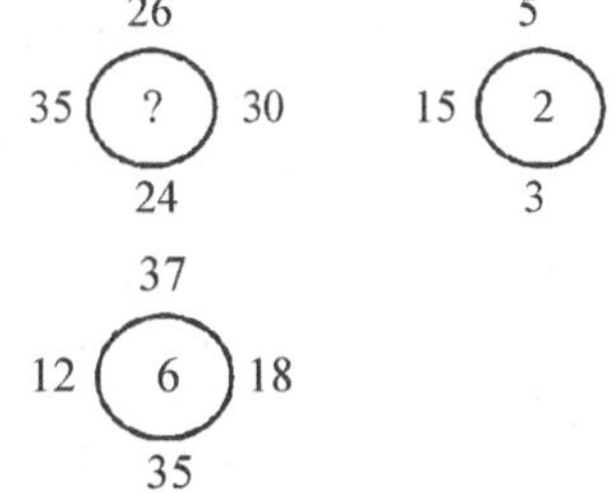

(a) 4   (b) 5
(c) 6   (d) 7

83.

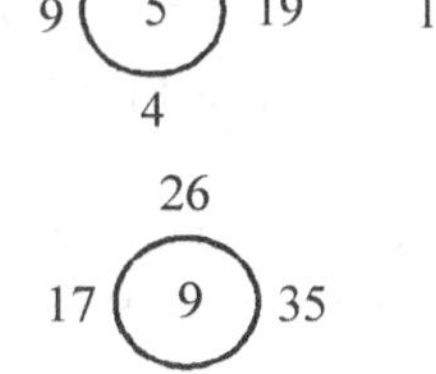

(a) 18   (b) 20
(c) 22   (d) 24

84.

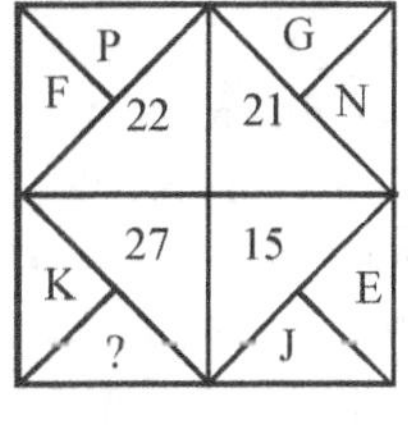

(a) M
(b) P
(c) 32
(d) None of these

85.

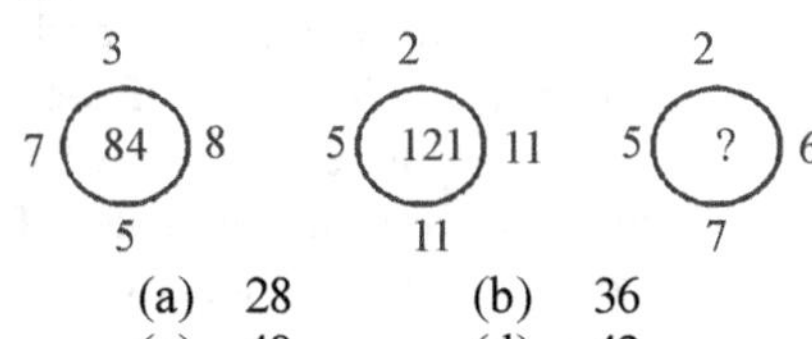

(a) 28   (b) 36
(c) 48   (d) 42

86.

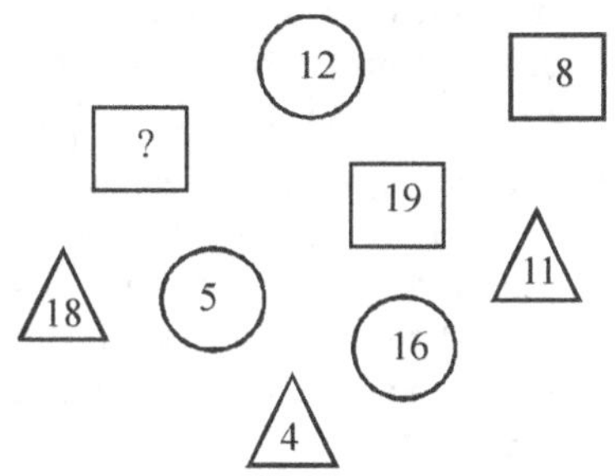

(a) 6   (b) 8
(c) 10   (d) 12

87.

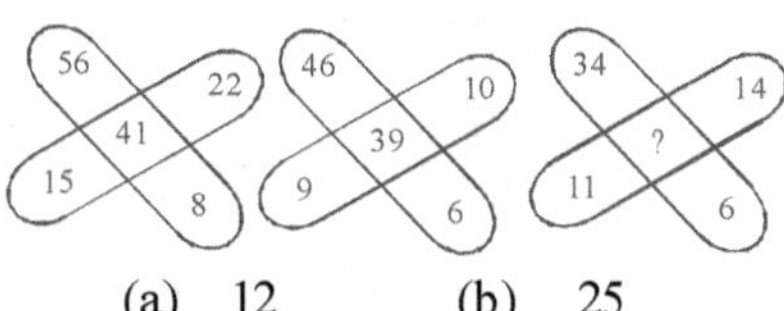

(a) 12   (b) 25
(c) 48   (d) 52

88.

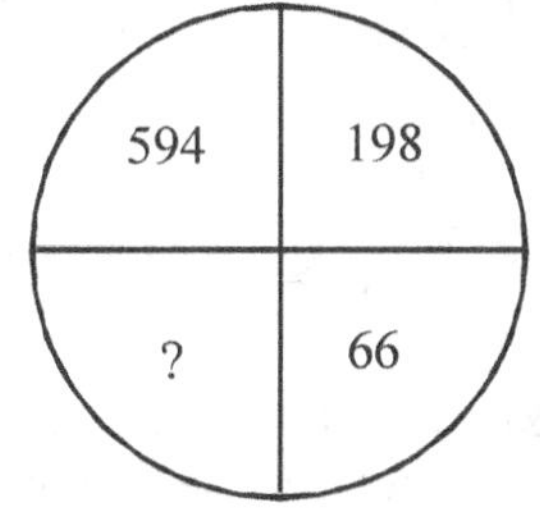

(a) 11   (b) 12
(c) 22   (d) 33

SOLUTIONS

1. **(b)** There is a gap of four letters between first and second, second and third letter of each term. Also there is a gap of 4 letters between the last letter of a term and the first letter of the next term.

2. **(d)** The first letters in odd numbered terms from the series J, I, H and in even numbered terms from the series K, L, M.

The sequence followed by the numbers is +2, +3, +4, +5, +6. The third letter of each term is moved two steps backward to obtain the third letter of the next term.

3. **(d)** There are two alternate series .

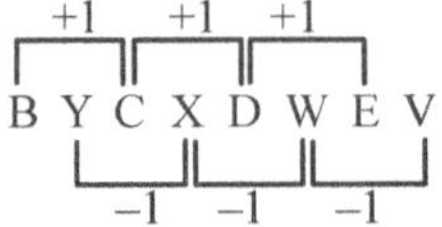

Series I : BCDE (natural order)

Series II : YXWV (reverse order)

4. **(d)** $3 = 2^2 - 1$,
$8 = 3^2 - 1$:
$35 = 6^2 - 1$,
$48 = 7^2 - 1$:
$? = 10^2 - 1$,
$120 = 11^2 - 1$.

5. **(b)** The difference between the letters increases at each step after beginning with two.

6. **(d)** The actual letters which are moving one step forward in the series are packed between B and D.

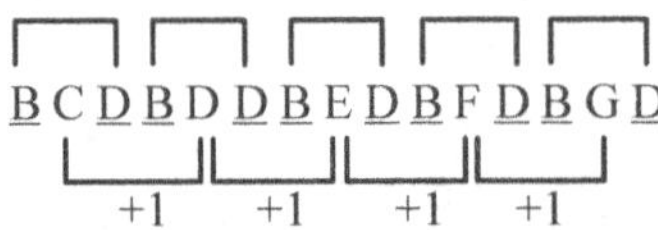

7. **(a)** The series is formed by moving the letters three and one steps forward alternately.

A D E H I L M P Q T U X Y
+3 +1 +3 +1 +3 +1 +3 +1 +3 +1 +3 +1

8. **(b)** The first number 3 is multiplied by 2 to get next number 6. The successive numbers are multiplied by 3, 4, 5, 6 etc.

Hence the number next to 360 × 6 = 2160.

9. **(a)** The sequence is × 2 – 1, × 2 + 3, × 2 – 5, × 2 + 7, × 2 – 9 etc.

The next number is 81 × 2 – 9 = 153.

10. **(d)** The given sequence comprises of three sequences

1, 4, 9, 16
(Square on 1, 2, 3, 4)

2, 3, 5, 7
(Prime number series)

10, 14, 18, 22
(Common difference 4)

The missing number belongs to series number three, so it is 18.

11. **(a)** The sequence is consisting of two series.

Z, W, T, Q,.......and S, O, K, G.

The logic is three steps backward and four step backward respectively.

12. **(d)** Three letters form a group. They are in natural series but the letters in each group are written backwards.

EDC   HGF   KJI   NML

13. **(c)** There are three alternate series.

A L W̱ B M X̱ C N Y̱

Series I : ABC

Series I : LMN

Series I : WXY

14. **(d)** The three series 0, 3, 8, 15; 2, 3, 4, 5; 2, 5, 10, 17 are considered.

15. **(b)** There are two series 2, 10, 26, 50, and 3, 15, 35, 63. Difference in the first and second series are 8, 16, 24, 32 etc, and 12, 20, 28, 36 etc.

16. **(b)** The difference of terms are 9, 13, 17, 21, 25 etc.

17. **(d)** $+2, +4, +8, +16, +32$.

18. **(a)** Given sequence consists of two series.

1, 7, 13, i.e., difference between consecutive nos is 6.

2, 7, 12, i.e., difference between consecutive nos is 5.

So, next number in the 1st series is 19.

19. **(c)** Add $1^2, 2^2, 3^2, 4^2, 5^2$ etc.

20. **(c)** First series : 4, 6, 8, 10

Second series : 6, 15, 28, ?

Differences in the second series are 9, 13, 17 etc.

Hence the next term is 28 + 17 = 45.

21. **(a)** The sequence is $0^3 + 1$, $1^3 + 1$, $2^3 + 1$, $3^3 + 1$, $4^3 + 1$, $5^3 + 1$ etc.

22. **(c)** P → R → T → V → X

3 → 5 → 8 → 12 → 17

C → F → 1 → L → O

23. **(a)** In each term the first letter is moved two steps forward, the second three steps forward and the third letter is moved one step backward to write the next term.

24. **(a)** These are two series in alternate places.

Z, X, V, T – and L, J, H, F, ...

25. **(c)** The terms exhibit the pattern $2^1, 2^2, 2^3$ and so on.

26. **(c)** Try the pattern $n^3 - 1$. n = 1, 2, ...

27. **(b)** Can you see that the pattern is $1^2, 2^3, 3^2, 4^3, 5^2, 6^3, 7^2$

28. **(d)** The terms exhibit the pattern $n^3 + 1$, n taking values 1, 2, 3.......

29. **(c)** $2 = 1^2 + 1^3$

$12 = 2^2 + 2^3$

$36 = 3^2 + 3^3$ and so on.

30. **(d)** Two sequences namely 25, 43, 44, 53, 71, 72

31. **(b)** Consider pairs of numbers:

24 : 6, 6 is one-fourth of 24 :

18, 9, 9 is half of 18;

36, 9 : 9 is one fourth of 36

32. **(b)** Each term is the sum of two preceding terms.

33. **(b)** $\times 2 \pm 1$. Thus $53 \times 2 + 1 =$

107

34. **(d)** Consecutive even number. Next term is 810.

35. **(d)** Preceding term is multiplied by 1, 2, 3, 4, 5 respectively and then 1 is added to the product

36. **(b)** Each difference is twice the previous difference.

37. **(b)** Triangular numbers, differences increase by 1.

38. **(b)** Two sequences of numbers are alter natively arranged.

39. **(d)** Numbers are in sets of three such that
$1^2 = 1, 2^3 = 8, 3^4 = 81$ and so on

40. **(b)** Preceding term is multiplied by 1, 2, 3, 4, 5 respectively to get the next term.

41. **(c)** Each number is 1 less than twice the preceding number.

42. **(d)** Numbers are in sets of three such that each set forms a pythagorean triple, i.e.

43. **(c)** Differences are $2^0.\ 2^1,\ 2^2,\ 2^3.$ and so on.

44. **(c)** The terms are
$1^1, 2^2, 3^3, 4^4$ and so on.

45. **(c)** $-$ abaaaba $-$ ab $-$ a
Option (c) i.e., aab provides the pattern a aba / aaba/ aaba

46. **(d)** Form groups of 3 numbers viz.
$$(1, 1, 1) = (1^1, 1^2, 1^3)$$
$$(2, 4, 8) = (2^1, 2^2, 2^3)$$
$$(3, -, -,) = (3^1, 3^2, 3^3)$$

47. **(c)** Each term is of the type

$n^2 + 1, n^2 - 1$, alternately, e.g.
$$2 = 1^2 + 1$$
$$3 = 2^2 - 1$$
$$10 = 3^2 + 1$$

48. **(b)** Two sequences of number appearing alternately. 2nd, 4th, 6th, 8th numbers are 1, 2, 4, 8, 16, 32
The other series is Fibonacci series.

49. **(d)** It is a combination of two series, namely
$24, 49, -94$; and $15, 31, 59, 58$
The two series correspond to x, $(2x + 1), (4x - 1), (4x - 2)$
Hence the missing term is
$4 \times 24 - 1 = 95$

50. **(d)** pattern is $2^2, 4^2 - 1, 4^2, 6^2 - 1, 6^2$ and so on.

51. **(d)** Terms taken alternately form two sequences.
These are
$$3, 24, 63\ ?$$
$$6, 30, 72, 132$$
$$3 = 2^2 - 1$$
$$6 = 2^2 + 2$$
$$24 = 5^2 - 1$$
$$30 = 5^2 + 5$$
$$63 = 8^2 - 1$$
$$72 = 8^2 + 8$$
Next term $= 11^2 - 1 = 120$

52. **(c)** Alternate terms from two sequences.

53. **(c)** Numbers are in sets of three: first set has middle term as the sum of the terms on its left and right: the second set has middle term as the difference and so on

54. **(a)** Alternate terms are cubes of even and odd numbers respectively.

55. **(b)** Second, fourth, sixth numbers are the sum of number on their left and right.

Quicker Method :

It consists of two alternate series. 5, 7, 8, 10 and 12, 15, 18

Next term in the second series is 21.

56. **(b)** Differences of the first set of differences are increasing by 1 viz.

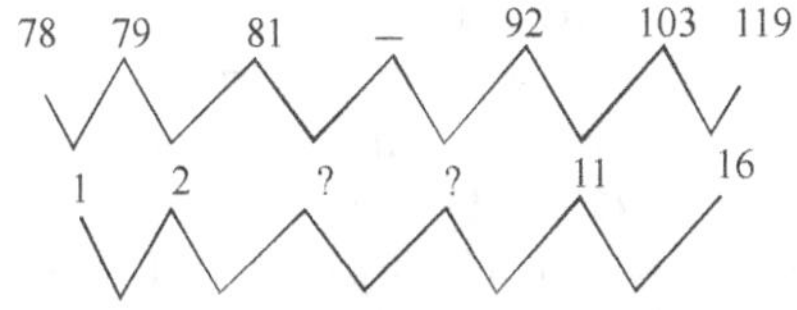

57. **(a)** b– a – bab – ab –

Option (a) i.e, abab provides the pattern baa bba / baa bb a

58. **(d)** a – baa – baa – ba

Option (d) i.e, bbb provides the pattern in which first six terms are laterally inverted as below. abbaab/ baabba

59. **(d)** a – bbc – aab – caaa – bca –

Option (d) i.e, aabba provides the pattern a abbca/ aab bca / aabbca/ a

60. **(c)** – baa – ba – aab –

Option (c) i.e, abbb provides the pattern a baabbabaabb

61. **(c)** abc – c–c– ba – bca

Option (c) i.e, baabc gives the

pattern abc/ cab /abc/ bca (abc rotate in cyclic order)

62. **(d)** –baa –bbb–ab–

Option (d) i.e, bbab provides the pattern b baa bb / bbaabb

63. **(d)** ab – a – dcacb – acd –

Option (5) i.e, cdbdb provides the pattern abcd/ abdc/ acdb

64. **(c)** Each number is of the form $n^3 - n$.e.g.

$336 = 7^3 - 7$

$210 = 6^3 - 6$

$120 = 5^3 - 5$

65. **(d)** Consider pair of numbers

$(1, 1) = (1, 1^3)$

$(2, 4) = (2, 2^2)$

$(3, 27) = (3, 3^3)$

$(4, 16) = (4, 4^2)$

Next number will be 5.

66. **(c)** The series is mno/nopq/ opqrs/pqrst

67. **(c)** Consider first three terms. Differences are 2, 4. In the next three, Differences are 6, 8. In the next three differences should be 10, 12.

68. **(a)** Add '1' and '0' to the alternate number to a series of odd-numbers in ascending order, viz.

$1 + 1, 3 + 0, 5 + 1, 7 + 0, 9 + 1, 11 + 0, 13 + 1$, etc. to get 2, 3, 6, 7, 10, 11, etc.

69. **(c)** The numbers in series are in the order of $3^2 - 1, 4^2 - 1, 5^2 - 1$, etc.

70. **(c)** It's the combination of two series,

$1, 2, 3, 4, 5, \ldots\ldots$ and $1^2, 2^2, 3^2, 4^2, \ldots$ etc., the numbers of the two series are placed alternatively.

71. **(d)** We have : $\sqrt{36}$ + $\sqrt{64}$ + $\sqrt{25}$ + $\sqrt{49}$ = 26 ;

$\sqrt{9}$ + $\sqrt{25}$ + $\sqrt{16}$ + $\sqrt{81}$ = 21

So, missing number

= $\sqrt{25}$ + $\sqrt{144}$ + $\sqrt{36}$ + $\sqrt{64}$

= (5 + 12 + 6 + 8) = 31

72. **(b)** We have (15 − 5) (2 + 6) = 80, (9 − 4) (7 + 6) = 65

So, missing number = (13 − 11) × (16 + 8) = 48.

73. **(a)** Add all the four numbers and then take its square root.

74. **(a)** Numbers on opposite sides of the central box are equal in magnitude but opposite in sign.

75. **(b)** $\dfrac{7 \times 4 \times 3}{6} = 14$;

$\dfrac{9 \times 2 \times 6}{6} = 18$

$\dfrac{12 \times 2 \times 4}{6} = 16$; $\dfrac{9 \times 4 \times 5}{6} = 30$

76. **(b)** $(7 \times 8) - (5 \times 4) = 36$

$(9 \times 3) - (5 \times 2) = 36$

$(8 \times 5) - (6 \times 3) = 22$

77. **(a)** The number in the center of each figure is the cube of the number of sides of the figure

78. **(b)** $7 \times 6 \times 1 \times 5 = 210$

79. **(a)** Subtract the sum of the even numbers from the sum of the odd numbers.

$7 + 9 = 16$ $9 + 3 = 12$

$2 + 4 = 6$ $4 + 6 = 10$

$16 - 6 = 10$ $12 - 10 = 2$

80. **(b)** Start at 1 and jump clockwise to alternate segments while adding 2, 4, 8, 16, 32, 64 in turn.

81. **(b)** Each side adds up to 50.

82. **(b)** The number inside the circle is the difference of the numbers on its left and right.

83. **(b)** The number at the centre is to be multiplied by 1, 2, 3, and 4, then subtract '1' from each to get the peripheral number.

84. **(b)** Putting A = 1, B = 2, C = 3, D = 4 ....

X = 24, Y = 25, Z = 26,

We have F + P = 6 + 16 = 22 :

G + N = 7 + 14 = 21

: J + E = 10 + 5 = 15.

Since K = 11, so value corresponding to missing letter

= (27 − 11) = 16

So, the missing letter is the 16th letter of the English alphabet, which is P.

85. **(d)** Multiply all the numbers around the circle and then divide it by 10 to get the number at the centre, viz.,

$\dfrac{7 \times 3 \times 8 \times 5}{10} = 84$

86. **(a)** This way, the sum of the numbers in the same shape totals 33.

87. **(b)** We have (56 + 15) − (22 + 8) = 41, (46 + 9) − (10 + 6) = 39

So, missing number = (34 + 11) − (14 + 6) = 25.

88. **(c)** Moving clockwise,

We have : 594 ÷ 3 = 198 : 198 ÷ 3 = 66.

So, missing number = 66 ÷ 3 = 22

Alphabet Test/ Coding-Decoding

ALPHABET TEST

In these types of questions, certain words are given. The candidate is required to arrange them in the order in which they are asked.

Illustration 1 :

How many letters are there in the word BACKLASH, each of which is as far away from the beginning of the word as it is from the beginning of the English alphabet ?

(a) None   (b) One

(c) Two   (d) Three

Sol. **(c)** Clearly, C and H are respectively the third and eighth letters in the word BACKLASH as well as in the English alphabet. Thus, there are two such letters.

ALPHABETICAL QUIBBLE

In this type of question, generally a letter series is given, be it the English alphabets from A to Z or a randomised sequence of letters. The candidate is then required to trace the letters satisfying certain given conditions as regards their position in the given sequence or the sequence obtained by performing certain given operations on the given sequence.

DIRECTIONS (Illustration 2) : The following question is based on the following alphabet series : A B C D E F G H I J K L M N O P Q R S T U V W X Y Z

Which letter will be the eighth to the right of the third letter of the second half of the English alphabet ?

(a) V   (b) W

(c) X   (d) Y

Sol. **(c)** Clearly, the first half of English alphabet has letters from A to M, and the second half has letters from N to Z.

The third letter of the second half is P, and the eighth letter to the right of P is X.

ALPHABETICAL ORDER

Arranging words in alphabetical order implies 'to arrange them in the order as they appear in a dictionary', i.e., as per the order in which the beginning letters of these words appear in the English alphabet.

First consider the first letter of each word. Arrange the words in the order in which these letters appear in the English alphabet.

In some cases, two or more words begin with the same letter. Such words should be arranged in the order of second letters in the alphabet.

DIRECTIONS (Illustration 3) : In each of the following questions, four words are given. Which of them will be the last if all of them are arranged alphabetically as in a dictionary?

(a)	Praise	(b)	Practical
(c)	Prank	(d)	Prayer

Sol. **(d)**   Practical, Praise, Prank, Prayer.

CODING

The word 'coding' stands for converting a **word from English language** into a certain pattern or expression.

Therefore, **code** is a sequence of letters/numbers, which is used in place of the original **word/series of numbers** that is coded.

Coding can be done for a group of letters (a word), a series of numbers or an **alphanumeric series** (*i.e.,* a series having both alphabets as well as numerals).

There are 4 types of coding methods :

I.   **Simple Arrangement.**

II.   **Direct Substitution.**

III.   **Pattern Substitution.**

IV.   **Alphanumeric coding.**

I.   **Simple Arrangement Method :** This is the most common & the simplest kind of coding. These codes are generally obtained by simply re-aligning the given alphabets in a word.

Illustration 4 :

In a code language, if TRAINS is coded as RTIASN, how will FLOWER be coded in the same language ?

(a)	LFOWER	(b)	LFWORE
(c)	WORELF	(d)	ERFLOW

Sol. (b)   TRAINS ⟶ RTIASN

In the above code, we can clearly observe that the code is obtained simply by interchanging the positions of 2 **consecutive alphabets** *i.e.,* TR becomes RT, AI becomes IA and NS becomes SN similarly,

FLOWER will be coded as (FL becomes LF, OW becomes WO and ER becomes RE) LFWORE.

FLOWER ⟶ LFWORE

Therefore, correct answer is option (b).

────────────────────────(**Quick Tips**)────────────────────────

Notes for simple arrangement :

(i)   Number of characters (letters / numbers / symbols) in the code should be same as that of the original word, otherwise coding is not possible.

(ii) Pay attention to the alignment of the word, *i.e,* if the letter/ number has changed its position from first to last & vice versa, a swap coding is possible.

For e.g. : in *e.g.* **3**, first group had 4 letters — 'FOUN' & there was a swap between letters at first & last position.

Swap coding

II.   Direct Substitution Method : When the characters, *i.e.,* letters of a word or numerals of a series are substituted by a coded character, *i.e.,* an alphabet, a numeral or a symbol & are placed in the coded word at similar positions as in the given / original word, it is known as direct substitution method.

These codes (substitutions) may either be in a direct fashion or in a jumbled fashion in order to make the questions tricky.

Illustration 5 :

In a code language, if SUGAR is coded as ZN and TEA is coded as FLD, how would you code GRATE in the same code language.

(a)   BNDFL   (b)   MBDFL
(c)   LDZMN   (d)   FLDZB

Sol. (b)   Original word :   S U G A R   T E A

Coded word :   Z N M D B   F L D

First we write the original words SUGAR & TEA and is corresponding alignment to these, we write down their codes respectively.

Therefore, we see that Z is coded for S, N for U, M for G, D for A and B for R, in the word SUGAR. While in the word TEA, F is substituted for T, L for E & D for A.

This implies that this code is in direct fashion as in both the words 'D' is coded for A.

Therefore, code for GRATE will be MBDFL.

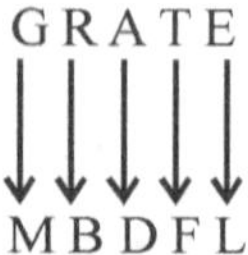

G R A T E

↓ ↓ ↓ ↓ ↓

M B D F L

So, correct answer option is (c).

──────────────────────────(**Quick Tips**)──────────────────────────

Notes for direct substitution :

(i)   If there are 2 words in the question for which codes are given and these 2 words have 1 or more same alphabets, then the codes for these alphabets will be the same as well.

(ii)   In case of confusion, note (a), *i.e.,* same codes in both the words for same alphabet, will help us identify that the question belongs to the category of **direct substitution.**

III. **Pattern Substitution Method :** This method involves the use of the alphabet series (A B C D E F ....X Y Z).

A certain word will be coded as certain other letters from the alphabet series following a certain pattern. It is further explained by examples.

Illustration 6 :

In a certain code language, the word 'RECTANGLE' is coded as TGEVCPING, then how is the word 'RHOMBUS' coded ?

(a)   TJOQDWV   (b)   UVWTJQN
(c)   TJQODWU   (d)   JTQOEWN

Sol.   (c) Each letter of the word RECTANGLE is moved two steps forward to obtain the corresponding letters of the code, *i.e.,*

R   E   C   T   A   N   G   L   E
│+2 │+2 │+2 │+2│+2 │+2 │+2│+2 │+2
↓   ↓   ↓   ↓   ↓   ↓   ↓   ↓   ↓
T   G   E   V   C   P   I   N   G

Similarly, we have :

R   H   O   M   B   U   S
│+2 │+2 │+2 │+2 │+2 │+2│+2
↓   ↓   ↓   ↓   ↓   ↓   ↓
T   J   Q   O   D   W   U

So, the desired code is 'TJQODWU'. So, option (c) is the correct answer.

IV. **Alpha-Numeric Series Coding:** Out of the entire alphabet series numbered 1 to 26, *i.e.,*

A	B	C	D	E	F	G	H	I	J	K
1	2	3	4	5	6	7	8	9	10	11

L	M	N	O	P	Q	R	S	T	U
12	13	14	15	16	17	18	19	20	21

V	W	X	Y	Z
22	23	24	25	26

it is difficult to remember each and every alphabets' numeric value, therefore, we just have to remember.

$E = 5, J = 10, O = 15, T = 20$ and $Y = 25$ which are multiples of 5.

In alphanumeric coding, the alphabets of the word are given and we code them in terms of their numeric value or some pattern according to their numeric values.

Illustration 7 :

If in a certain code language, 'MIRROR' is coded as '139181815', how will 'APPLE' be coded in the same language ?

(a)   11616125   (b)   3984145

(c)   1162254   (d)   11213147

Sol.   (a)   As we can see from the alphabet series, numeric values for the alphabets M is 13, I is 9, R is 18 and O is 15.

Similarly, for the word APPLE, $A = 1, P = 16, P = 16, L = 12$ & $E = 5$. So, the code is 11616125. Therefore, option (1) is the correct answer.

DECODING

The word decoding stands for converting a certain pattern or expressions, *i.e.,* the code, to a word from English language or a certain series of numbers.

In other words, decoding refers to the process of converting the code back to the original word.

Similar to coding, there are 4 types of Decoding Methods :

I.   **Simple Arrangement**

II.   **Direct Substitution**

III.   **Pattern Substitution**

IV.   **Alphanumeric Decoding**

We would first like you to go back and revise the four types of CODING methods before we move on.

I.   **Simple Arrangement Method :** Under this, the code will be obtained simply by re-arrangement of the alphabets of the word.

The questions will test you on decoding these codes.

Illustration 8 :

In a certain language, 'SIMPLE' is written as 'ISPMEL' and 'CHAPTER' is written as 'HCPARET'. Then 'LFWORE' stands for which word ?
(a)   LOWFER   (b)   FLOREW
(c)   FLOWER   (d)   WORFEL

Sol. (c)   SIMPLE ——→ ISPMEL

The word 'SIMPLE' is of 6 letters and so is the code given in the question. Therefore, we have to follow the pattern of the word 'SIMPLE'.

In the above code, we can clearly observe that the code is obtained simply by inter changing the positions of consecutive alphabets, *i.e.,*

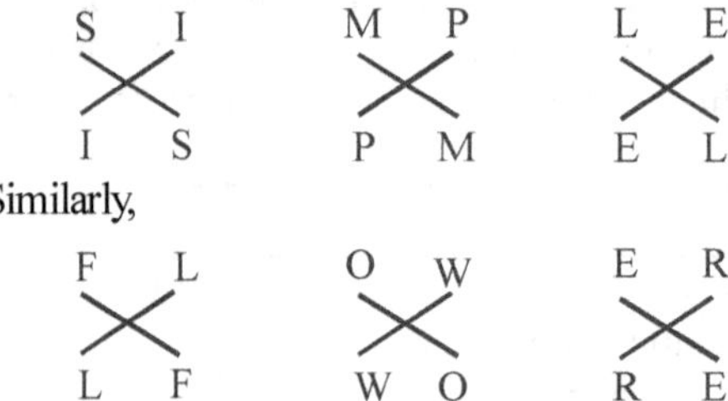

Similarly,

Hence, option (3) is the correct answer. 'FLOWER' is the word for which the code is given.

II.   Direct Substitution Method : In these kind of questions, there will be one or more words given in the question for which codes will be given either in direct fashion or in jumbled up fashion. We'll discuss both.

We will be asked to find out the original word (s) for the given code(s).

Illustration 9 :

In a certain code language, if P O U R I N G is written as x f n p l o m, S A M P L E is written as z e h x c j and W H I T E N E R is written as a t l k j o j p.

Then which word is written as 'hjecz' ?
(a)   LEAMS   (b)   SMEAL
(c)   MEALS   (d)   MALES

Sol. (c) The codes for the three words are direct substitution of the small alphabets for the capital ones, because 'N' & 'I' are codes as 'o' & 'l' respectively in both POURING as well as WHITENER, while 'E' is written as 'j' both the times in the word WHITENER and also in the word SAMPLE.

Words	P	O	U	R	I	N	G	S	A	M	P	L	E	W	H	I	T	E	N	E	R
Codes	x	f	n	p	l	o	m	z	e	h	x	c	j	a	t	l	k	j	o	j	p

Letter	P	O	U	R	I	N	G	S	A	M	L	E	W	H	T
Codes :	x	f	n	p	l	o	m	z	e	h	c	j	a	t	k

Therefore, the code 'h j e c z' stands for MEALS.

deriving the word from the code (see arrows)
Hence, option (3) is the correct answer.

── **Quick Tips** ──

(i)   Spotout the common letters in the wrds and try to find the code for the common letters first.

(ii) As soon as you find the codes for some letters, tick those letters as well as codes so you don't keep checking them again & again. This will save your time & save you from any kind of confusion while solving the questions.

Illustration 10 :

ZGCX :

(a)   WORE   (b)   WEAR
(c)   MERE   (d)   WERE

Sol. **(b)**   For the code letters Z, G, C, X the alphabets are

$$Z \quad G \quad C \quad X$$
$$\downarrow \quad \downarrow \quad \downarrow \quad \downarrow$$
$$W \quad E/R \quad A \quad E/R$$

Therefore, the word from the given options is 'WEAR'. Correct option is (2).

III.   Pattern Substitution Method

Under this method, a code will be given to you, you will have to recognize the pattern the code is following.

The pattern may be moving a few alphabets forward, a few alphabets backward or alternate forward & backward.

Illustration 11 :

If, in a certain language, POWERFUL is coded as QQZIWLBT, then which word is coded as ECQGJXZ ?

(a)   DANCERS   (b)   HARMLESS
(c)   PRACTISE   (d)   DANGERS

Sol. **(a)**   The pattern followed by the code is moving up in an increasing order.

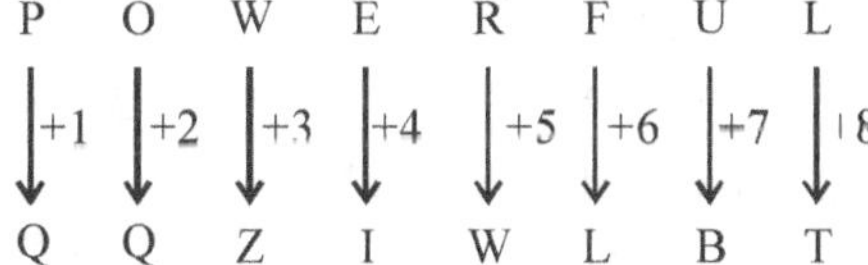

First method : similarly, the code given will also follow the same pattern. Therefore, we subtract or move the alphabets of the code backwards to form the word.

$$
\begin{array}{ccccccc}
D & A & N & C & E & R & S \\
\downarrow{-1} & \downarrow{-2} & \downarrow{-3} & \downarrow{-4} & \downarrow{-5} & \downarrow{-6} & \downarrow{-7} \\
E & C & Q & G & J & X & Z
\end{array}
$$

Second method : We can also go by the options, *i.e.,* check each option one by one and see if it forms the code given in the questions using the same pattern as coded in the word 'POWERFUL'.

IV. Alpha-Numeric Decoding

This is similar to alpha-numeric coding, with the only difference that we have to derive the code from a given word in case of alpha- numeric coding. While in decoding, we have to derive the word from the code following the alphabet series (ABCDEFG. .... PQRSTUVWXYZ).

Illustration 12 :

If the code in a certain language, for PAPER = 56 and SHEET = 57, then for which of the following words is the code 88 ?

(a) IRON   (b) PUPPET
(c) HELMETS   (d) PARROT

Sol. (d) As we know the values of each alphabet in the alphabet series, so we can unlock the codes.

PAPER $\longrightarrow$ P = 16, A = 1, P = 16, E = 5, R = 18

$$16 + 1 + 16 + 5 + 18 = 54$$

SHEET $\longrightarrow$ S = 19, H = 8, E = 5, E = 5, T = 20

$$19 + 8 + 5 + 5 + 20 = 57$$

Now, to find the word for the code 88, we have to check all the options.
Option (1)

IRON $\longrightarrow$ I = 9, R = 18, O = 15, N = 14

$$9 + 18 + 15 + 14 = 56$$

Option (2)

PUPPET $\rightarrow$ P = 16, U = 21, P = 16, P = 16, E = 5, T = 20,
$$16 + 21 + 16 + 16 + 5 + 20 = 94$$

Option (3)

HELMETS $\rightarrow$ H = 8, E = 5, L = 12, M = 13, E = 5, T = 20, S = 19
$$8 + 5 + 12 + 13 + 5 + 20 + 19 = 82$$

Option (4)

PARROT $\rightarrow$ P = 16, A = 1, R = 18, R = 18, O = 15, T = 20
$$16 + 1 + 18 + 18 + 15 + 20 = 88$$

EXERCISE

1. If the first three letters of the word COMPREHENSION are reversed, then the last three letters are added and then the remaining letters are reversed and added, then which letter will be exactly in the middle. ?
   (a) H   (b) N
   (c) R   (d) S

2. If the first and second letters in the word DEPRESSION were interchanged, also the third and the fourth letters, the fifth and the sixth letters and so on, which of the following would be the seventh letter from the right ?
   (a) R   (b) O
   (c) S
   (d) None of these

3. If the positions of the third and tenth letters of the word DOCUMENTION are interchanged, and likewise the positions of the fourth and seventh letters, the second and sixth letters is interchanged, which of the following will be eleventh from the right end ?
   (a) C   (b) I
   (c) T   (d) U

4. Arrange the given words in alphabetical order and tick the one that comes in the 2nd position.
   (a) Restrict   (b) Rocket
   (c) Robber   (d) Radom

5. Select the combination of numbers so that letters arranged accordingly will form a meaningful word.
   R   A   C   E   T

   1   2   3   4   5
   (a) 1, 2, 3, 4, 5
   (b) 3, 2, 1, 4, 5
   (c) 5, 2, 3, 4, 1
   (d) 5, 1, 2, 3, 4

6. Rearrange the first four letters, in any way, of the word DECISION. Find how many words can be formed by using all the four words.
   (a) One
   (b) Two
   (c) Three
   (d) More than three

7. The letters of the word NUMKIPP are in disorder. If they are arranged in proper order, the name of a vegetable is formed. What is the last letter of the word so formed?
   (a) K   (b) M
   (c) N   (d) P

8. If by arranging the letters of the word NABMODINT, the name of a game is formed, what are the first and the last letters of the word so formed?
   (a) B, T   (b) B, N
   (c) N, D   (d) M, T

9. If with the third, fourth, fifth, seventh and tenth letters of the word 'PERSONALITY', a meaningful word is formed, then first letter of the word is the answer. If no word is possible then X is the answer.
   (a) O   (b) T
   (c) R   (d) S

10. A meaningful word starting with A is made from the first, the second, the fourth, the fifth and the sixth letters of the word 'CONTRACT'. Which of the following is the middle letter of the word?
   (a)   C   (b)   O
   (c)   R   (d)   T

11. If in a certain language, POPULAR is coded as QPQVMBS, which word would be coded as GBNPVT ?
   (a)   FARMER
   (b)   FAMOUS
   (c)   FRAMES
   (d)   FAMOTH

12. If in a certain language, GRASP is coded as BMVNK, which word would be coded as CRANE ?
   (a)   EUDQH   (b)   HWFSJ
   (c)   GVERI   (d)   XMVIZ

13. If SIMPLE is coded as TJNQMF, then SJQQMF stands for ?
   (a)   PIPPLE   (b)   RIPPLE
   (c)   DIMPLE   (d)   PIMPLE

14. What does the code RGMARAM stands for ?
   (a)   DRUMMER
   (b)   GRAMMAR
   (c)   REPAIRS
   (d)   PRIMARY

15. What is the original word for the code UMBMIA?
   (a)   UMBRELLA
   (b)   BOMBAY
   (c)   MAMMIA
   (d)   MUMBAI

16. In the same language, IMRRSRO's code for ?
   (a)   MIRRORS
   (b)   MRRRSIO
   (c)   MANAGER
   (d)   METALLIC

17. How many as are there in the following series which are immediately followed by B as well as immediately proceded by Z?
   A M B Z A N A A B Z A B
   A Z B A P Z A B A Z A B
   (a)   Nil   (b)   One
   (c)   Two   (d)   Three

DIRECTIONS (Qs. 18-20) : Arrange the given words in the sequence in which they occur in the dictionary and then choose the correct sequence.

18.   1. Page   2. Pagan   3. Palisade
         4. Pageant   5. Palate
   (a)   1, 4, 2, 3, 5
   (b)   2, 4, 1, 3, 5
   (c)   2, 1, 4, 5, 3
   (d)   1, 4, 2, 5, 3

19.   1.   Wrinkle   2.   Wriggle
         3.   Writhe   4.   Wretch
         5.   Wrath
   (a)   4, 5, 1, 2, 3
   (b)   5, 4, 2, 1, 3
   (c)   4, 2, 5, 1, 3
   (d)   5, 2, 1, 3, 4

20.   1. Brook   2. Bandit
         3. Boisterous 4. Baffle
         5. Bright
   (a)   4, 2, 3, 5, 1
   (b)   2, 4, 3, 1, 5
   (c)   2, 4, 3, 5, 1
   (d)   4, 2, 3, 1, 5

DIRECTIONS (Qs. 21-25) : Find which one word cannot be made from the letters of the given word.

21. UNCONSCIOUS
   (a)   SON   (b)   COIN
   (c)   SUN   (d)   NOSE

22. INTERNATIONAL
   (a)   ORIENTAL
   (b)   TERMINAL
   (c)   LATTER
   (d)   RATIONALE

23. CREDENTIAL
    (a) DENTAL   (b) CREATE
    (c) TRAIN   (d) CREAM

24. TEACHERS
    (a) REACH   (b) CHAIR
    (c) CHEER   (d) SEARCH

25. CONTEMPORARY
    (a) PARROT
    (b) COMPANY
    (c) CARPENTER
    (d) PRAYER

26. If in a certain code, 'COVET is written as 'FRYHW', which word should be written as 'SHDUO'?
    (a) QUAKE   (b) REPAY
    (c) VKGXR   (d) REARL

27. If the for TOWN is 'UQZR', then what will be the code for 'WKOPFML'?
    (a) OWKPFML
    (b) VILLAGE
    (c) FASTEST
    (d) DEVELOP

28. If in a code, ALTERED is written as ZOGVIVW, then in the same code, how is IVOZGVW written as?
    (a) FEATHER
    (b) DEARST
    (c) RELATED
    (d) BELATED

29. How many such pairs of letters are there in the word CORPORATE each of which has as many letters in the same sequence between them in the word as in the english alphabet?
    (a) None   (b) One
    (c) Two   (d) Three

30. If the last four letters of the word 'CONCENTRATION' are written in reverse order followed by next two in the reverse order and next three in the reverse order and then followed by the first four in the reverse order, counting from the end which letter would be eighth in the new arrangement?
    (a) N   (b) T
    (c) E   (d) R

31. If it is possible to make a meaningful word with the third, fifth, eight and tenth letters of the word 'DISTRIBUTE', which of the following will be the third letter of that word? If no such word can be made give X as the answer.
    (a) S   (b) R
    (c) E   (d) X

32. How many independent words can 'HEARTLESS' be divided into without changing the order of the letters and using each letter only once?
    (a) Two   (b) Three
    (c) Four   (d) Five

33. How many independent words can 'STAINLESS' be divided into without changing the order of the letters and using each letter only once?
    (a) Nil   (b) One
    (c) Two   (d) Three

34. Select the combination of numbers so that the letters arranged accordingly will form a meaningful word.
V A R S T E
    (a) 2, 3, 1, 6, 4, 5
    (b) 4, 5, 2, 3, 1, 6
    (c) 6, 3, 4, 5, 2, 1
    (d) 3, 2, 4, 5, 6, 1

35. If in a certain code, HAT is 782, RABBIT is 681192. Then how will HABIT be coded as?
    (a) 78139   (b) 78192
    (c) 68192   (d) 78129

36. In a certain code, ELEPHANT is written as TNPEAHLE, the CROCODILE will be written as ?
(a) RCCOOIDEL
(b) ELCOOIDRC
(c) ELCIOODRC
(d) ELCOIODRC

DIRECTIONS (Qs. 37 & 38) : In a certain code language, '782' means 'Flowers are beautiful', '692' means 'Roses are red', '628' means 'Roses are beautiful'.

37. Which number denotes 'Flowers' ?
(a) 8   (b) 7
(c) 2   (d) 6

38. What does number '9' denote ?
(a) Roses   (b) Flowers
(c) Red   (d) are

39. If CAT is 48, Z is 52. Then what is TEA equal to ?
(a) 48   (b) 52
(c) 60   (d) 50

40. If HELMET is written as IFMNFU. Then how will CHOCOLATE be written as ?
(a) DIDPMPBUF
(b) EIDPMPBUF
(c) DIPDPMBFU
(d) DIPDPMBUF

41. If DRINK = 6, POLLUTION = 10, then GOVERNMENT is equal to ?
(a) 8   (b) 10
(c) 12   (d) 11

42. If FAIR is written as IENX. Then TAPE will be written as ?
(a) WEVL   (b) WEUK
(c) WFUK   (d) XEUK

43. If DELHI is coded as 73541 and CALCUTTA coded as 82589662, how can CALICUT be written ?
(a) 5279431   (b) 5978213
(c) 5473628   (d) 8251896

44. In a certain language '+ , ?' means 'where are you', '@ – ,' means 'we are here', and '+ @ ×' means 'you come here'. What is the code for 'where' ?
(a) +   (b) ÷
(c) ?   (d) @

45. If VISHAL is coded as 22102111517, then what will be the code for SACHIN ?
(a) 1925311191
(b) 1295111319
(c) 1925111319
(d) 1952111319

46. In a certain code, 3456 is coded as ROPE, 15526 is coded as APPLE. Then how is 54613 coded as ?
(a) POEAR   (b) PROEA
(c) PEORA   (d) RPOEA

47. In a certain code if FRIEND is written as DNEIRF. Then, what will be the code for DESERT ?
(a) TRESED   (b) DSERET
(c) TRSEED   (d) TESERD

48. In a certain code, if AFFAIR is FAAFRI, then FERRARIS is coded as ?
(a) EFRRARIS
(b) EFRRRASI
(c) EFRRRAIS
(d) EFRRARSI

49. In a certain code, APPLE is XNNZM and BAT is HXC, then BATTLE will be coded as ?
(a) XHCCZH
(b) HXCCZM
(c) HXCCMZ
(d) HXMCCZ

50. In a certain code, RADIO is XZOPL and SHEET is NBGGI, then HEATER is coded as ?
(a) BNGZIX   (b) BGZGIX
(c) BGZIGX   (d) GZBIXZ

51. In a certain code, if BLACK is KCALB then THEFT is ?
    (a) TFEHT   (b) FHETT
    (c) TEHFT   (d) TFHET

52. In a certain code BOOK is TLLC and TRICK is NAGDC, then BRICK is coded as -
    (a) NAGDC   (b) TAGLC
    (c) TALCD   (d) TAGDC

53. If COME is code as BNLD then DANGER will be coded as
    (a) EBOHIS
    (b) CZMGER
    (c) CZMFDQ
    (d) DANFDQ

DIRECTIONS (Qs. 54-56): In a certain code, 'il be pee' means 'roses are blue', 'silk hee' means 'red flowers' and 'pee mit hee' means 'flowers are vegetables.

54. How is 'red written in that code ?
    (a) hee
    (b) silk
    (c) be
    (d) cannot be determined

55. How is 'roses' written in that code ?
    (a) il
    (b) pee
    (c) be
    (d) cannot be determined

56. How is 'vegetables are red flowers' written in this code ?
    (a) pee silk mit hee
    (b) silk peehee be
    (c) il silk mit hee
    (d) none

SOLUTIONS

1. **(d)** Clearly, we have :
COMPREHENSION → (COM) (PREHENS) (ION)
→ MOCIONSNEHERP
The middle letter is the seventh letter, which is S.

2. **(d)** The new letter sequence is EDRPSEISNO.
The seventh letter from the right is P.

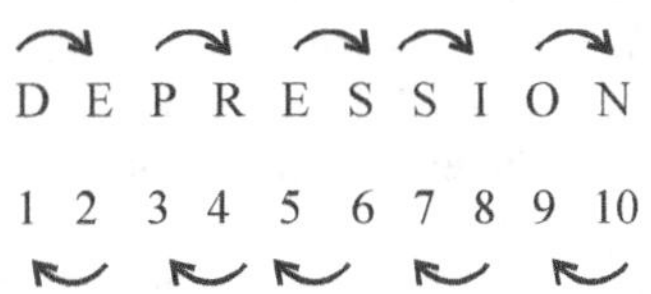

3. **(c)**

D O C U M E N T A T I O N
1 2 3 4 5 6 7 8 9 10 11 12 13

4. **(a)** Arranging the words in alphabetical order, we have Random, Restrict, Robber, Rocket.
So the word in the 2nd position is Restrict and the correct answer is (a)

5. **(d)** Clearly, the given letters, when arranged in the order 5, 1, 2, 3, 4 from the word 'TRACE'.

6. **(a)** The first four letters are D, E, C, I and only word DICE can be formed so the answer is (a)

7. **(c)** The name of the vegetable is PUMPKIN. The last letter is N.

8. **(b)** The name of the game is BADMINTON.

9. **(c)** The respective letters of the given word are R, S, O, A and T. The word formed is ROAST. So the first letter is R.

10. **(d)** The respective letters of the word 'CONTRACT' are C, O, T, R, A. The word formed is ACTOR, in which the middle letter is T.

11. **(b)**

P O P U L A R
+1 +1 +1 +1 +1 +1 +1
Q P Q V M B S

F A M O U S
−1 −1 −1 −1 −1 −1
G B N P V T

Thus, FAMOUS is the answer.

12. **(b)**

G R A S P
−5 −5 −5 −5 −5
B M V N K

H W F S J
+5 +5 +5 +5 +5
C R A N E

Thus, HWFSJ is the answer.

13. **(b)** PATTERN
SUBSTITUTION (+ 1)

14. **(b)** GRAMMAR

15. **(d)** MUMBAI

16. **(a)** MIRRORS

17. **(d)** A M B Z A N A A B Z A̲ B
A Z B A P Z A̲ B A Z A̲ B

18. **(c)**   **19.** **(b)**   **20.** **(a)**

21. **(d)**   **22.** **(b)**   **23.** **(d)**

24. **(b)**   **25.** **(c)**

26. **(d)** In the first code, 'C' has been coded as + 2 alphabets, 'O' has been coded as +2 so on & so forth. Similarly PEARL can be coded as SHDUO.

27. **(b)** Each letter of the word 'TOWN' is moved 1, 2, 3, & 4 steps forward, i.e., 'T' is moved 1 step, 'O' 2 steps, W 3 steps & N 4 steps, to obtain the code. So in "village", V is coded as W, I as K, L as O, again L as P, A as F, G as M and E as L. Thus the code for **village** becomes WKOPFML.

28. **(c)**

A L T E R E D
↓ ↓ ↓ ↓ ↓ ↓ ↓
Z O G V I V W

R E L A T E D
↑ ↑ ↑ ↑ ↑ ↑ ↑
I V O Z G V W

Thus, RELATED is the answer.

29. **(c)**

C O R P O R A T E

Three pairs — (P, R), (R, T) and (P, O) have as many letters between them in the word as in the English alphabet. But since the letters must be in the same sequence in the word as in English alphabet, so that desire pairs are (P, R) and (R, T) only.

30. **(d)** The new letter sequence is NOITARTNECNOC
The eighth letter from the end is R.

31. **(b)** The word formed by S, R, U and E is SURE, USER.

32. **(b)** The words are HE, ART, LESS

33. **(c)** Only two such words can be formed. The words are STAIN and LESS.

34. **(b)** Clearly the given letters, when arranged in the order 4, 5, 2, 3, 1, 6 form the word 'STRAVE'.

35. **(b)** Type – Direct substitution (Direct fashion)

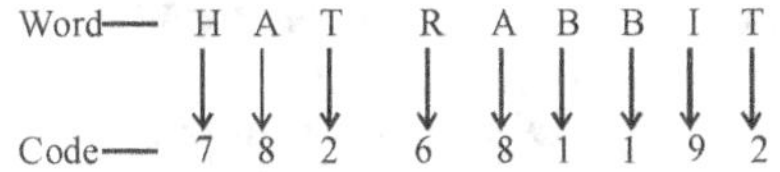

Word— H A T R A B B I T
Code— 7 8 2 6 8 1 1 9 2

Thus the code for the given word

H A B I T
7 8 1 9 2

Thus option (b) is the correct answer.

36. **(b)** Type – Simple Arrangement (Swap Coding)
Positions of T and E and L and N are swapped.
Also, positions of second E and P and H and A are swapped.
Therefore, for CROCODILE the common in all the three sentences. Therefore, the digit '2' is the representation for 'are'.
Similarly, on the code side '8' is the digit common in 1st & 3rd codes, therefore, '8' stands for 'beautiful'.
Thus '7' is the representation for 'flowers'.
Also, the digit '6' is common in 2nd & 3rd codes and so is the word 'roses'. Therefore, '6' stands for 'roses'. Thus '9' stands for 'red'.

37. **(b)**

38. **(c)** Red.

39. **(b)** Alphanumeric coding type.

Word	Code value (alphabet series)	Final code
CAT	C = 3, A = 1, T = 20 3 + 1 + 20 = 24	24 × 2 = 48
Z	26	26 × 2 = 52
TEA	T = 20, E = 5, A = 1 20 + 5 + 1 = 26	26 × 2 = 52

40. **(d)** Type – Pattern substitution (+1)

Word — H E L M E T
         +1 +1 +1 +1 +1 +1
Code — I F M N F U

∴ C H O C O L A T E
   +1 +1 +1 +1 +1 +1 +1 +1 +1
   D I P D P M B U F

41. **(d)** Type – Alphanumeric series type.
Code for 'DRINK' = 6 Because no. of letters = 5
5 + 1 = '6', *i.e.,* the code.
Code for 'POLLUTION' = 10 Because no. of letters = 9
9 + 1 = '10', *i.e.,* the code.
Code for 'GOVERNMENT' = 11 Because no. of letters = 10
10 + 1 = '11', *i.e.,* the code.

42. **(b)** Type – Pattern substitution (moving forward in ascending order).

Word — F A I R T A P E
        +3 +4 +5 +6 +3 +4 +5 +6
Code — I E N X W E U K

43. **(d)** Type – Direct substitution (direct fashion)
So, code for CALICUT – 8251896.

44. **(c)** Type – Direct substitution (Jumbled fashion).

S.No.	Code	Sentence
1.	+ ÷ ?	Where are you
2.	@ – ÷	We are here
3.	+ @ ×	You come here

As we can see, that 'where' is only in sentence 1. ['Where' is the word for which we have to find the code.] Therefore, we need to gather the codes for 'are' & 'you' to find out the code for 'where'.

Sentence 1 & 2 have the word 'are' in common and the symbol '÷' in common. Therefore, '÷' is the symbol for 'are'.

Sentence 1 & 3 have the word 'you' in common and the symbol '+' in common. Therefore '+' stands for 'you'. Thus '?' represents 'where'.

45. **(c)** Type – Alphanumeric coding.

Word ⟶	V	I	S	H	A	L
Value in ⟶ alphabet series	22	9	19	8	1	12

		+1	+2	+3	+4	+5
Code	22	10	21	11	5	17

similarly,	S	A	C	H	I	N
for the word	19	1	3	8	9	14
		+1	+2	+3	+4	+5
Final code	19	2	5	11	13	19

Thus code is 1925111319, option (c).

46. **(a)** Type – Direct coding (Direct fashion)
$5 \rightarrow P, 4 \rightarrow O, 6 \rightarrow E, 1 \rightarrow A, 3 \rightarrow R.$
Therefore, 54613 is coded as POEAR.

47. **(a)** Type – Simple arrangement (SWAP CODING)
Interchange F and D, R and N and I and E.
Similarly, DESERT is coded as TRESED.

48. **(b)** Type – Simple Arrangement (Swap coding).

In the word AFFAIR, the positions of first A & first F are interchanged second A & second F are interchanged and I and R are interchanged.
Similarly, RERRARIS is coded as EFRRRASI.

49. **(b)** Direct Substitution.
50. **(c)** Direct Substitution.
51. **(a)** Simple arrangement (Swap Coding)
52. **(d)** Direct Substitution.
53. **(c)** Pattern Substitution (–1).

Word —	C	O	M	E		D	A	N	G	E	R
	↓–1	↓–1	↓–1	↓–1		↓–1	↓–1	↓–1	↓–1	↓–1	↓–1
Code —	B	N	L	D		C	Z	M	F	D	Q

Thus required code is 'CZMFDQ'.

Solutions 54 to 56:

Type Direct coding (Jumbled fashion)

S. No.	Code	Sentence
1.	il be pee	roses are blue
2.	silk hee	red flowers
3.	pee mit hee	flowers are vegetables.

Common word in sentences 1 & 3 → 'are' and code → 'pee'
Common word in sentences 2 & 3 → 'flowers' and code → 'hee'.
Therefore,

Codes	Words
pee	are
hee	flowers
silk	red
niit	vegetables
il	roses / blue
be	blue / rose

54. **(b)** silk.
55. **(d)** il or be, cannot be determined.
56. **(a)** niit silk hee pee.

Directions, Clock & Calender

DIRECTIONS

There are four directions North, South, East and West. The word NEWS came from North, East, West and South. There are four regions :

North-East (I); South-East (IV); North-West (II); South-West (III). The directions OP, OS, OQ and OR are North East direction; North-West direction; South-West and South-East direction.

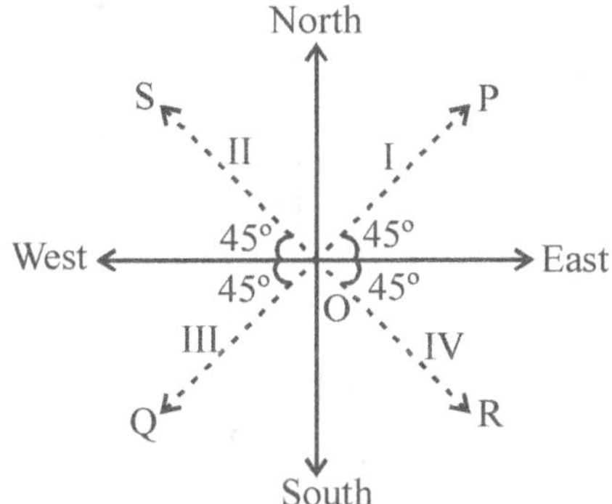

The candidate must distinguish between the regions and directions i.e. between North-East region and North-East direction.

If you move with your face east-wards, your left hand is towards north and your right hand is towards south. Similarly the positions of the directions of the hands can be fixed when you move in any of the other three directions.

To solve the question, first draw the direction figure

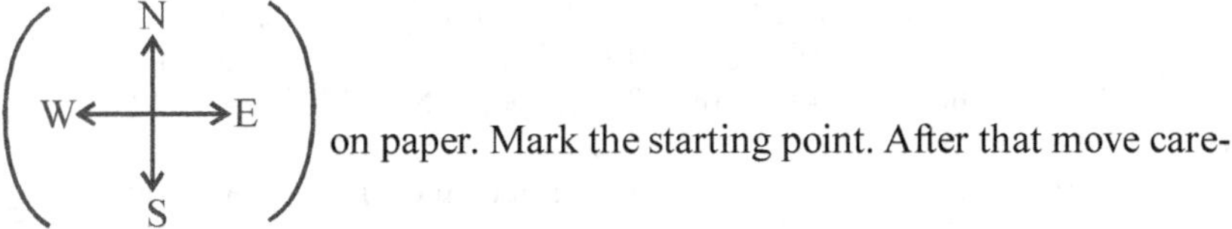

on paper. Mark the starting point. After that move carefully according to the directions given in the question.

Illustration 1:

Four persons stationed at the four corners of a square piece as shown in the diagram. P starts crossing the field diagonally. After walking half the distance, he turns right, walks some distance and turns left.

Which direction is P facing now ?

(a) North-east
(b) North-west
(c) North
(d) South-east
(e) South-west

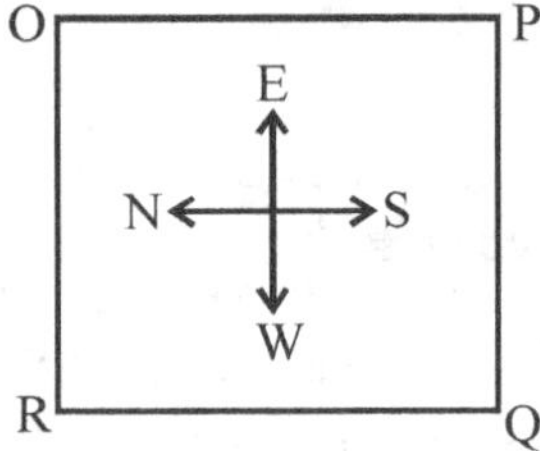

***Sol.* (b)**   The route of P is shown in the diagram.
Clearly the direction of P is North-west.

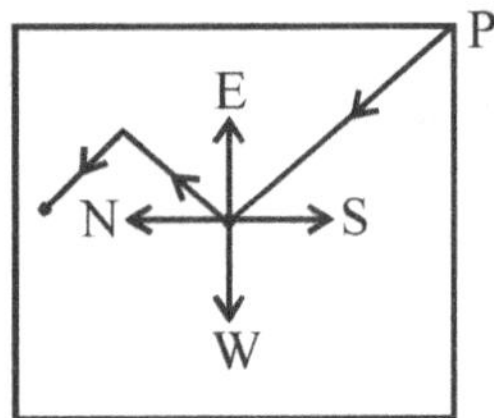

CALENDER

REMEMBER FOLLOWING POINTS

We are supposed to find the day of the week on a given date.
For this, we use the concept of odd days.

(i)   Odd Days : In a given period, the number of days more than the complete weeks are called odd days.

(ii)   Leap Year :
(1) Every year divisible by 4 is a leap year, if it is not a century.
(2) Every 4th century (i.e., divisible by 400) is a leap year and no other century is a leap year.
Note : A leap year has 366 days.
Examples.
1. Each of the years 1948, 2004, 1676 etc. has been a leap year.
2. Each of the years 400, 800, 1200, 1600, 2000 etc. is a leap year.
3. None of the years 2001, 2002, 2003, 2005, 1800, 2100 is a leap year.

(iii)   Ordinary Year :
The year which is not a leap year is called an ordinary year. An ordinary year has 365 days.

(iv)   Counting of odd days :
(a) 1 ordinary year = 365 days = (52 weeks + 1 day)
∴ 1 ordinary year has 1 odd day.

(2) 1 leap year = 366 days = (52 weeks + 2 days).
$\therefore$ 1 leap year has 2 odd days.
(3) 100 years = 76 ordinary years + 24 leap years
= (76 × 1 + 24 × 2) odd days = 124 odd days.
= (17 weeks + 5 days) ≡ 5 odd days.
$\therefore$ Number of odd days in 100 years = 5
Number of odd days in 200 years = (5 × 2) ≡ 3 odd days.
Number of odd days in 300 years = (5 × 3) ≡ 1 odd day.
Number of odd days in 400 years = (5 × 4 + 1) ≡ 0 odd days.
Similarly, each one of 800 years, 1200 years, 1600 years, 2000 years etc. has 0 odd days.

(v) First January 1 AD was Monday. Therefore, we must count days from Sunday, i.e. Sunday for 0 odd days, Monday for 1 odd day, Tuesday for 2 odd days and so on.

(vi) February in an ordinary year gives no odd day, but in a leap year gives one odd day.

Illustration 2:

What was the day of the week on 15th August, 1947 ?

Sol. 15th August, 1947 = (1946 years + Period from 1.1.1947 to 15.8.1947)
Odd days in 1600 years = 0
Odd days in 300 years = (5 × 3) = 15 ≡ 1
46 years = (11 leap years + 35 ordinary years)
= (11 × 2 + 35 × 1) odd days = 57 odd days
= (8 weeks + 1 day) = 1 odd day.
$\therefore$ Odd days in 1946 years = (0 + 1 + 1) = 2.
Jan. Feb. March April May June July Aug.
(31 + 28 + 31 + 30 + 31 + 30 + 31 + 15) = 227 days.
227 days = (32 weeks + 3 days) ≡ 3 odd days.
Total number of odd days = (2 + 3) = 5.
Hence, the required day is Friday.

CLOCK

REMEMBER THE FOLLOWING POINTS

The face of the dial of a watch is a circle whose circumference is divided into 60 equal parts, called minute spaces.

A clock has two hands, the smaller one is called the hour hand or short hand while the larger one is called the minute hand or long hand.

(i) In 60 minutes, the minute hand gains 55 minutes on the hour hand.

(ii) 1 minute space = $\dfrac{360°}{60}$.

(As 360° of the circle is divided into 60 minutes).

(iii) In one minute, the hour hand moves $\dfrac{360}{12 \times 60} = \dfrac{360}{720} = \dfrac{1°}{2}$

(As there are 12 hours of 60 minutes each)

Thus, in one minute the minute hand gains $5\dfrac{1}{2}^{\circ}$ over the hour hand.

(iv) In every hour, both the hands coincide once.

(v) The hands are in the same straight line when they are coincident or opposite to each other.

(vi) When the two hands are at right angles, they are 15 minute spaces apart.

(vii) The hands coincide 11 times in every 12 hours (between 11 and 1 O'clock there is a common position at 12 O'clock). Hence, the hands coincide 22 times in a day.

(viii) The hands of a clock are at right angles twice in every hour, but in 12 hours they are at right angles 22 times since there are two common positions in every 12 hours.

(ix) When the hands are in opposite directions, they are 30 minute spaces apart.

(x) Angle traced by hour hand in 12 hrs = 360°.

(xi) Angle traced by minute hand in 60 min. = 360°.

EXERCISE

1. A child is looking for his father. He went 90 metres in the East before turning to his right. He went 20 metres before turning to his right again to look for his father at his uncle's place 30 metres from this point. His father was not there. From here he went 100 metres to the North before meeting his father in a street. How far did the son meet his father from the starting point ?
(a) 80 metres (b) 100 metres
(c) 140 metres(d) 260 metres

2. If A to the south of B and C is to the east of B, in what direction is A with respect to C ?
(a) North-east
(b) North-west
(c) South-east
(d) South-west

3. A,B,C and D are playing cards. A and B are partners. D faces towards North. If A faces towards west, then who faces towards south?
(a) B
(b) C
(c) D
(4) Data inadequate

4. Divya journeys 10 km to east then 10 km to south-west. He turns again and journeys 10 km to North-West. Which direction is he in from the starting point ?
(a) South   (b) North
(c) West   (d) East

5. Sobha was facing East. She walked 20 metres. Turning left she moved 15 metres and then turning right moved 25 metres. Finally, she turned right and moved 15 metres more. How far is she from her starting point?
(a) 25 metres (b) 35 metres
(c) 50 metres (d) 45 metres

6. Jatin leaves his house and walks 12 km towards North. He turns right and walks another 12 km. He turns right again, walks 12 km more and turns left to walk 5 km. How far is he from his home and in which direction ?
   - (a) 7 km East (b) 10 km East
   - (c) 17 km East (d) 24 km East

7. Deepak starts walking straight towards east. After walking 75 metres, he turns to the left and walks 25 metres straight. Again he turns to the left, walks a distance of 40 metres straight, again he turns to the left and walks a distance of 25 metres. How far is he from the starting point ?
   - (a) 25 metres
   - (b) 50 Metres
   - (c) 115 Metres
   - (d) 35 Metres

8. A rat runs 20' towards East and turns to right, runs 10' and turns to right, runs 9' and again turns to left, runs 5' and then turns to left, runs 12' and finally turns to left and runs 6' Now, which direction is the rat facing ?
   - (a) East (b) West
   - (c) North (d) South

9. Ramakant walks northwards. After a while, he turns to his right and a little further to his left. Finally, after walking a distance of one kilometre, he turns to his left again. In which direction is he moving now ?
   - (a) North (b) South
   - (c) East (d) West

10. Raj travelled from a point X straight to Y at a distance of 80 metres. He turned right and walked 50 metres, then again turned right and walked 70 metres. Finally, he turned right

and walked 50 metres. How far is he from the starting point
   - (a) 10 metres (b) 20 metres
   - (c) 50 metres (d) 70 metres

11. P, Q, R, S, T, U, V and W are sitting around a round table in the same order, for group discussion at equal distance. Their positions are clockwise. If V sits in the north, then what will be the position of S?
   - (a) East
   - (b) South-east
   - (c) South
   - (d) South-west

12. If all the directions are rotated, i.e., if North is changed to West and East to North and so on, then what will come in place of North-West ?
   - (a) South-West
   - (b) North-East
   - (c) East-North
   - (d) East-West

13. If a person is walking towards North, what direction should he follow so that he is walking towards West ?
   - (a) right, right, left
   - (b) left, left, right
   - (c) left, right, left
   - (d) left, left, left

14. Two friends start a race, and together they run for 50 mts. Jack turns right and runs 60 mts while Bunny turns left and runs 40 mts. Then Jack turns left and runs 50 mts while Bunny turns right and runs 50 mts. How far are the two friends now from each other
   - (a) 60 mts (b) 20 mts
   - (c) 100 mts (d) 150 mts

15. If the two hands in a clock are 3 minutes divisions apart, then the angle between them is
   - (a) 3° (b) 18°
   - (c) 24° (d) 60°

16. What will be the acute angle between hands of a clock at 2 : 30?
 (a) 105°   (b) 115°
 (c) 95°   (d) 135°

17. A clock gains 15 minutes per day. It is set right at 12 noon. What time will it show at 4.00 am, the next day?
 (a) 4 : 10 am   (b) 4 : 45 am
 (c) 4 : 20 am   (d) 5 : 00 am

18. What is the angle between the 2 hands of the clock at 8:24 pm?
 (a) 100°   (b) 107°
 (c) 106°   (d) 108°

19. If a clock strikes 12 in 33 seconds, it will strike 6 in how many seconds?

 (a) $\dfrac{33}{2}$ (b) 15

 (c) 12   (d) 22

20. At 12 O'clock, the minute hand is point East. At 4:30, in which direction will the hour hand point ?
 (a) North-West
 (b) South-West
 (c) South
 (d) South-West

21. A clock loses $\dfrac{1}{2}$% on true time during one week and gains $\dfrac{1}{4}$% on true time during the next week. If it is set right at 12 O'clock on Saturday morning, what time will it indicate at the end of second week ?
 (a) 11 : 34   (b) 11 : 48
 (c) 12 : 15   (d) 13 : 02

22. At what time between 9 and 10 will the hands of a watch be together ?
 (a) 45 minutes past 9
 (b) 50 minutes past 9

 (c) $49\dfrac{1}{11}$ minutes past 9

 (d) $48\dfrac{2}{11}$ minutes past 9

23. Between 2 O'clock to 10 O'clock, how many times the hands of a clock are at right angle ?
 (a) 14   (b) 12
 (c) 16   (d) 15

24. The year next to 1988 having the same calendar as that of 1988 is –
 (a) 1990   (b) 1992
 (c) 1993   (d) 1995

25. The first republic day of India was celebrated on 26th January, 1950. It was –
 (a) Monday   (b) Tuesday
 (c) Thursday (d) Friday

26. On January 12, 1980, it was Saturday. The day of the week on January 12, 1979 was –
 (a) Saturday (b) Friday
 (c) Sunday   (d) Thursday

27. The number of odd days in a leap year is –
 (a) 1   (b) 2
 (c) 3   (d) 4

28. The year next to 1991 having the same calendar as that of 1990 is –
 (a) 1998   (b) 2001
 (c) 2002   (d) 2003

29. Find the exact time between 7 am and 8 am when the two hands of a watch meet ?
 (a) 7 hrs 35 min
 (b) 7 hrs 36.99 min
 (c) 7 hrs 38.18 min
 (d) 7 hrs 42.6 min

30. Monday falls on 4th April, 1998. What was the day 3rd November, 1987 ?
   (a) Monday   (b) Sunday
   (c) Tuesday (4) Wednesday

31. A watch which gains 5 seconds in 3 minutes was set right at 7 a.m. In the afternoon of the same day, when the watch indicated quarter past 4 O'clock, the true time is –
   (a) 4 p.m.

   (b) $59\dfrac{7}{12}$ minutes past 3

   (c) $58\dfrac{7}{11}$ minutes past 3

   (d) $2\dfrac{3}{11}$ minutes past 4

32. Smt. Indira Gandhi died on 31st October, 1984. The day of the week was –
   (a) Monday
   (b) Tuesday
   (c) Wednesday
   (d) Friday

33. How many times in a day, the two hands of a clock coincide?
   (a) 11   (b) 12
   (c) 22   (d) 24

34. When the time is 4.20, the angle between the hands of the clock is –
   (a) 20°   (b) 15°
   (c) 12 ½°   (d) 10°

SOLUTIONS

1. **(b)** The movements of the child from A to E are as shown in fig

Clearly, the child meets his father at E.

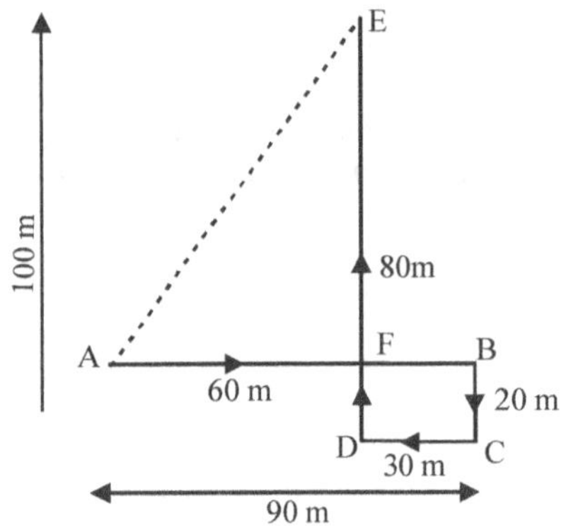

Now AF = (AB – FB) = (AB – DC) = (90 – 30) m = 60 m.
EF = (DE – DF) = (DE – BC) = (100 – 20) m = 80 m.
∴ Required distance

$$= AE = \sqrt{AF^2 + EF^2}$$

$$= \sqrt{(60)^2 + (80)^2}$$

$$= \sqrt{3600 + 6400} = \sqrt{10000}$$

$$= 100 \text{ m.}$$

2. **(d)** Clearly comparing the direction of A w.r.t C in the second diagram with that in the first diagram, A will be south-west of C.

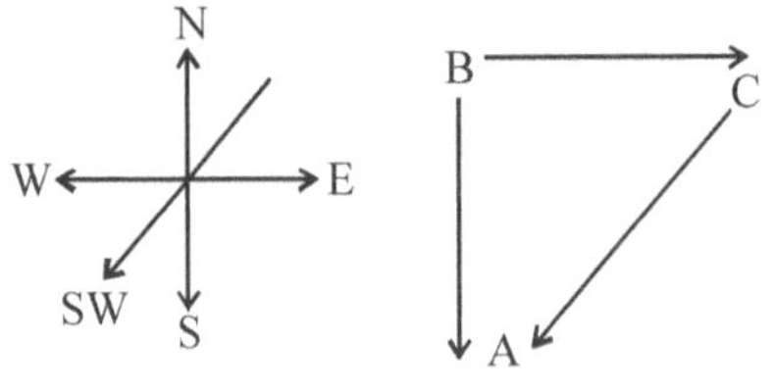

3. **(b)** As per the data, D faces North. A faces towards west. So, its partner B will face towards A and hence towards East. So, C who will face D will face towards south.

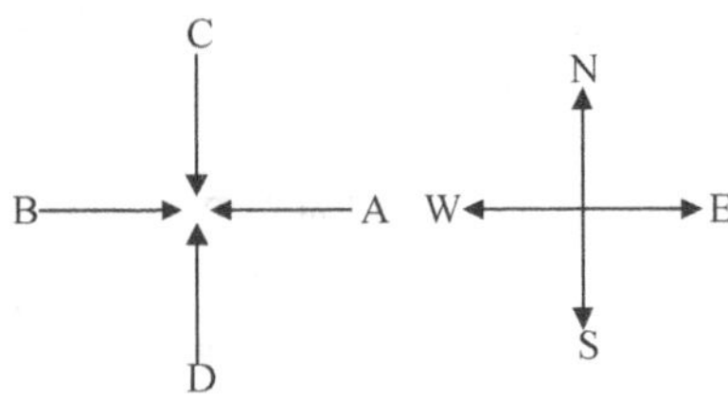

4. **(c)**

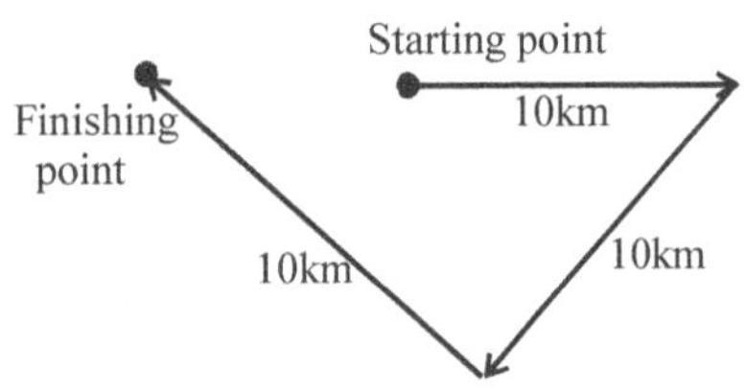

5. **(d)**

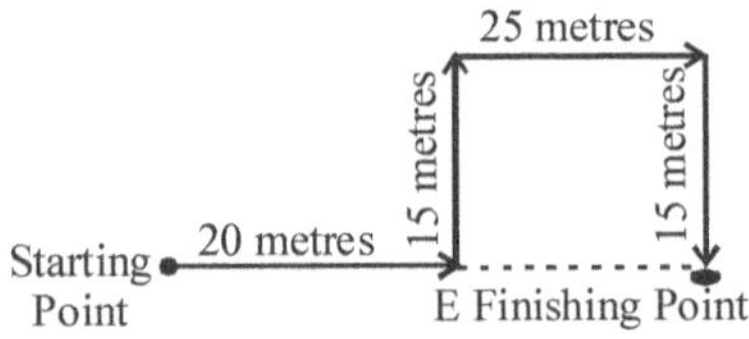

Shobha turns left after walking 20 metres towards East. Now she walks 15 metres towards North. She turns right towards East again and walks 25 metres further. Finally turning right towards South, she walks 15 metres. The distance moved towards North and towards South is same, i.e., 15 metres. So, Shobha is 20 + 25 metres = 45 metres away from her starting point.

6. **(c)** (12 km + 5 km = 17 km)

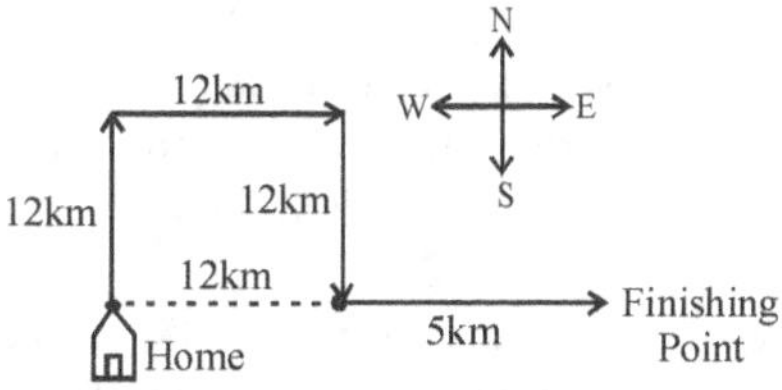

7. **(d)** The movements of Deepak are as shown in fig.

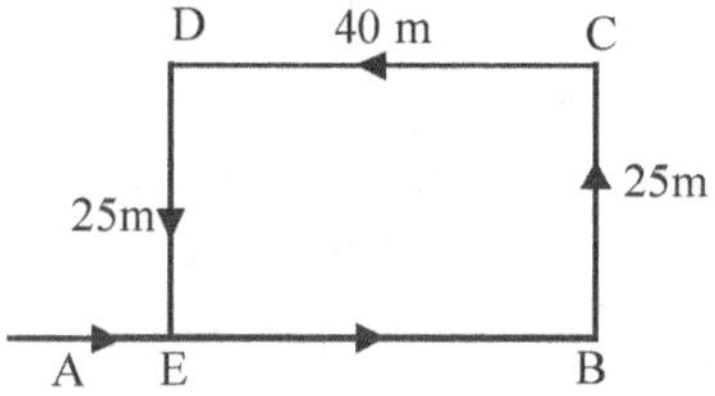

Clearly, FB = DC = 40 m .

∴ Deepak's distance from the starting point A

= (AB – EB) = (75 – 40) m = 35m.

8. **(c)** The movements of the rat from A to G are as shown in fig.

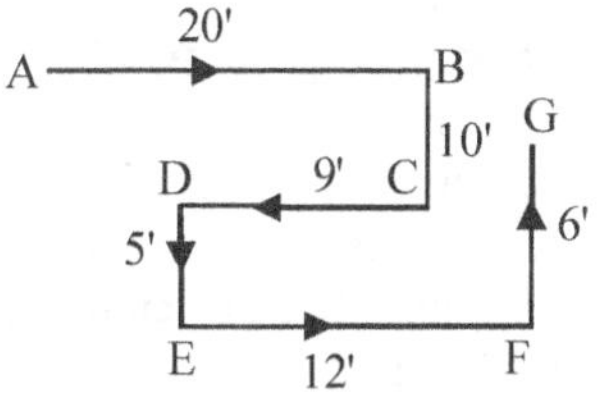

Clearly, it is finally walking in the direction FG i.e., North

9. **(d)** The movements of Ramakant are as shown in fig.

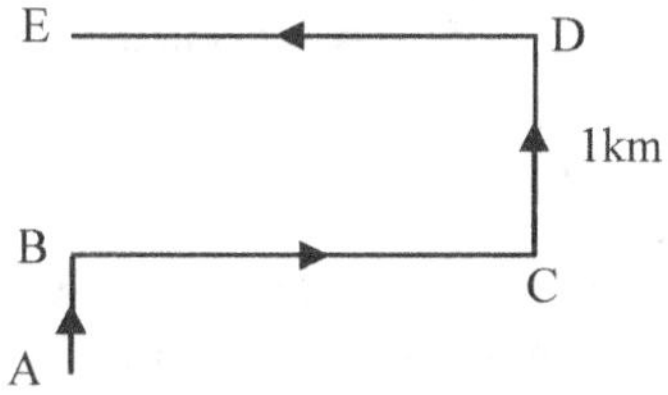

Clearly he is finally walking in the direction DE i.e, west

10. **(a)** The movements of Raj are as shown in fig (X to Y, Y to A, A to B , B to C).

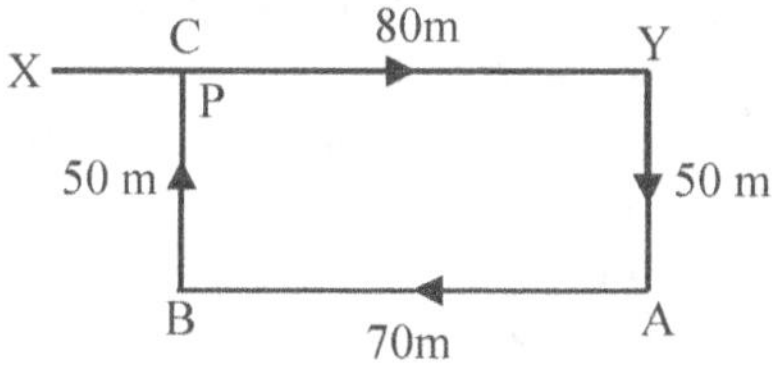

∴ Raj's distance from the starting point

= XC = (XY – YC) = (XY – BA)

= (80 – 70) m = 10 m.

11. **(d)** Clearly, the seating arrangement is as shown in the adjoining figure. So, S is at the south-west position.

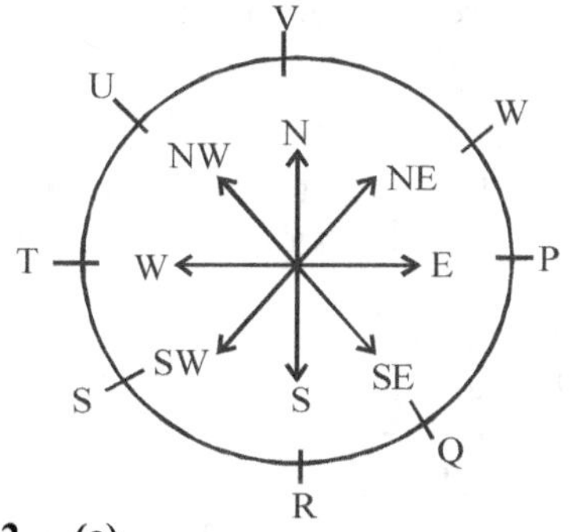

12. **(a)**

13. **(c)** The directions to be followed will be :

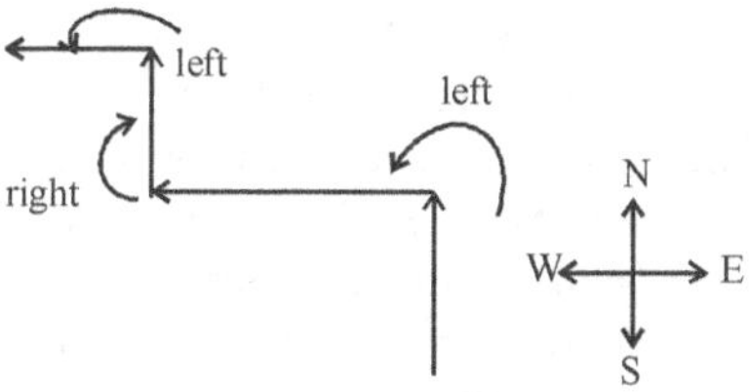

14. **(c)** The track of both the friends is

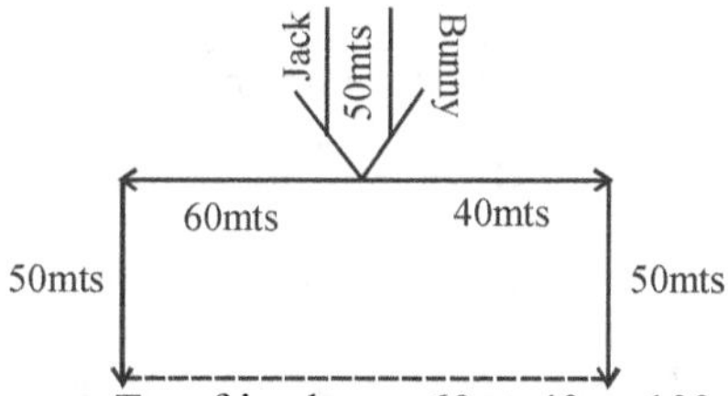

Two friends are 60 + 40 = 100 mts apart

15. **(b)** In a clock, each minute makes 6°

$\therefore$ 3 minutes will make $6 \times 3 = 18°$

16. **(a)**

17. **(a)** The clock gains 15 min in 24 hours.

Therefore, in 16 hours, it will gain 10 minutes.

Hence, the time shown by the clock will be 4.10 am.

18. **(d)** Required angle = 240 – 24 × (11/2) = 240 –132 = 108°.

19. **(b)** In order to strike 12, there are 11 intervals of equal time

$= \dfrac{33}{11} = 3$ seconds each

Therefore, to strike 6 it has 5 equal intervals, it requires 5 × 3 = 15 sec.

20. **(d)**

21. **(a)** Loss = 0.005 × 7 × 24 hrs. = 0.84 hrs.

Gain = 0.42 hrs.

Overall loss = 0.42 hrs. = 25 min. 12 sec.

$\therefore$ Time shown at end of 2nd week = 11.34 a.m.

i.e., 11 hr 34 min 48 sec.

22. **(c)** To be together between 9 and 10, the minute hand has to gain 45 minute spaces.

Now, 55 min. spaces are gained in 60 minutes.

$\therefore$ 45 min. spaces are gained

in $\left(\dfrac{60}{55} \times 45\right)$ min. or $49\dfrac{1}{11}$ min.

So, the hands are together at

$49\dfrac{1}{11}$ min. past 9.

23. **(a)** Between 2 and 4 O'clock, 8 and 10 O'clock, the hands are

at right thrice in each case. Between 4 and 8'O clock, the hands are at right angles.

So total number of times the hands are at right angles

= 3 + 3 + (2 × 4) = 14.

24. **(c)** Starting with 1988, we go on counting the number of odd days till the sum is divisible by 7.

Years → 1988 1989 1990 1991 1992

Odd days → 2   1   1   1   2

= 7 i.e. odd days

$\therefore$ Calendar for 1993 the same as that of 1988.

25. **(c)**

26. **(b)**

27. **(b)** A leap year has (52 weeks + 2 days). So, the number of odd days in a leap year is 2.

28. **(c)**

29. **(c)** 55 min spaces are gained in 60 min

$\Rightarrow$ 35 min spaces will be gained in 38.18 min.

$\Rightarrow$ Answer = 7 hrs + 38.18 min.

30. **(c)** Counting the number of days after 3rd November, 1987, we have :

Nov.   Dec.   Jan.   Feb. March   April

days 27 + 31 + 31 + 29 +   31 + 4

=   153 days containing 6 odd days.

31. **(a)**

32. **(c)**

33. **(c)** The hands coincide 11 times in every 12 hours (between 11 and 1 O'clock there is a common position at 12 O'clock). Hence, the hands coincide 22 times in a day.

34. **(d)**

CHAPTER 5

Number Test & Ranking Test

Number test

In this type of question, generally a set, group or series of numerals is given and the candidate is required to find out how many times a number satisfying the conditions specified in the question occurs.

Illustration 1:

In the series given below, how many 8s are there each of which is exactly divisible by its immediate preceding as well as succeeding numbers ?

2 8 3 8 2 4 8 2 4 8 6 8 2 8 2 4 8 3 8 2 8 6

(a)   One   (b)   Two

(c)   Three   (d)   Four

Sol. **(b)**   Clearly, we may mark such sets of 3 numbers, in which the middle number is 8 and each of the two numbers on both sides of it is a factor of 8, as shown.

2 8 3 8 2 4 8 2 4 8 6 8 2 8 2 4 8 3 8 2 8 6

so there are two such 8s.

RANKING TEST

Generally, the number of persons are arranged in either ascending or descending order of their performance in a certain activity.

Let there be n persons who qualified in a certain event. A particular man Rohan is one of them whose rank from the top i.e, top rank T_r is 14 th and his rank from the other side i.e, from the bottom (B_r) is 26th. Then clearly the number of persons who qualify is $T_r + B_r - 1$ i.e, $14 + 26 - 1 = 39$.

$$\Rightarrow \qquad n = T_r + B_r - 1 \qquad ......(1)$$
$$T_r = (n + 1) - B_r \qquad ....(2)$$
$$\text{and} \qquad B_r = (n + 1) - T_r \qquad ....(3)$$

these rules (1), (ii) and (iii) are very useful in problems on ranks

---

Illustration 2:

Sunita ranked 11 th from txhe top and 27th from the bottom in a class. How may student are in the class ?

(a)   38   (b)   28

(c)   40   (d)   37

Sol. **(d)** $T_r = 11, B_r = 27$.

$\therefore$ Number of students in the class $= 11 + 27$
$- 1 = 37$.

──────────────── **Useful Tips** ────────────────

1.   Position of person from top

= [Total no. of persons – position of person from down] + 1.

2.   Position of person from bottom

= [Total no. of persons – position of person from up]+1.

3.   Position of person from right

= [Total no. of persons – position of person from left]+1

4.   Position of person from left

= [Total no. of persons – position of person from right] + 1.

5.   Total no. of persons

= [Position of person from top/ right + position of person from bottom / left] – 1.

6.   If two persons are on a definite position from up and down or left and right) and they interchange their ranks, then

(1)   Total no. of persons in order

= [First position of first person + second position of second person] – 1

(2)   Second position of first person or second position of second person = Difference of the two positions of second person + first position of second person.

= Difference of the two positions of first person + First position of second person.

EXERCISE

1.   Manish ranked sixteenth from the top and twenty-nineth from the bottom among those who has passed an examination. Six boys did not participate in the examination and five failed in it. How many boys were there in the class?

(a)   40   (b)   44
(c)   50   (d)   55

2.   Roshan ranked 11 th from the top and thirty one from the bottom in a class. How many students are there in the class?

(a)   42   (b)   43
(c)   41   (d)   40

3.   If a test score goes up 15% from x to 69, what was the previous test score ?

(a)   52   (b)   60
(c)   65   (d)   68

4.   What will be the difference between the sum of the odd digits and the sum of the even digits in the number 857423

(a) 0	(b) 1		
(c) 2	(d) 4		

5. A number is greater than 3 but less than 8. Also, it is greater than 6 but less than 10. The number is

(a) 5   (b) 6
(c) 7   (d) 8

6. If it is possible to make a number which is perfect square of a two-digit odd number with the second, the sixth and the ninth digits of the number 187642539, which of the following is the digit in the unit's place of that two-digit odd number ?

(a) 1   (b) 7
(c) 9
(d) No such number can be made

7. How many combinations of two-digit numbers having 8 can be made from the following numbers ?

8, 5, 2, 1, 7, 6

(a) 9   (b) 10
(c) 11   (d) 12

8. How many numbers amongst the numbers 9 to 54 are there which are exactly divisible by 9 but not by 3?

(a) 8   (b) 6
(c) 5   (d) Nil

9. In a row of boys facing the North, A is sixteenth from the left end and C is sixteenth from the right end. B, who is fourth to the right of A, is fifth to the left of C in the row. How many boys are there in the row ?

(a) 39   (b) 40
(c) 41   (d) 42

10. In a class of 60, where girls are twice that of boys, kamal ranked seventeenth from the top. If there are 9 girls ahead of kamal, how many boys are after him in rank ?

(a) 3   (b) 7
(c) 12   (d) 23

11. In a queue, A is eighteenth from the front while B is sixteenth from the back. If C is twentieth from the front and is exactly in the middle of A and B, then how many persons are there is the queue ?

(a) 45   (b) 46
(c) 47   (d) 48

12. In a row of 21 girls, when monika was shifted by four place towards the right, she became 12 th from the left end. What was her earlier position from the right end of the row ?

(a) 9th   (b) 10th
(c) 11th   (d) 14 th

13. The positions of the first and the second digits in the number 94316875 are interchanged. Similarly, the positions of the third and fourth digits are interchanged and so on. Which of the following will be the third to the left of the seventh digit from the left end after the rearrangement ?

(a) 1   (b) 4
(c) 6
(d) None of these

14. A bus for Delhi leaves every thirty minutes from a bus stand. An enquiry clerk told a passenger that the bus had already left ten minutes ago and the next bus will leave at 9.35 a.m. At what time did the enquiry clerk give this information to the passenger ?

(a) 9.10 a.m.   (b) 8.55 a.m.
(c) 9.08 a.m.   (d) 9.15 a.m.

15. Ram and Sham are ranked 13th and 14th respectively in a class of 23. What are their ranks from the last respectively?

(a) 10 th : 11th
(b) 11 th; 12 th
(c) 11th ; 10 th
(d) None of these

16. How many 5s are there in the following sequence which are immediately followed by 3 but not immediately preceded by 7?

8 9 5 3 2 5 3 8 5 5 6 8 7 3 3 5 7 7 5 3 6 5 3 3 5 7 3 8

(a) One   (b) Two
(c) Three   (d) Four

17. How many even numbers are there in the following sequence of number which are immediately followed by an odd number as well as immediately preceded by an even number?

8 6 7 6 8 9 3 2 7 5 3 4 2 2 3 5 5 2 2 8 1 1 9

(a) One   (b) Three
(c) Four   (d) Six

18. In the following series of numbers, find out how many times 1, 3 and 7 have appeared together, 7 being in the middle and 1 and 3 on either side of 7.

2 9 7 3 1 7 3 7 7 1 3 3 1 7 3 8 5 7 1 3 7 7 1 7 3 9 0 6

(a) 3
(b) 4
(c) 5
(d) More than 5

19. In the series;

6 4 1 2 2 8 7 4 2 1 5 3 8 6 2 1 7 1 4 1 3 2 8 6

How many pairs of alternate numbers have a difference of 2?

(a) One   (b) Two
(c) Three   (d) Four

Rules: If there are N persons standing in a row and ranks of a person both from the top and from the bottom are Tr and Br, then the rules are

(i) $N = Tr + Br - 1$
(ii) $Tr = (N + 1) - Brand$
(iii) $Br = (N + 1) - Tr.$

20. Sarita is at 27th position from the top in a class of 43 students. What is her rank from the other side?

(a) 16th   (b) 17th
(c) 15th   (d) 21th

21. Anmol finds that he is twelfth from the right in a line of boys and fourth from the left, how many boys should be added to the line such that there are 35 boys in the line?

(a) 19   (b) 13
(c) 14   (d) 20

22. In a row of students, Deepak is seventh from the left and Madhu is twelfth from the right. If they interchange their positions, Deepak becomes twenty-second from the left. How many students are there in the row?

(a) 19   (b) 31
(c) 33
(d) Can't be found

23. If the boy before yesterday was Thursday, when will be Sunday?

(a) Today
(b) Two days after today
(c) Tomorrow
(d) Day after tomorrow

24. Standing on the platform, Amit told Sunita that Aligarh was more that 10 km but less than 15 km from there. Sunita knew that it was more than 12 km but less than 14 km from there. If both of them were correct, which of the following could be the distance of Aligarh from the platform?

(a) 11 km   (b) 12 km
(c) 13 km   (d) 14 km

25. In the following sequence of instructions, 1 stands for Run, 2 stands for Stop, 3 stands for Go, 4 stands for Sit and 5 stands for Wait. If the sequence were to continue, which instruction will come next?

4 4 5 4 5 3 4 5 3 1 4 5 3 1 2 4 5 4 5 3 4 5 3

(a) Wait   (b) Sit
(c) Run   (d) Stop

26. In a class of 60, the number of girls are twice that of boys. Kamal ranked seventeenth from the top. If there are nine girls ahead of Kamal, how many boys are after him in rank?
(a) 3   (b) 7
(c) 12   (d) 23

27. If Thursday was the day after the day before yesterday five days ago, what is the least number of days ago when Sunday was three days before the day after tomorrow?
(a) Two   (b) Three
(c) Four   (d) Five

28. A bus for Delhi leaves every 30 minutes from a bus stand. An enquiry clerk told a passenger that the bus had already left 10 minutes ago and the next bus will leave at 9:35 am. At what time did the enquiry clerk give this information to the passenger?
(a) 9.10 am   (b) 9.15 am
(c) 8.55 am   (d) 8.08 am

29. Rakesh is on 9th position from upwards and on 38th position from downwards in a class. How many students are in class?
(a) 47   (b) 45
(c) 46   (d) 48

30. Sarita is on 11th place from upwards in a group of 45 girls. If we start counting from downwards, what will be her place?
(a) 36th
(b) 34th
(c) 35th
(d) Can not be determined

31. Some boys are sitting in a line. Mahendra is on 17th place from left and Surendra is on 18th place from right. There are 8 boys in between them. How many boys are there in the line?
(a) 43   (b) 42
(c) 41   (d) 44

32. In a row of students, Ramesh is 9th from the left and Suman is 6th from the right. When they both interchange their positions then Ramesh will be 15th from the left. What will be the position of Suman from the right?
(a) 12th   (b) 13th
(c) 15th   (d) 6th

33. In a row of 21 girls, when monika was shifted by four place towards the right, she became 12 th from the left end. What was her earlier positions from the right end of the row ?
(a) 9th   (b) 10th
(c) 11th   (d) 14th

34. Ram and Sham are ranked 13th and 14th respectively is a class of 23. What are their ranks from the last respectively?
(a) 10th : 11th
(b) 11th; 12th
(c) 11th ; 10th
(d) None of these

35. Manisha ranked sixteenth from the top and twenty-nineth from the bottom among those who has passed an examination. Six boys did not participate in the examination and five failed in it. How many boys were there in the class.?
(a) 40   (b) 44
(c) 50   (d) 55

36. In the first and second digits in the sequence 5 9 8 13 2 7 4 3 8 are interchanged. Also the third and fourth digits, the fifth and sixth digits and so on, which digit would be the seventh counting to your left ?
(a) 1   (b) 4
(c) 7   (d) 8

37. Raman is 7 ranks ahead of Suman in a class of 39. If Suman's rank is seventeenth from the last. What is Raman's rank from the start ?
(a)   14 th   (b)   15 th
(c)   16 th   (d)   17 th

38. Mohan and Ramesh are ranked seventh and eleventh respectively from the top in a class of 41 students. What will be their respective ranks from the bottom in the class
(a)   30 th and 34th
(b)   34 th and 30th
(c)   35 th and 31 st
(d)   36 th and 32 nd

39. Manish is fourteenth from the right end in a row of 40 boys. What is his position from the left end ?
(a)   24th   (b)   25th
(c)   26th   (d)   27th

40. In a row of girls. Rita and monika occupy the ninth place from the right end and tenth place from the left end respectively. If the interchange their places, then Rita and monika occupy seventh place from the right and eighteenth place from the left respectively How many girls are there in the row ?
(a)   25   (b)   26
(c)   27
(d)   Data inadequate

SOLUTIONS

1. **(d)** Number of boys who passed $= 16 + 29 - 1 = 44$
$\therefore$ Total number of boys in the class $= 44 + 6 + 5 = 55$

2. **(c)** $T_r = 11, B_r = 31$
$\Rightarrow$ no. of students $= T_r + B_r - 1 = 11 + 31 - 1 = 41$

3. **(b)** $69 = 60 + (15\% \text{ of } 60)$

4. **(b)** Required difference
$= (5 + 7 + 3) - (8 + 4 + 2) = 15 - 14 = 1.$

5. **(c)** According to first condition, the number is greater than 3 but less than 8. Such numbers are 4, 5, 6, 7.
According to the second condition, the number is greater than 6 but less than 10. Such numbers are 7, 8, 9.
Clearly, the required number is the number satisfying both the above conditions, i.e, 7.

6. **(b)** The 2nd, 6th and 9th digits of the number 187642539 are 8, 2 and 9 respectively.
The perfect square of a two-digit odd number, formed using these digits, is 289 and $289 = 17^2$.

7. **(c)** The possible two-digit number are
88, 85, 82, 81, 87, 86, 58,, 28, 18, 78, 68
These are 11 in number.

8. **(d)** Any number divisible by 9 is also divisible by 3.

9. **(b)**

Clearly, according to the given conditions, there are 15 boys to the left of A , as well as to the right of C. Also, B lies between A and C such that there are 3 boys between A and B and 4 boys between B and C. So, number of boys in the row
$= (15 + 1 + 3 + 1 + 4 + 1 + 15) = 40.$

10. **(c)** Let the number of boys be x. Then, number of girls = 2x.
$\therefore$ $x + 2x = 60$ or $3x = 60$ or $x = 20$.
So, number of boys = 20 and number of girls = 40.
Number of students behind Kamal in rank
$(60 - 17) = 43$.
Number of girls ahead of Kamal in rank = 9.
Number of girls behind Kamal in rank = $(40 - 9) = 31$
$\therefore$ Number of boys behind Kamal in rank = $(43 - 31) = 12$.

11. **(c)** A is 18th from front and C is 24th
Number of persons between A and C = 6.
Since C is exactly in middle of A and B, so number of persons between C and B = 6.

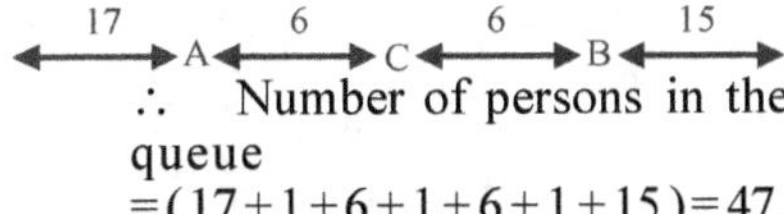

$\therefore$ Number of persons in the queue
$= (17 + 1 + 6 + 1 + 6 + 1 + 15) = 47$.

12. **(d)** The change of place by Monika can be shown as under.

1 2 3 4 5 6 7 8 9 10 11 M 13 14 15 16 17 18 19 20 21

Clearly, Monika's earlier position was 8th from the left and 14th from the right end.

13. **(d)** Changing the positions of the digits as mentioned, we get the number : 49138657.
The seventh digit from the left end of this number is 5.
The third digit to the left of 5 is 3.

14. **(d)** The next bus will leave at 9.35 a.m. This means that the previous bus had left at 9.05 a.m. But it happened ten minutes before the clerk gave the information to the passenger. Thus, the enquiry clerk gave the information at 9.15 a.m.

15. **(c)** Ram's rank from last = 23 – 13 + 1 = 11th
Sham's rank from last = 23 – 14 + 1 = 10th

16. **(c)** The numbers satisfying the given conditions, can be seen as follow: 8 9 5 3 2 5 3 8 5 5 6 8 7 3 3 5 7 7 5 3 6 5 3 3 5 7 3 8
Clearly there are three such numbers.

17. **(c)** 8 6 7 6 8 9 3 2 7 5 3 4 2 2 3 5 5 2 2 8 1 1 9

18. **(a)** 2 9 7 3 1 7 3 7 7 1 3 3 1 7 3 8 5 7 1 3 7 7 1 7 3 9 0 6

19. **(b)** Clearly there are two such pairs only namely (4, 2); (1, 3)

20. **(b)** Sarita rank from the bottom = $(43 + 1) - 27 = 17$.

21. **(d)** Clearly, number of boys in a line = 12 + 4 – 1 = 15
$\therefore$ Number of boys to be added = 35 – 15 = 20.

22. **(c)** Deepak's new position is 22nd from left. But it is the same as Madhu's earlier position i.e. 12th from the right.
$\therefore$ there are (22 + 12 – 1) i.e. 33 boys in the row.

23. **(c)** If day before yesterday was Thursday, so today is Saturday. So tomorrow will be Sunday.

24. **(c)** Clearly, according to Sunita, the distance was more than 12 km but less than 14 km which is 13 km.

25. **(c)** The given sequence may be analysed as under:
4, 45, 453, 4531, 45312, 45, 453, 453
Following the above sequence, the next number is 1 which stands for 'run'.

26. **(c)** Clearly there are 20 boys and 40 girls. Number of students behind Kamal in rank = 60 – 17 = 43
Number of girls ahead of Kamal in rank = 9.

∴ Number of girls behind Kamal in rank $= 40 - 9 = 31$.

∴ Number of boys behind Kamal in rank $= 43 - 31 = 12$.

27. **(a)** Day after the day before yesterday is yesterday. Now, five days ago, yesterday was Thursday. So five days ago it was Friday.

∴ Today is Wednesday. Now three days before the day after tomorrow is yesterday. Now it is on Monday that we say yesterday was Sunday.

28. **(b)** The next bus will leave at 9.35 am. This means that the previous bus had left at 9.05 am but that happened 10 minutes before the clerk gave the information to the passenger. Thus the enquiry clerk gave the information at 9.15 am.

29. **(c)** Total students
= [Rakesh's position from upwards + Rakesh's position from downwards] – 1
$= [9 + 38] - 1 = 46$

30. **(c)** Sarita's place from downwards

$$= \left[\frac{\text{Total}}{\text{girls}} - \frac{\text{Sarita's place}}{\text{from upwards}} \right] + 1 =$$

$[45 - 11] + 1 = 35\text{th}$

31. **(a)** Total boys

$$= \left[\begin{array}{ccc} \text{Mahendra's} & & \text{Surendra's} \\ \text{place} & + & \text{place} \\ \text{from left} & & \text{from right} \end{array} \right]$$

$$+ \left[\begin{array}{c} \text{Boys between} \\ \text{them} \end{array} \right]$$

$= [17 + 18] + 8 = 43$

32. **(a)** Position of Suman from right

$$= \left[\begin{array}{cc} \text{Difference of} & + & \text{First position} \\ \text{Ramesh's position} & & \text{of Suman} \end{array} \right]$$

$= [(15 - 9) + 6] = 12\text{th}$

33. **(d)** The change of place by Monika can be shown as under.

1 2 3 4 5 6 7 8 9 10 11 M 13 14 15 16 17 18 19 20 21

Clearly, Monika's earlier position was 8th from the left and 14th from the right end.

34. **(c)** Rank of Ram from the last
$= 23 - 13 + 1 = 11$
and Rank of Shyam from the last
$= 23 - 14 + 1 = 10$

35. **(d)** Number of boys who passed $= 16 + 29 - 1 = 44$
∴ Total number of boys in the class $= 44 + 6 + 5 = 55$

36. **(d)** The new sequence becomes 9 5 1 8 2 3 4 7 8 3 counting to the left, the seventh number is 8.

37. **(c)** Suman is 17th from the last and Raman is 7 ranks ahead of Suman. So Raman is 24 th from the last.

∴ Raman rank from the start is $39 + 1 - 24$ i.e, 16 th

38. **(c)** Rank of Mohan from the bottom $= (41 + 1) - 7 = 35$ th.
Rank of Ramesh from the bottom $= (41 + 1) - 11 = 31$ st.

39. **(d)** Clearly, number of boys towards the left of Manish $= (40 - 14) = 26$.
So, Manish is 27th from the left end.

40. **(b)** Since Rita and Monika exchange places, so Rita's new position is the same as Monika's earlier positions. This position is 17 th from the right and 10th from the left
∴ Number of girls in the row $= (16 + 1 + 9) = 26$.

Blood Relations

While attempting questions on blood relations, one should be clear of all the relation patterns that can exist between any two individuals.

These type of questions are given mainly to test one's relationship ability.

Mother's or father's son	Brother
Mother's or father's daughter	Sister
Mother's or father's brother	Uncle
Mother's or father's sister	Aunt
Mother's or father's father	Grandfather
Mother's or father's mother	Grandmother
Son's wife	Daughter-in-law
Daughter's husband	Son-in-law
Husband's or wife's sister	Sister-in-law
Husband's or wife's brother	Brother-in-law
Brother's son	Nephew
Brother's daughter	Niece
Uncle or aunt's son or daughter	Cousin
Sister's husband	Brother-in-law
Brother's wife	Sister-in-law
Grandson's or Grand daughter's daughter	Great granddaughter

A relation on the mother's side is called maternal while that on the father's side is called paternal. Thus, mother's brother is maternal uncle while father's brother is paternal uncle.

To solve problems on relationship you can construct family tree.

To build a family tree, certain standard notations are used to indicate a relationship between the members of the family. It is not necessary to follow them implicity; you can formulate your own notations to draw the family tree quickly and accurately

1. A is male   A

2. A is a female   

3.	Sex of A not known	A
4.	A and B are married to each other	A = B
5.	A and B are siblings	A ⟷ B

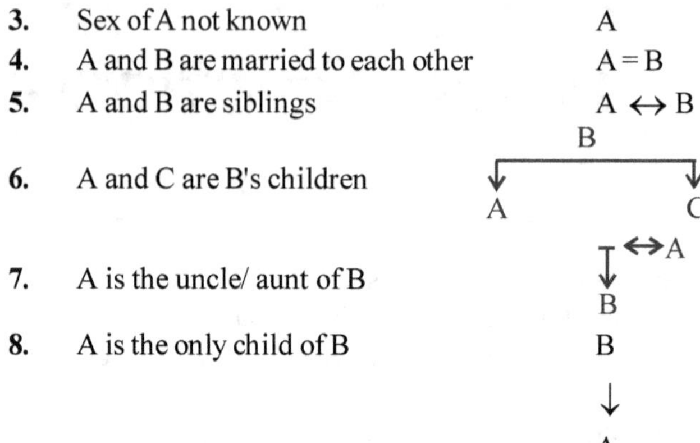

6.   A and C are B's children

7.   A is the uncle/ aunt of B

8.   A is the only child of B

To make a family tree from the given data, we will first identify the males and the females in the family and then try to put each member in their respective position in the tree. For example A, B, C, D, E and F are related to each other as given here, B is F's daughter-in-law. D is A's only grand child. C is D's only uncle. A has only 2 children F and C, one male and one female (not necessarily in the same order). E is the father of C.

(i)   Who is the grandmother of D ?

(ii)   Who is the mother-in-law of B?

(iii)   When a girl G is married into the family, what is the relationship between G and D?

Step I : Identify the elements A, B, C, D, E and F,

From the given conditions we can determine who are the males/ females in the above group.

(a)   B is F's daughter-in-law   Ⓑ

(b)   C is D's only uncle   

(c)   A has 2 children F and C, one male   Ⓕ

and one female, Since C is male, F is Female.

Step II : Try to identify the positions of the members in the family tree. For this , determine the number of generations involved from the statements. D is A's only grand child. Thus, we know that there are three generations.

Step III : Use the conditions to arrange A , B , C , D , E and F in these three generations.

(a) B is F 's daughter-in-law,

(b) D is A 's only grandchild

(c) C is D's uncle.

(d) A has only two children

F and C, one male and one female.

(e) E is C's father.

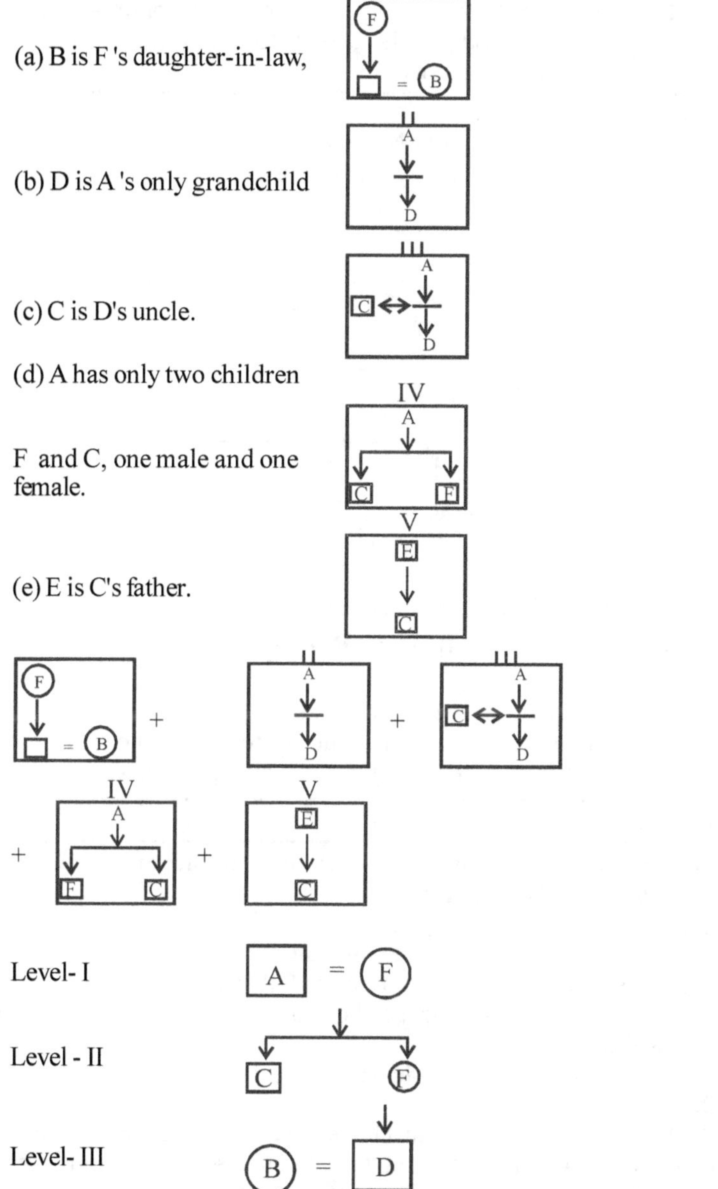

Level- I

Level - II

Level- III

Question (i) and (ii) can be answered easily by looking at the family tree. A is the grandmother of D and F is the mother-in -law of B. For question (iii), C is the only male in the family who is unmarried. G will be married to C and hence she will be D's aunt.

DIRECTIONS (Illustration 1) : Abra is Rambo's daughter. Shintu is Rambo's sister. Shintu's daughter is called Cabra and son is called Dabra. Limba is Cabra's maternal Aunt.

Abra is Limba's

(a)   Aunt   (b)   Nephew
(c)   Uncle   (d)   None of these

Sol. **(d)**

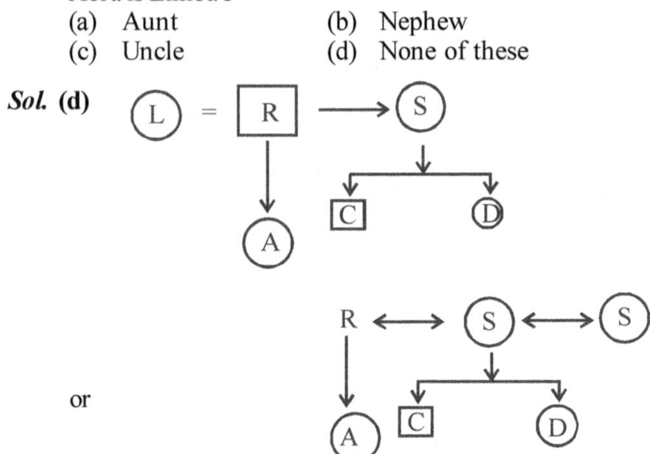

or

Abra can be Limba's niece or daughter.

PROBLEMS IN DECIDING RELATIONSHIP

TYPE 1 :

In this type of question, a roundabout description is given in the form of certain small relationships and you are required to analyse the whole chain of relations and decipher the direct relationship between the persons concerned.

Illustration 2:

Anil introduces Rohit as the son of the only brother of his father's wife. How is Rohit related to Anil ?

(a)   Cousin   (b)   Son
(c)   Uncle   (d)   Son-in-law

Sol.   **(a)**   The relations may be analysed as follows.

Father's wife– mother, Mother's brother — Uncle; Uncle's son— Cousin.

So, Rohit is Anil's cousin. Hence, the answer is (a)

TYPE 2 :

In this type of question, mutual blood relations of more than two persons are mentioned. The candidate is required to analyse the given information, work out a family chart and then answer the given questions.

DIRECTIONS (Illustration 3) : Read the following information carefully and answer the questions given below.

There are six children playing football, namely A,B,C,D, E and F. A and E are brothers. F is the sister of E. C is the only son of A's uncle. B and D are the daughter of the brother of C's father.

How is C related to F ?

(a) Cousin   (b) Brother son

(c) Son   (d) Uncle

Sol. **(a)** F is E's and hence A's sister. So, C is also the son of F's uncle and is, therefore, F's Cousin.

TYPE 3:

Coded Relations

In such questions, the relationships are represented by certain specific codes or symbols. The candidate is then required to analyse some given codes to determine the relationship between a set of persons, or to express a given relationship in the coded form.

DIRECTIONS (Illustration 4) : Study the information given below and answer the questions that follow :

A + B ' means 'A is the daughter of B; A – B ' means ' A is the husband of B'. A × B means A is the brother of B.

If P + Q – R, which of the following is true ?

(a) R is the mother of P.

(b) R is the sister in -law of P.

(c) R is the aunt of P.

(d) R is the mother in- law of P.

Sol. **(a)** P + Q – R means P is the daughter of Q who is the husband of R i.e, R is the mother of P.

--- (Useful Tips) ---

1. The only son of your father — Yourself
2. Wife of the father —Mother
3. The only son of grand father or grand mother – father
4. The only daughter-in-law of grand father or grand mother – Mother
5. Mother-in-law of mother –Grand mother
6. Father-in-law of mother – Grand father
7. The only daughter of the father –Sister
8. Son of the father of the sister – Brother
9. Son of the only son of the father –son
10. Son of the only son of grand father – Brother
11. Daughter of the only son of Grand father – Sister

EXERCISE

DIRECTIONS (Qs. 1 to 5) : Read the following information carefully to answer the questions.

(i)   'A $ B' means 'A' is mother of B'

(ii)   A' # B' means "A' is father of B'

(iii)   'A @ B' Means 'A' is husband of B'

(iv)   'A % B' means A is daughter of B'

1. P @ Q $ M # T indicates what relationship of P with T
   (a) Paternal grandmother
   (b) Maternal grandmother
   (c) Paternal grandfather
   (d) Maternal grandfather

2. Which of the following expressions indicates 'R is the sister of H'?
   (a) H $ D @ F # R
   (b) R % D @ F $ H
   (c) R $ D @ F # H
   (d) H % D @ F $ R

3. If F @ D % K # H, then how is F related to H?
   (a) Brother-in-law
   (b) Sister
   (c) Sister-in-law
   (d) Cannot be determined

4. Which of the following expressions indicates 'H is the brother of N'?
   (a) H # R $ D $ N
   (b) N % F @ D $ H # R
   (c) N% F @ D $ H
   (d) N% F @ D % H

5. If G $ M @ K, how is K related to G?
   (a) Daughter-in-law
   (b) Mother-in-law
   (c) Daughter
   (d) Aunt

6. A lady said, ' The person standing there is my grandfather's only son's daughter' How is the lady related to the standing person?
   (a) Sister   (b) Mother
   (c) Aunt   (d) Cousin

7. Given that
   1. A is the mother of B
   2. C is the son of A
   3. D is the brother of E
   4. E is the daughter of B.
   The grandmother of D is
   (a) A   (b) B
   (c) C   (d) E

8. Deepak said to Nitin, " That boy playing football is the younger of the two brothers of the daughter of my father's wife " How is the boy playing football related to Deepak ?
   (a) Son   (b) Brother
   (c) Cousin   (d) Niece

9. Pointing out to a lady, a girl said " she is the daughter-in-law of the grandmother of my father's only son." How is the lady related to the girl ?
   (a) Sister-in-law
   (b) Mother
   (c) Aunt
   (d) Mother-in-law

10. A and B are brothers. C and D are sisters A's son is D's brother. How is B related to C
    (a) Father
    (b) Brother
    (c) Grand father
    (d) Uncle

11. Pointing out to a photograph, a man tells his friend, " she is the daughter of the only son of my father's wife. How is the girls

related to the man in the photograph?

(a) Daughter (b) Cousin
(c) Mother (d) Sister

12. X' is the wife of 'Y' and 'Y' and Y' is the brother of 'Z' , 'Z' is the son of 'P' . How is 'P' related to 'X'

(a) Sister (b) Aunt
(c) Brother (d) Father

13. Ajay is the brother of Vijay. Mili is the sister of Ajay. Sanjay is the brother of Rahul and Mehul is the daughter of Vijay. Who is Sanjay's Uncle ?

(a) Rahul

(b) Ajay

(c) Mehul

(d) Data inadequate

14. If S – T means 'S' is the wife of 'T' is S + T means 'S' is the daughter of 'T' and S ÷ T means 'S' is the son of 'T' What will M + J ÷ K means ?

(a) 'K' is the father of 'M'
(b) M' is the grand daughter
(c) 'J' is wife of 'K'
(d) 'K' and 'M' are brothers

15. A man pointing to a photograph says. "The lady in the photograph is my nephew's maternal grandmother". How is the lady in the photograph related to the man's sister who has no other sister.

(a) Cousin
(b) Sister-in-law
(c) Mother
(d) Mother-in-law

16. Pointing to Kapil, shilpa said, His mothers's brother is the father of my son Ashish" How is kapil related to shilpa
(a) Sister-in-law
(b) Nephew
(c) Niece
(d) Aunt

17. A is the uncle of B, who is the daughter of C and C is the daughter-in-law of P. How is A related to P?
(a) Brother
(b) Son
(c) Son-in-law
(d) Data inadequate

18. E is the son of A. D is the son of B. E is married to C. C is B's daughter. How is D related to E?
(a) Brother
(b) Uncle
(c) Father-in-law
(d) Brother-in-law

DIRECTIONS (Qs. 19 to 20) : Study the following information and answer the questions given below.
'P = Q' means Q is the father of P'
'P * Q' means 'P' is the sister of Q'
'P ? Q' means Q is the mother of P'
'P $ Q means P is the brother of Q'
'P ς Q' means Q is the son of P'
'P x Q' means 'P is the daughter of

19. Which of the following is not correct ?
(a) R x S ? T means R is the granddaughter of T.
(b) P = Q ? R means R is the grandmother of P.
(c) L $ M * O means O is the sister of L.
(d) M * O P ς P = Q means Q and O are husband and wife.

20. If P $Q means P is the father of Q, P # Q means P is mother Q,& P * Q means P is the sister of then how is related to N if N # L $ P * Q
(a) grandson
(b) grand daughter
(c) nephew
(d) data inadequate

21. A is the brother of B, C is the brother of A . To establish a relationship between B & C, which of the following information is required.

I   Sex of C

II.   Sex of B

(a) Only I is required

(b) Only II is required

(c) Both I and II are required

(d) Neither required

22. Pointing towards a man in the photograph, lady said the father of his brother is the only son of my mother " How is the man related to lady ?

(a) Brother   (b) Son

(c) Cousin   (d) Nephew

23. Soni, who is Dubey's daughter, says to Preeti, "Your mother Shyama is the yougest sister of my father, Dubey's Father's child is Prabhat". How is Prabhat related to Preeti ?

(a) Uncle

(b) Father

(c) Grandmother

(d) Father in law

24. Pointing towards a man in the photograph, Arachana said, " He is the son of only son of may grandmother". "How is man related to Archana ?

(a) Cousin   (b) Nephew

(c) Brother   (d) Son

25. Pointing towards a woman in the photograph, Rajesh said "the only daughter of her grandfather (Paternal) is my wife". How is Rajesh related to that woman

(a) Uncle (Fufa)

(b) Father

(c) Maternal uncle

(d) Brother

DIRECTIONS (Qs. 26-27) : Read the following information and answer the questions that follow:

S and R are brothers. T is daughter of S. U is the spouse of R and mother of Q. P is the daughter of V, who is the spouse of T.

26. Who is the grand father of P ?

(a) U   (b) S

(c) R   (d) V

27. Who is the cousin of Q ?

(a) T   (b) V

(c) R   (d) P

SOLUTIONS

1. **(c)** P @ Q $ # T means P is the husband of Q who is the mother of M who is the father of T i.e, is the father of T' s father i.e, P is T' paternal grandfather.

2. **(b)** R is the sister of H means R is the daughter of the father of H i.e., R is the daughter of the husband (say D) of the mother (say F) of H i.e, R % D @ F $ H.

3. **(a)** F @ D % K # H means F is the husband of D who is the daughter of K who is the father of H i.e, F is the husband of D who is the sister of H i.e, F is H's F is H's brother in-law.

4. **(b)** H is the brother of N means N is the daughter of H's father and H is a male i.e, N is the daughter of the husband (say F) i.e, N % F @ D $ H # R or N% F @ D $ H @ R. husband of some other person (say, F) or the father (say, D) of H and H is the father or husband of some other person (say, R) i.e, N% F @ D $ H # R or N% F @ D$ H @ R.

5. **(a)** G $ M @ K means G is the mother of M who is the husband of K i.e, K is the wife of G's son i.e, K is G's daughter-in-law

6. **(a)**

Grandfather

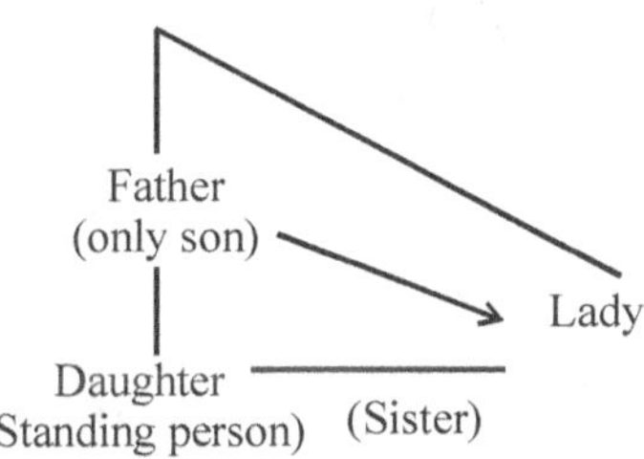

Lady's grandfather's son is lady's father and father's daughter will only be lady's sister.

7. **(a)** D is the brother of E and E is the daughter of B. This means that D is the son of B. Also, A is the mother of B. So, A is the grandmother of D.

8. **(b)** Father's Wife — Mother; Mother's daughter — Sister Deepak's sister's younger brother— Deepak's brother.

9. **(b)** Girl's Father's only son— Girl's brother Grandmother of Girl's brother – Girl's Grandmother; Daughter-in-law of girl's grandmother — Girls' mother.

10. **(d)** Studying the statements carefully, was find that B is the brother of A and A's son is the brother of D, so D is the daughter of A. Since C and D are sister, so C is also the daughter of A. The B is the uncle of C. The answer is (d)

11. **(a)** Father's wife means mother ; mother's only son means himself and thus the girls is the daughter of the man.

12. **(d)** The relationship chart, based on the given problem can be worked out as given below.

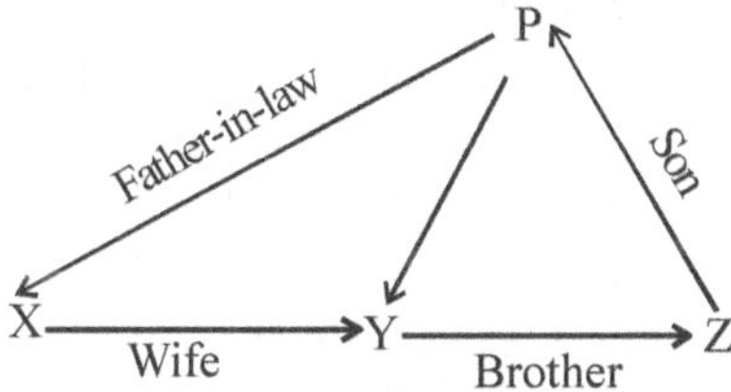

'Y' is the brother of 'Z' who is son of "P' So. Z' is also the son of 'P' When 'P' is the father of 'Y' and X' is the wife of 'Y' then 'P is the father-in-law of 'X'

13. **(d)**

1. Mili —→ Ajay —→ Vijay —→ Mehul
  (Sister)   (Brother)

(daughter)

2. Sanjay —————→ Rahul
            (brother)

There are two sets of relationship information given is incomplete and no relation can be established between the two sets.

14. **(b)** M + J means 'M' is the

daughter of 'J' J + K means 'J' is the son of 'K'

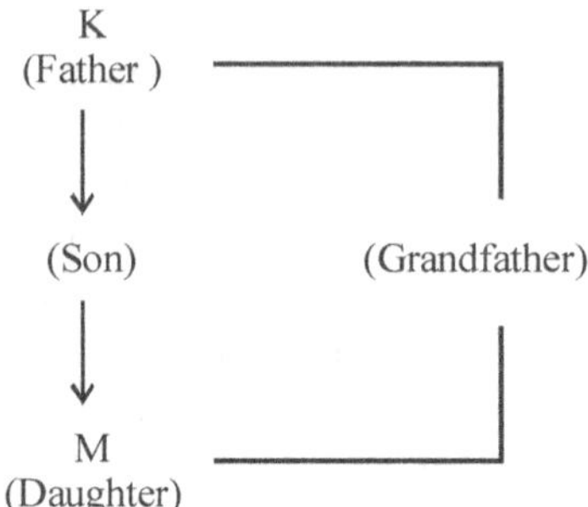

15. **(c)** Clearly, the lady is the grandmother of man's sister's son i.e, the mother of the mother of man's sister's son i.e, the mother of man's sister.

16. **(b)** Father of shilpa's son— Shilpa's husband.

So, kapil is the son of sister of shilpa's husband. Thus, Kapil is shilpa's nephew.

17. **(b)** B is the daughter of C and C is the daughter in law of P. So P is the grandfather of B. Also, A is uncle of B i.e, A is the brother of B's father. Thus, A is the son of P.

18. **(d)** C is B's daughter and D is B's son. So, D is the brother of C.E is a male married to C so, E is the husband of C, whose brother is D. Thus, D But D is the brother in-law of E.

19. **(c)** R x S ? T means R is the daughter of S whose mother is T i.e, R is the granddaughter of T.

P = Q ? R means R is the mother of Q who is the father of P i.e, R is the grandmother of P.

L$M * O means L is the brother of M who is the sister of O i.e, L is the brother of O i.e, O is the brother of sister of L.

M * O S P = Q means Q is the father of the son (P) of O i.e, Q is the father and O is the mother of P i.e Q and O are husband and wife.

20. **(d)** The sex of Q is not given hence the exact relation ship between N & Q cannot be established.

21. **(b)** It is clear that C is the Brother of B but how B is related to C depends on the sex of B.

22. **(d)** The father of his brother means " his father" is the only son of my mother means " my brother" It means lady's is the father's sister of the man's father.

23. **(a)** Preeti's mother Shyama is youngest sister of Dubey & Sister of Prabhat. Therefore Prabhat is Preeti's uncle.

24. **(c)** Only son of Archana's grandfather means Archana's father & his son is Archana's brother.

25. **(a)** Rajesh is the husband of woman's father's sister.

26. **(b)** P is the daughter of V, who is spouse of T. T is the daughter of S. So, T is the mother and V is the father of P. Therefore, S is the grandfather of P.

27. **(a).** R and S are brothers. Q is the child of R and T is the child of S. So, cousin of Q is T.

CHAPTER 7

Mathematical Operations/ Quantitative Reasoning

MATHEMATICAL OPERATIONS

This section deals with questions on simple mathematical operations. There are four fundamental operations, namely :

Additions i.e, + ; Subtraction i.e, – ;

Multiplication i.e, X ; and Division i.e. , ÷

There are also statements such as Less than i.e. <, greater than i.e. >, and equal to i.e =, not equal to i.e $\neq$, etc.

Such operations are represented by symbols different from the usual ones. The questions involving these operations are coded using artificial symbols. The candidate has to make a substitution of the real signs and solve the equation accordingly.

We always, while solving a mathematical expression, proceed according to the rule B O D M A S.

i.e, B for Brackets ; O for ' of (literally multiplication),

D for division ; M for multiplication , A for additions and S for subtraction in sequence.

PROBLEM-SOLVING BY SUBSTITUTION

In this type, you are provided with substitutes for various mathematical symbols or numbers. Followed by a question involving calculation of an expression or choosing the correct/ incorrect equations. The candidate is required to put in the real signs or numerals in the given equation and then solve the questions as required.

Illustration 1 :

If L stands for +, M stands for –, N stands for x, P stands for ÷ , then 14 N 10 L 42 P 2 M 8 = ?

(a) 153 (b) 216

(c) 248 (d) 251

Sol. **(a)** Using the proper signs, we get

Given expression

$= 14 \times 10 + 42 \div 2 - 8 = 14 \times 10 + 21 - 8$

$= 140 + 21 - 8 = 161 - 8 = 153.$

QUANTITATIVE REASONING

Arithmetical Reasoning tests the ability to solve basic arithmetic problems encountered in everyday life. These problems require basic mathematical skills like addition, subtraction, multiplication, division etc. The tests include operations with whole numbers, rational numbers, ratio and proportion, interest and percentage, and measurement. Arithmetical reasoning is one factor that helps characterize mathematics comprehension, and it also assesses logical thinking.

EXAMPLE 1.

The total of the ages of Amar, Akbar and Anthony is 80 years. What was the total of their ages three years ago ?

(a)   71 years   (b)   72 years

(c)   74 years   (d)   77 years

Sol.   (a)   Required sum = (80 – 3 x 3) years = (80 – 9) years

$$= 71 \text{ years.}$$

EXERCISE

1.   In the following questions which one of the four interchanges in signs and numbers would make the given equation correct ?
$(3 \div 4) + 2 = 2$
(a)   + and ÷, 2 and 3
(b)   + and ÷, 2 and 4
(c)   + and ÷, 3 and 4
(d)   No interchanges, 3 and 4

2.   If A stands for +, B stands for – , C stands for x, then what is the value of $(10 \text{ C} 4) + (4 \text{ C } 4) \text{ B } 6$?
(a)   60   (b)   56
(c)   50   (d)   20

3.   If P denotes ÷, Q denotes ×, R denotes + and S denotes –, then the value of $18 \text{ Q } 12 \text{ P } 4 \text{ R } 5 \text{ S } 6$ when simplified gives
(a)   36   (b)   53
(c)   59   (d)   65

4.   If + means ÷ ,– means ×, ÷ means + and × means –, then
$36 \times 8 + 4 \div 6 + 2 - 3 = ?$
(a)   2   (b)   18
(c)   43   (d) $6\dfrac{1}{2}$

5.   It being given that :> denotes +, < denotes –, + denotes ÷, – denotes =, = denotes 'less than' and × denotes 'greater than' , find which of the following is a correct statement:
(a) $3 + 2 > 4 = 9 + 3 < 1$
(b) $3 > 2 > 4 = 18 + 3 < 2$
(c) $3 > 2 < 4 \times 8 + 4 < 2$
(d) $3 + 2 < 4 \times 9 + 3 < 3$

6.   If L denotes ×, M denotes ÷ , P denotes + and Q denotes –, than $8 \text{ P } 36 \text{ M } 6 \text{ Q } 6 \text{ M } 2 \text{ L } 3 = ?$
(a) $\dfrac{13}{6}$ (b) $-\dfrac{1}{6}$
(c) $14\dfrac{1}{2}$ (d)   5

7.   If × stands for' addition', < for 'substraction', + stands for 'division', > for 'multiplication', –, stands for 'equal to', ÷ for 'greater than' and = stands for 'less than', state which of the following is true ?
(a) $3 \times 2 < 4 \div 16 > 2 + 4$
(b) $5 > 2 + 2 = 10 < 4 \times 2$

    (c) $3 \times 4 > 2 - 9 + 3 < 3$
    (d) $5 \times 3 < 7 \div 8 + 4 \times 1$

8. If + means ×. × means −, ÷ means + and − means ÷, then which of the following gives the result of
$175 - 25 \div 5 \div 20 \times 3 + 10$?
    (a) 77   (b) 160
    (c) 240   (d) 2370

9. If $20 - 10$ means 200, $8 \div 4$ means 12, 6×2 means 4 then
$100 - 10 \times 1000 \div 1000 + 100 \times 10 = ?$
    (a) 0   (b) 20
    (c) 1000   (d) 1900

10. If ' + ' means ' divided by', '−' means ' added to', 'x' means ' subtracted from' and ÷ means ' multiplied by', then what is the value of $24 \div 12 - 18 + 9$?
    (a) -25 (b) 0.72
    (c) 15.30   (d) 290

11. If × means ÷, − means × , ÷ means + and + means − then
$(3 - 15 \div 19) \times 8 + 6 = ?$
    (a) -1 (b) 2
    (c) 4   (d) 8

12. If ÷ means +, − means ÷, × means − and + means ×, then $=$
$$\frac{(36 \times 4) - 8 \times 4}{4 + 8 \times 2 + 16 \div 1} \; ?$$
    (a) 0   (b) 8
    (c) 12   (d) 16

13. IF P means ' division', T means ' additions', M means ' subtraction and D means multiplication', then what will be the value of the expressions 12 M 12 D 28 P 7 T 15 ?
    (a) -30 (b) -15
    (c) 15   (d) −21

14. If A stands for +, B stands for − , C stands for ×, then what is the value of $(10 \, C \, 4) \, A \, (4 \, C \, 4) \, B \, 6$?
    (a) 60   (b) 56
    (c) 50   (d) 46

15. If → stands for ' addition'; ← stands for ' subtraction' ; ↑ stands for ' division '; ↓ stands for ' multiplication' ; ↗ stands for equal to', then which of the following alternatives is correct ?
    (a) $7 \leftarrow 43 \uparrow 6 \downarrow 1 \nearrow 4$
    (b) $3 \downarrow 6 \uparrow 2 \rightarrow 3 \leftarrow 6 \nearrow 5$
    (c) $5 \rightarrow 7 \leftarrow 3 \uparrow 2 \nearrow 5$
    (d) $2 \downarrow 5 \leftarrow 6 \rightarrow 2 \nearrow 6$

16. Of 'x' Stands for ' addition' 'z' for subtraction' '+' for division' > for multiplication' '−' for equal to' '+' for ' greater than' and '=' for ' less than' state which of the following is true. ?
    (a) $3 \, x \, 4 > 2 - 9 + 3 < 3$
    (b) $5 \, x \, 3 < 7 \div 8 + 4 \, x \, 1$
    (c) $5 > 2 + 2 = 10 < 4 \, x \, 8$
    (d) $3 \, x \, 2 < 4 \div 16 > 2 + 4$

17. If the given interchanges namely : signs + and ÷ and numbers 2 and 4 are made in signs and numbers, which one of the following four equations would be correct ?
    (a) $2 + 4 \div 3 = 3$
    (b) $4 + 2 \div 6 = 1.5$
    (c) $4 \div 2 + 3 = 4$
    (d) $2 + 4 \div 6 = 8.$

18. Which one of the four interchanges in signs and numbers would make the given equation correct ?
$3 + 5 - 2 = 0$
    (a) + and −, 2 and 3
    (b) + and −, 2 and 5
    (c) + and − , 3 and 5
    (d) None of these

19. The letters L, M, N, O, P, R, S and T in their order are substituted by nine integers 1 to 9 but not in that order. 4 is

assigned to P. The difference between P and T is 5. The difference between N and T is 3. What is the integer assigned to N?
(a) 4   (b) 5
(c) 6   (d) 7

20. The 30 members of a club decided to play a badminton singles tournament. Every time a member loses a game he is out of the tournament. There are no ties. What is the minimum number of matches that must be played to determine the winner?
(a) 15   (b) 29
(c) 61
(d) None of these

21. A tailor had a number of shirt pieces to cut from a roll of fabric. He cut each roll of equal length into 10 pieces. He cut at the rate of 45 cuts a minute. How many rolls would be cut in 24 minutes?
(a) 32 rolls   (b) 54 rolls
(c) 108 rolls   (d) 120 rolls

22. In a class of 60 students, the number of boys and girls participating in the annual sports is in the ratio 3 : 2 respectively. The number of girls not participating in the sports is 5 more than the number of boys not participating in the sports. If the number of boys participating in the sports is 15, then how many girls are there in the class?
(a) 20   (b) 25
(c) 30
(d) Data inadequate

23. At a dinner party every two guests used a bowl of rice between them, every three guests used a bowl of daal between them and every four used a bowl of meat between

them. There were altogether 65 dishes. How many guests were present at the party ?
(a) 60   (b) 65
(c) 90
(d) None of these

24. In a family, each daughter has the same number of brothers as she has sisters and each son has twice as many sisters as he has brothers. How many sons are there in the family?
(a) 2   (b) 3
(c) 4   (d) 5

25. In a garden, there are 10 rows and 12 columns of mango trees. The distance between the two trees is 2 metres and a distance of one metre is left from all sides of the boundary of the garden. The length of the garden is
(a) 20 m   (b) 22 m
(c) 24 m   (d) 26 m

26. In a family, the father took 1/4 of the cake and he had 3 times as much as each of the other members had. The total number of family members is
(a) 3   (b) 7
(c) 10   (d) 12

27. In three coloured boxes - Red, Green and Blue, 108 balls are placed. There are twice as many balls in the green and red boxes combined as there are in the blue box and twice as many in the blue box as there are in the red box. How many balls are there in the green box ?
(a) 18
(b) 36
(c) 45
(d) None of these

28. A, B, C, D and E play a game of cards. A says to B, "If you give me 3 cards, you will have as many as I have at this moment

while if D takes 5 cards from you, he will have as many as E has." A and C together have twice as many cards as E has. B and D together also have the same number of cards as A and C taken together. If together they have 150 cards, how many cards has C got ?
(a) 28   (b) 29
(c) 31   (d) 35

29. A man wears socks of two colours - Black and brown. He has altogether 20 black socks and 20 brown socks in a drawer. Supposing he has to take out the socks in the dark, how many must he take out to be sure that he has a matching pair ?
(a) 3   (b) 20
(c) 39
(d) None of these

30. I have a few sweets to be distributed. If I keep 2, 3 or 4 in a pack, I am left with one sweet. If I keep 5 in a pack, I am left with none. What is the minimum number of sweets I have to pack and distribute ?
(a) 25   (b) 37
(c) 54   (d) 65

31. Mr. X, a mathematician, defines a number as 'connected with 6 if it is divisible by 6 or if the sum of its digits is 6, or if 6 is one of the digits of the number. Other numbers are all 'not connected with 6'. As per this definition, the number of integers from 1 to 60 (both inclusive) which are not connected with 6 is
(a) 18   (b) 22
(c) 42   (d) 43

32. A player holds 13 cards of four suits, of which seven are black and six are red. There are twice as many diamonds as spades

and twice as many hearts as diamonds. How many clubs does he hold ?
(a) 4   (b) 5
(c) 6   (d) 7

33. Nitin's age was equal to square of some number last year and the following year it would be cube of a number. If again Nitin's age has to be equal to the cube of some number, then for how long he will have to wait?
(a) 10 years   (b) 38 years
(c) 39 years   (d) 64 years

34. At the end of a business conference the ten people present all shake hands with each other once. How many handshakes will there be altogether ?
(a) 20   (b) 45
(c) 55   (d) 90

35. Anand, David, Karim and Mano are fans of games. Each has a different favourite game among hockey, chess, cricket and football. David doesn't watch cricket and hockey matches. Anand doesn't like hockey, chess and cricket. Mano doesn't watch cricket. Which is favourite game of Karim?
(a) chess   (b) cricket
(c) football   (d) hockey

36. David gets on the elevator at the 11th floor of a building and rides up at the rate of 57 floors per minute. At the same time. Albert gets on an elevator at the 51st floor of the same building and rides down at the rate of 63 floors per minute. If they continue travelling at these rates, then at which floor will their paths cross?
(a) 19   (b) 28
(c) 30   (d) 37

37. A fibres 5 shots to B's 3 but A kills only once in 3 shots while B kills once in 2 shots. When B has missed 27 times, A has killed
(a) 30 birds   (b) 60 birds
(c) 72 birds   (d) 90 birds

38. First bunch of bananas has (1/4) again as many bananas as a second bunch. If the second bunch has 3 bananas less than the first bunch, then the number of bananas in the first bunch is
(a) 9   (b) 10
(c) 12   (d) 15

39. A boy's age is one fourth of his father's age. The sum of the boy's age and his father's age is 35. What will be father's age after 8 years?

(a) 15   (b) 28
(c) 35   (d) 36

40. If 1 candle in box number 1 is placed in box number 2, then box-2 has twice the number of candles that box 1 has.
If 1 candle from box-2 is placed in box-1, the box-2 and box-1 have the same number of candles.
How many candles were there in box-1 and box-2 ?

Box--1 Box-2
Box-1 Box-2

(a) $\boxed{5}:\boxed{3}$ (b) $\boxed{7}:\boxed{5}$
(c) $\boxed{6}:\boxed{4}$ (d) $\boxed{5}:\boxed{7}$

SOLUTIONS

1. **(a)** On interchanging + and ÷ and b and c, we get the equations as $(2 + 4) \div 3 = 2$ or $6 \div 3 = 2$ or $2 = 2$, which is true.

2. **(c)** Given expression = $(10 \times 4) + (4 \times 4) - 6 = 50$

3. **(b)** Using correct symbols, we have
Given expression = $18 \times 12 \div 4 + 5 - 6$
$= 18 \times 3 + 5 - 6 = 54 + 5 - 6 = 53$

4. **(c)** Using the proper signs, we get:
$36 - 8 4 + 6 \div 2 \times 3 = 36 - 2 + 3 \times 3 = 36 - 2 + 9 = 45 - 2 = 43$

5. **(c)** Using proper notations, we have:
(a) given statement is $3 \div 2 + 4 < 9 \div 3 - 1$ or $\dfrac{11}{2} < 2$,
which is not true.

(b) given statement is $3 + 2 + 4 < 18 \div 3 - 2$ or $9 < 4$, which is not true.

(c) given statement is $3 + 2 - 4 > 8 \div 4 - 2$ or $1 > 0$, which is true.

(d) given statement is $3 \div 2 - 4 > 9 \div 3 - 3$ or $-\dfrac{5}{2} > 0$, which is not true . So, the statement (c) is true.

6. **(d)** Using the correct symbols, we have:
Given expression $= 8 + 36 \div 6 - 6 \div 2 \times 3 = 8 + 6 - 3 \times 3 = 5$

7. **(b)** Using the proper notations in (b), we get the statement as $5 \times 2 \div 2 < 10 - 4 + 2$ or $5 < 8$, which is true.

8. **(a)** Using the proper signs in the given expression, we get

$175 \div 5 \times 20 - 3 \times 10 = 7 + 5 \times 20$
$- 3 \times 10$
$= 7 + 100 - 30 = 107 - 30 = 77.$

9. **(a)** Given that : $20 - 10 = 200.$
But, actually $20 \times 10 = 200$, so $-$ means $\times$.
Given that $8 \div 4 = 12$, But actually $8 + 4 = 12.$
So, $\div$ means $+$.
Given that : $6 \times 2 = 4$ But actually $6 - 2 = 4.$
So, $\times$ means $-$
Thus, in the given mathematical language $-$ means $\times$,
$\div$ means $+$ and $\times$ means $-$ So, $\div$
Given expression
$= 100 \times 10 - 1000 + 1000 \div 100 - 10$
$1000 - 1000 + 10 - 10 = 0.$

10. **(d)** Using the correct symbols, we have
Given expression $= 24 \times 12 + 18$
$\div 9 = 288 + 2 = 290.$

11. **(b)** Using the correct symbols, we have
Given expression $= (3 \times 15 + 19)$
$\div 8 - 6$
$= 64 \div 8 - 6 = 8 - 6 = 2.$

12. **(a)** Using the correct symbols, we have
Given expression
$= \dfrac{(36 - 4) \div 8 - 4}{4 \times 8 - 2 \times 16 + 1} = \dfrac{32 \div 8 - 4}{32 - 32 + 1}$
$= \dfrac{4 - 4}{0 + 1} = 0.$

13. **(d)** Using the correct symbols, we have
Given expression,
$= 12 - 12 \times 28 \div 7 + 15$
$= 12 - 12 \times 4 + 15$
$= 12 - 48 + 15 = 27 - 48$
$= -21.$

14. **(c)** Using the correct symbols, we have
Given expression,
$= (10 \times 4) + (4 \times 4) - 6$
$= 40 + 16 - 6$
$= 56 - 6 = 50.$

15. **(d)** Using the proper notations in (4), we get the statement as
$2 \times 5 - 6 + 2 = 6$ or $10 - 6 + 2 = 6$
or $6 = 6$, which is true.

16. **(c)** Using the proper notations in (3), we get the statement as $5 \times 2 \div 2 < 10 - 4 + 8$ or $5 \times 1 < 18 - 4$ or $5 < 14$, which is true.

17. **(d)** Interchanging $(+$ and $\div)$ and $(2$ and $4)$, we get :
(1) $4 \div 2 + 3 = 3$ or $5 = 3$, which is false
(2) $2 \div 4 + 6 = 1.5$ or $6.5 = 1.5,$ which is false.

(3) $2 + 4 \div 3 = 4$ or $\dfrac{10}{3} = 4,$

which is false.
(4) $4 \div 2 + 6 = 8$ or $8 = 8$, which is true.

18. **(a)** By making the interchanges given in (1), we get the equation as $2 - 5 + 3 = 0$ or $0 = 0$ which is true.
By making the interchanges given in (b), we get the equation as
$3 - 2 + 5 = 0$ or $6 = 0$, which is false.
By making the interchanges given in (c), we get the equation as
$5 - 3 + 2 = 4$ or $4 = 0$ which is not true.
So, the answer is (a).

19. **(c)** $P = 4$
Difference between P and T $= 5$
Hence, T is assigned $= 9$
Difference between N and T $= 3$
Hence, N is assigned $= 6$

20. **(b)** Clearly, every member except one (i.e. the winner) must lose one game to decide the winner. Thus, minimum number of matches to be played $= 30 - 1 = 29$.

21. **(d)** Number of cuts made to cut a roll into 10 pieces = 9. Therefore required number of rolls $= (45 \times 24)/9 = 120$.

22. **(c)**

23. **(a)** Let the number of guests be x. Then number of bowls of

rice $= \dfrac{x}{2}$; number of bowls of

dal $= \dfrac{x}{3}$; number of bowls of

meat $= \dfrac{x}{4}$.

$$\therefore \frac{x}{2} + \frac{x}{3} + \frac{x}{4} = 65$$

$$\Leftrightarrow \frac{6x + 4x + 3x}{12} = 65 \Leftrightarrow 13x = 65 \times 12$$

$$\Leftrightarrow x = \left(\frac{65 \times 12}{13}\right) = 60$$

24. **(b)** Let d and s represent the number of daughters and sons respectively.
Then, we have :
d – 1 = s and 2 (s – 1) = d.
Solving these two equations, we get: d = 4, s = 3.

25. **(c)** Each row contains 12 plants.
There are 11 gapes between the two corner trees (11×2) metres and 1 metre on each side is left.
Therefore Length $= (22 + 2)$ m = 24 m.

26. **(c)** Let there be (x + 1) members. Then,

Father's share $= \dfrac{1}{4}$, share of each other member

$$= \frac{3}{4x}.$$

$$\therefore \ 3\left(\frac{3}{4x}\right) = \frac{1}{4} \Leftrightarrow 4x = 36$$
$$\Leftrightarrow x = 9$$

Hence, total number of family member = 10.

27. **(d)** Let R, G and B represent the number of balls in red, green and blue boxes respectively.
Then, R + G + B = 108 ...(i)
G + R = 2B   ...(ii)
B = 2R   ...(iii)
From (ii) and (iii), we have G + R $= 2 \times 2R = 4R$ or G = 3R.
Putting G = 3R and B = 2R in (i), we get:
R + 3R + 2R = 108 6R = 108 R = 18.
Therefore Number of balls in green box $= G = 3R = (3 \times 18) = 54$.

28. **(a)**

29. **(a)** Since there are socks of only two colours, so two out of any three socks must always be of the same colour.

30. **(a)** Clearly, the required number would be such that it leaves a remainder of 1 when divided by 2, 3 or 4 and no remainder when divided by 5. Such a number is 25.

31. **(d)** Numbers from 1 to 60, which are divisible by 6 are : 6,12,18, 24, 30, 36,42, 48, 54, 60.There are 10 such numbers.

Numbers from 1 to 60, the sum of whose digits is 6 are : 6, 15, 24, 33, 42, 51, 60.

There are 7 such numbers of which 4 are common to the above ones. So, there are 3such uncommon numbers.

Numbers from 1 to 60, which have 6 as one of the digits are 6, 16, 26, 36, 46, 56, 60.

Clearly, there are 4 such uncommon numbers.

So, numbers 'not connected with 6'

$= 60 - (10 + 3 + 4) = 43.$

32. **(c)** Clearly, the black cards are either clubs or spades while the red cards are either diamonds or hearts.

Let the number of spades be x.

Then, number of clubs $= (7 - x)$.

Number of diamonds = 2 x number of spades = 2x;

Number of hearts = 2 x number of diamonds = 4x.

Total number of cards $= x + 2x + 4x + 7 - x - 6x + 7.$

Therefore $6x + 7 = 13 \Leftrightarrow 6x = 6 \Leftrightarrow x - 1.$

Hence, number of clubs $= (7 - x) = 6.$

33. **(b)**

34. **(b)** Clearly, total number of handshakes $= (9 + 8 + 7 + 6 + 5 + 4 + 3 + 2 + 1) - 45.$

35. **(b)**

36. **(c)** Suppose their paths cross after x minutes.

Then, $11 + 57x = 51 - 63x \Leftrightarrow 120$

$x = 10 \Leftrightarrow x = \dfrac{1}{3}$

Number of floors covered by David in $\dfrac{1}{3}$ min

$= \left(\dfrac{1}{3} \times 57\right) = 19.$

So, their paths cross at (11 + 19)th i.e., 30th floor.

37. **(a)** Let the total number of shots be x. then,

Shots fired by A $= \dfrac{5}{8}x$; Shots fired by B $= \dfrac{3}{8}x$

Killing shots by A $= \dfrac{1}{3}$ of $\dfrac{5}{8}x$

$= \dfrac{5x}{24}$;

Shots missed by B $= \dfrac{1}{2}$ of $\dfrac{3}{8}x$

$= \dfrac{3x}{16}.$

$\therefore \dfrac{3x}{16} = 27$

or $x = \left(\dfrac{27 \times 16}{3}\right) = 144$

Birds killed by A

$= \dfrac{5x}{24} = \left(\dfrac{5}{24} \times 144\right) = 30$

38. **(d)**

39. **(d)**

40. **(d)**

Non-Verbal Reasoning

FORMATION OF FIGURES

In this topic, a question is one of the following types :

I. Formation of triangles/square/rectangle etc. either by joining of three figures after choosing them from the given five figures or by joining any other pieces after selecting them from given alternatives.

II. Making up a figure from given components.

III. Making up a three dimensional figure by paper folding.

IV. Rearrangement of the parts of given figure.

V. Fragmentation of key figure into simple pieces.

TYPE-I: Formation of triangles/square/rectangle etc. either by joining of three figures after choosing them from the given five figures or by joining any other pieces after selecting them from given alternatives.

EXAMPLE 1.

A set of five figures (A), (B), (C), (D) and (E) are followed by four combinations as the alternatives. Select the alternative which represents the combination of figures which if fitted together, will form a complete triangle.

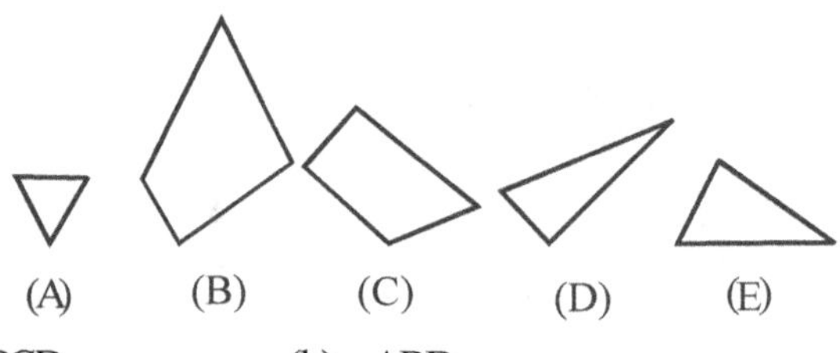

(A)   (B)   (C)   (D)   (E)

(a) BCD   (b) ABD
(c) CDE   (d) ABE

Sol.

(d) If figures A, B and E are fitted together, the resultant figure will be

a triangle.

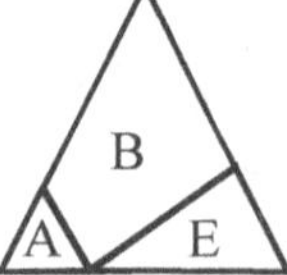

TYPE-II: Making up a figure from given components

EXAMPLE **2.**

Find out which of the alternatives (a), (b), (c) and (d) can be formed from the pieces given in box 'X'.

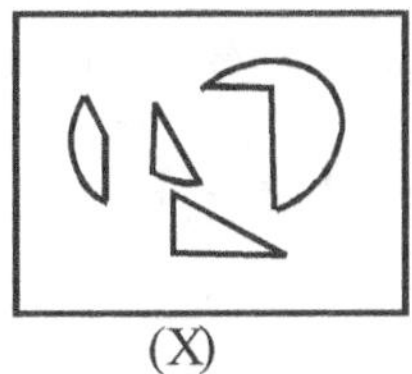

(X)

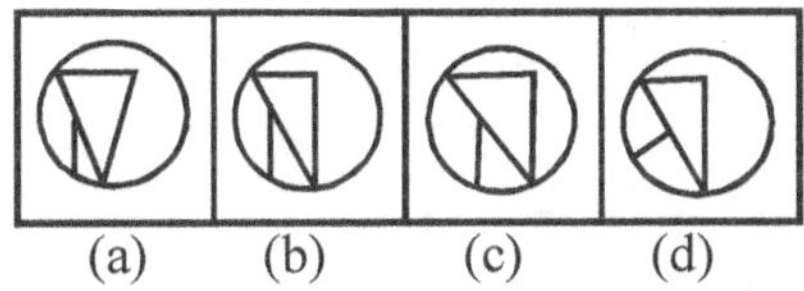

(a)　　　　(b)　　　　(c)　　　　(d)

Sol. (b)

TYPE-III: Making up a three dimensional figure by paper folding.

In this type, we have to analyze when a paper folded along the lines, how a three dimensional figure look like. Sometimes, a key figure is given which is made by folding one of the four figures given in alternatives. We have to determine which figure can be used to create the key figure.

EXAMPLE **3.**

A figure 'X' is given. You have to choose the correct figure, given in the alternatives, when folded along the lines, will produce the given figure 'X'.

(X)

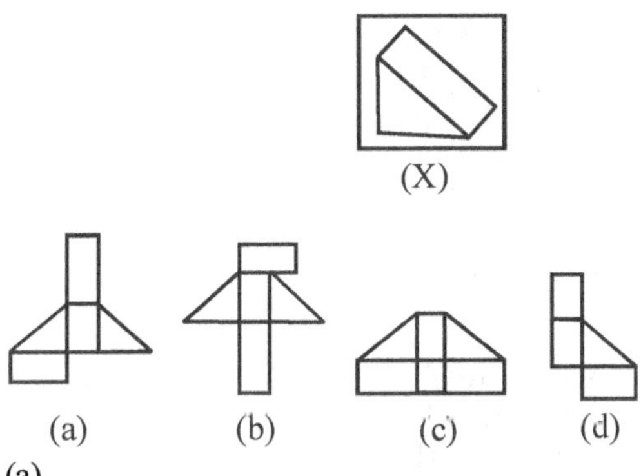

(a)　　　　(b)　　　　(c)　　　　(d)

Sol. (a)

TYPE-IV: Fragmentation of key figure into simple pieces.

This type is opposite to TYPE-II. In this type, a key figure is given and every alternatives has different pieces. We have to select the set of pieces that can make the given key figure.

EXAMPLE 4.

Find out which of the alternatives will exactly make up the key figure (X)

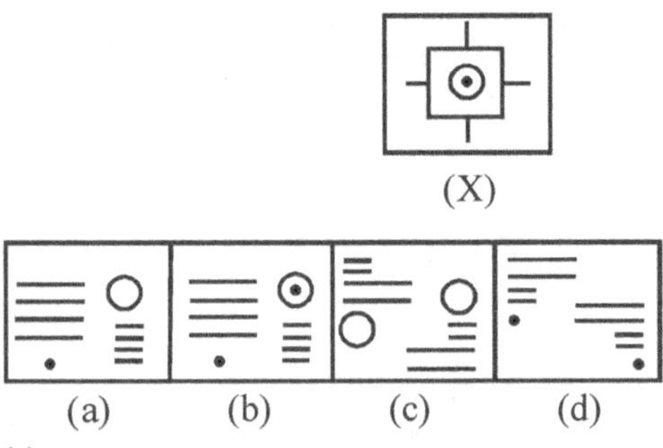

(X)

(a)   (b)   (c)   (d)

Sol.   (a)

COUNTING OF FIGURES PROBLEM

EXAMPLE 5.

How many triangles are there in the given diagram?

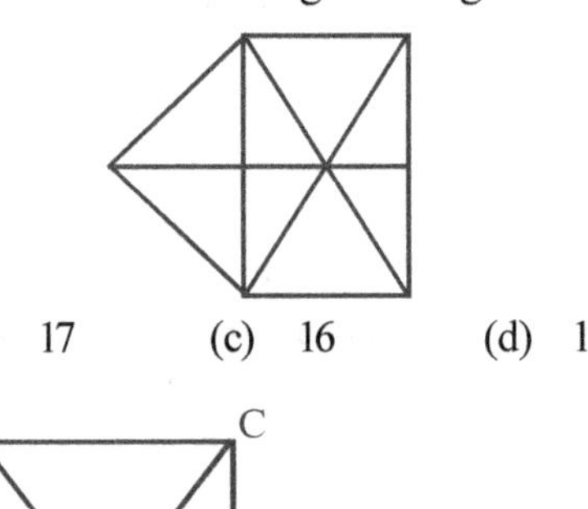

(a)   18   (b)   17   (c)   16   (d)   15

Sol. (b)

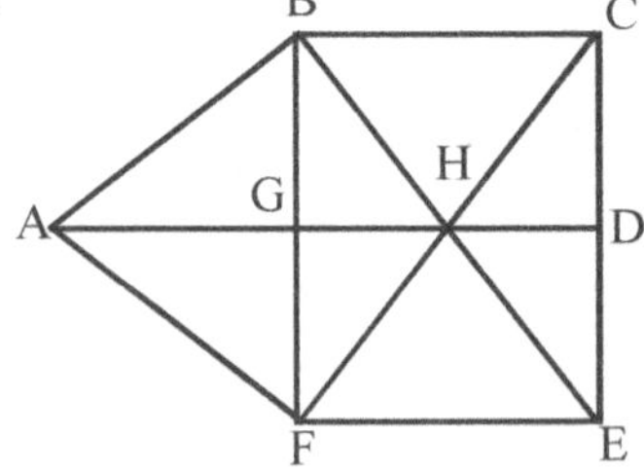

The triangles are:

△ABF: △AGB : △AGF : △BFC;

△BCE : △CEF : △BFE : △HBC;

△HCE : △HEF : △HBF : △BGH;

△FGH : △HCD : △HDE : △AFH;

△ABH ;

EXERCISE

DIRECTIONS (Qs. 1 to 8) : In each of following questions select that combination of parts (A), (B), (C), (D) and (E) which if fitted together will form an equilateral triangle.

1.

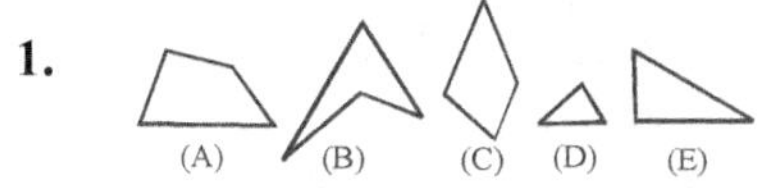

(a) ABC	(b) BCD
(c) ABD	(d) ABE

2.

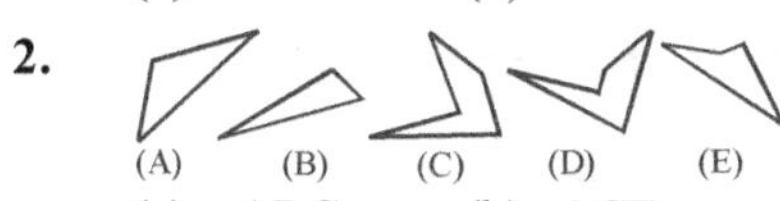

(a) ABC	(b) ACE
(c) BCD	(d) BDE

3.

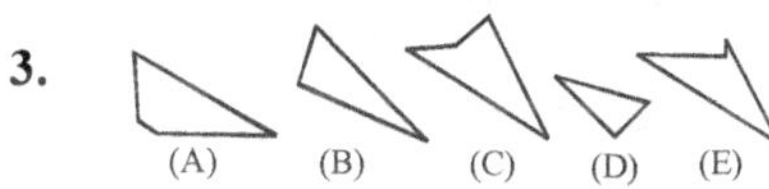

(a) ABE	(b) BCE
(c) ADE	(d) BDE

4.

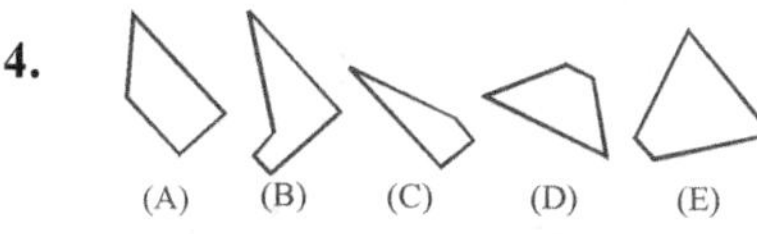

(a) ABD	(b) BCE
(c) ACD	(d) BDE

5.

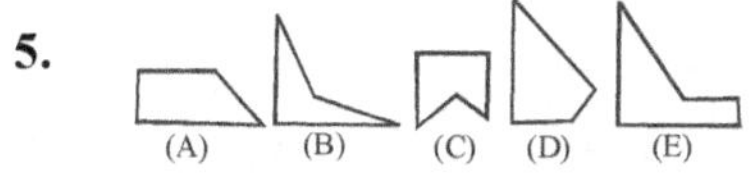

(a) ACD	(b) ABD
(c) BCD	(d) CDE

6.

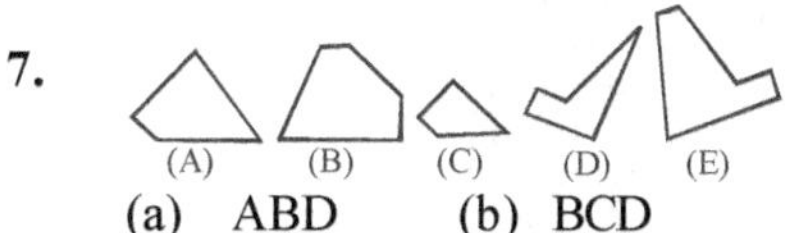

(a) ABC	(b) BCD
(c) ACD	(d) CDE

7.

(a) ABD	(b) BCD
(c) BDE	(d) ADE

8.

(a) ABC	(b) BCE
(c) BDE	(d) ADE

DIRECTIONS (Qs. 9 to 12): a key figure (X) is given followed by four alternative figures. You will have to select one figure from the alternatives which fits exactly into key figure (X) to form a perfect square.

9.

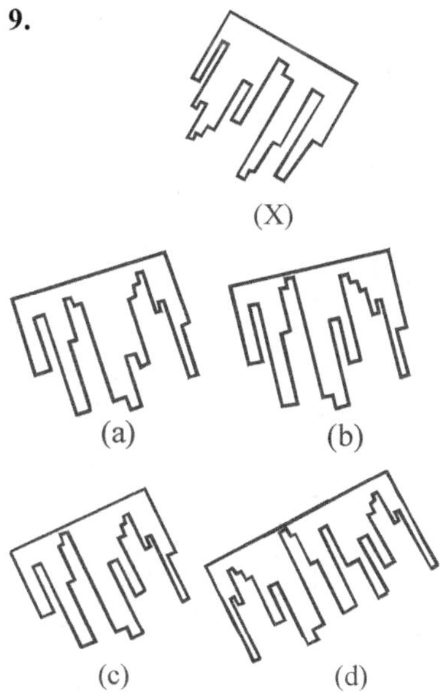

(X)

(a)   (b)

(c)   (d)

10.

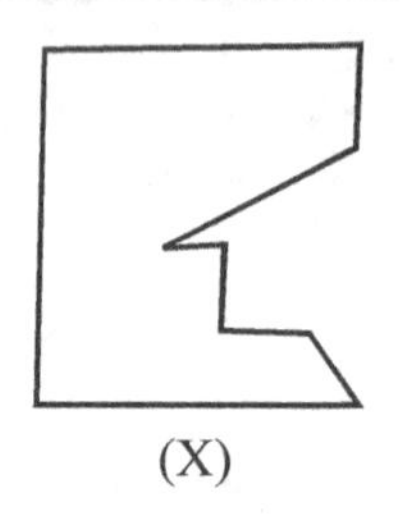

(X)

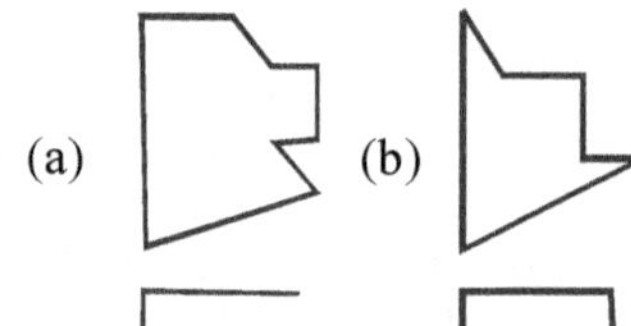

(a)   (b)

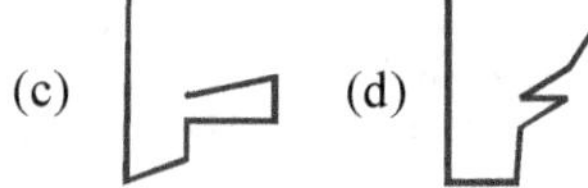

(c)   (d)

11.

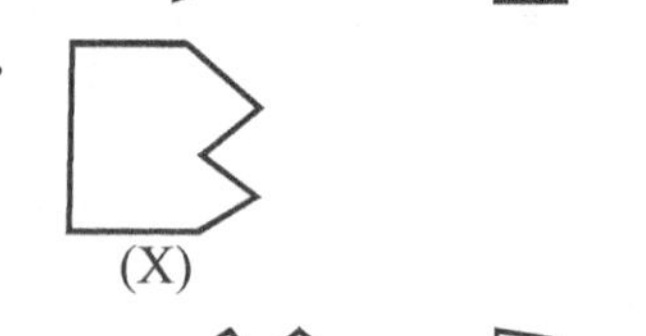

(X)

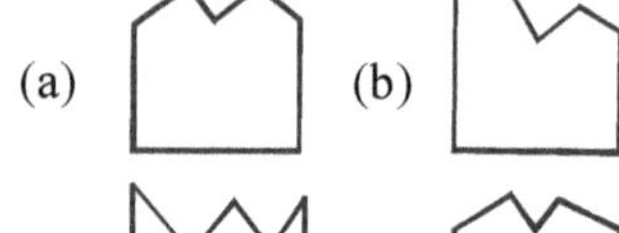

(a)   (b)

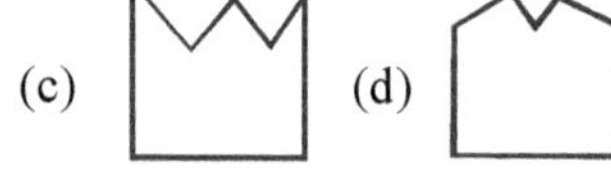

(c)   (d)

12.

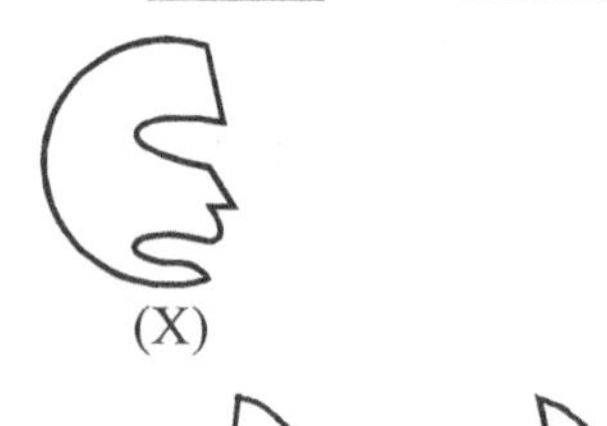

(X)

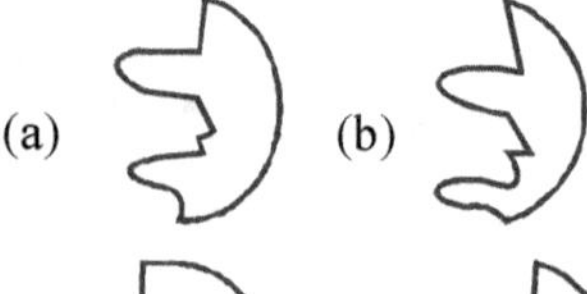

(a)   (b)

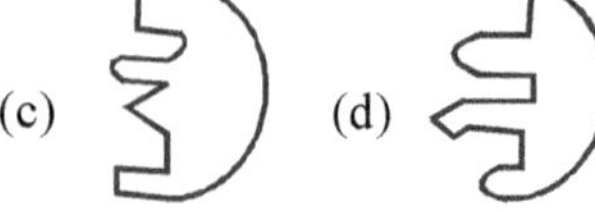

(c)   (d)

DIRECTIONS (Qs. 13 to 18) : In each of following questions find out which of the figures (a), (b), (c) and (d) can be formed from the pieces given in (X).

13.

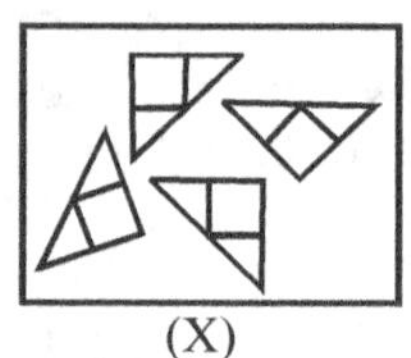

(X)

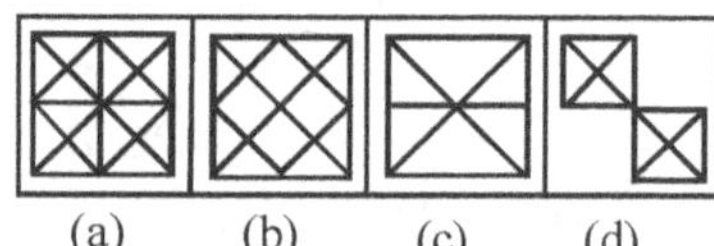

(a)   (b)   (c)   (d)

14.

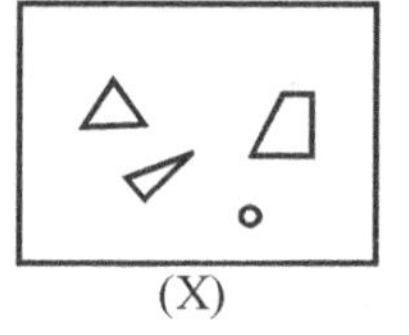

(X)

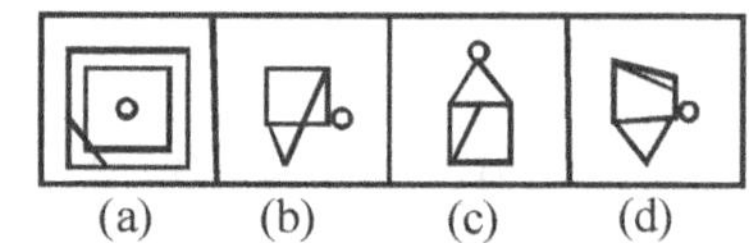

(a)   (b)   (c)   (d)

15.

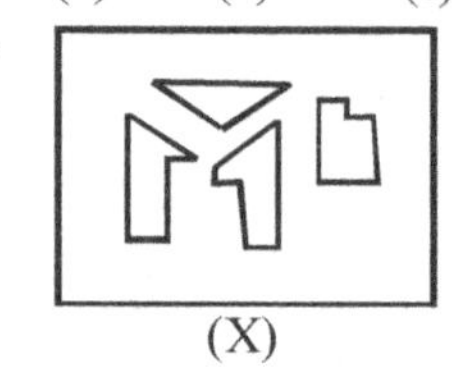

(X)

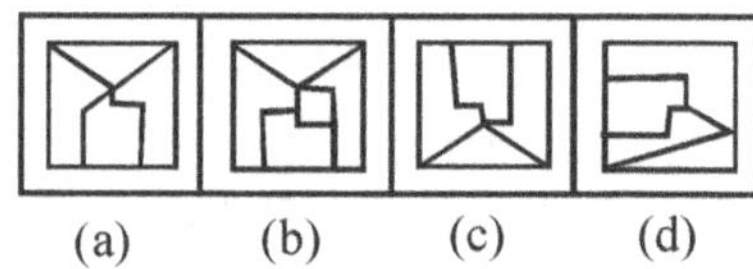

(a)   (b)   (c)   (d)

16.

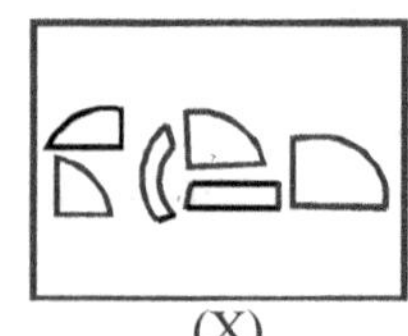

(X)

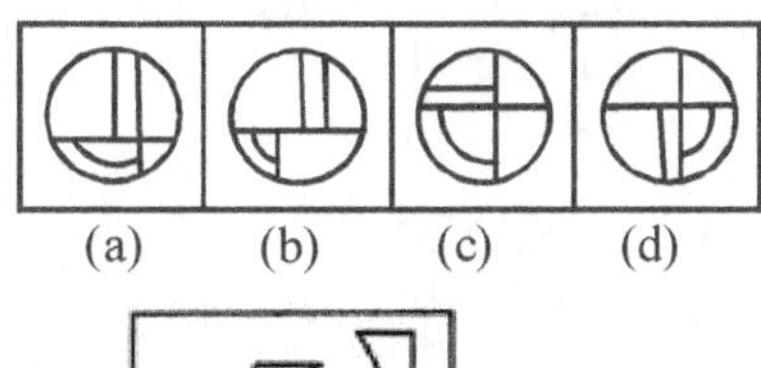

   (a)   (b)   (c)   (d)

17.

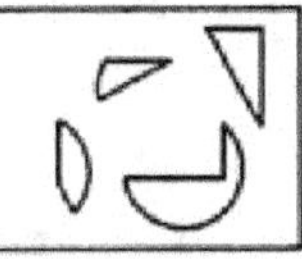

(X)

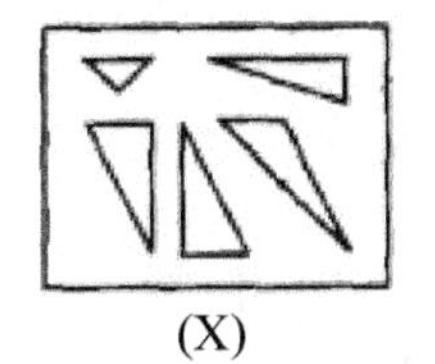

   (a)   (b)   (c)   (d)

18.

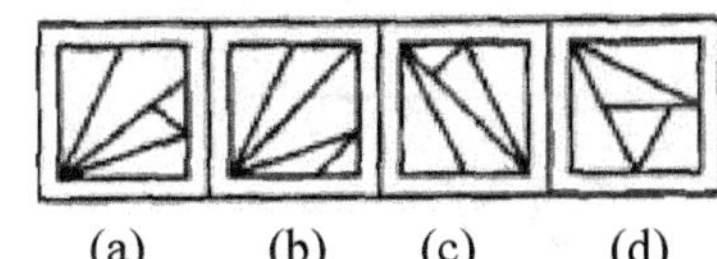

(X)

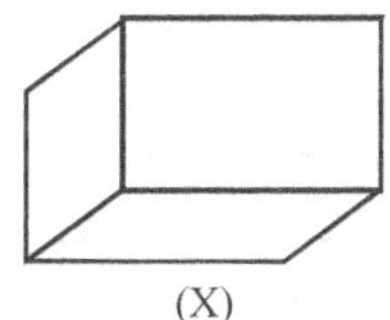

   (a)   (b)   (c)   (d)

19. In this question, which of the following figures (a), (b), (c), (d) when folded along the lines, will produce the given figure 'X'.

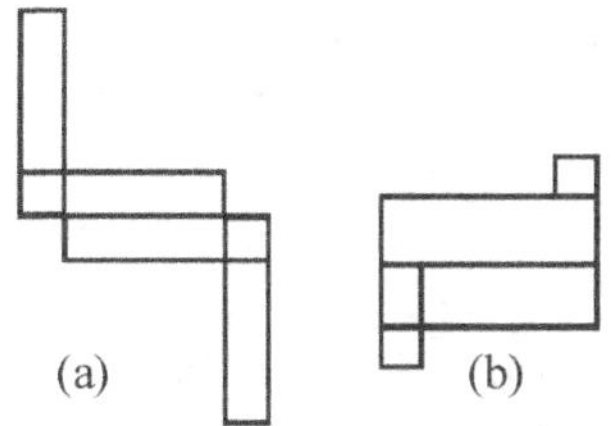

(X)

   (a)   (b)

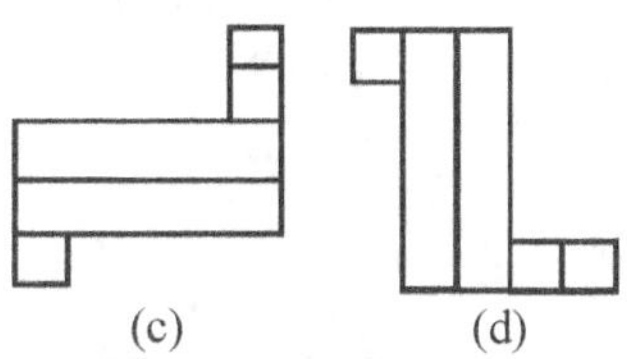

   (c)   (d)

20. How many triangles are there in the following figure?

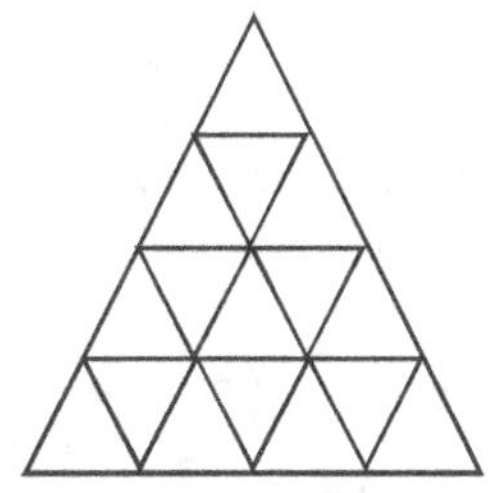

(a) 29   (b) 27
(c) 23   (d) 30

21. How many triangles are there in the given figure?

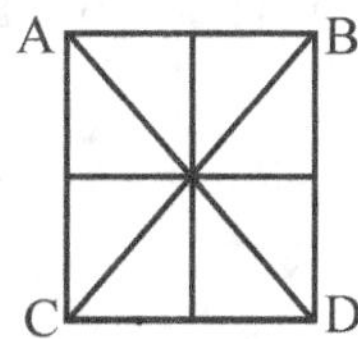

(a) 16   (b) 14
(c) 8   (d) 12

22. How many triangles are there in the given figure?

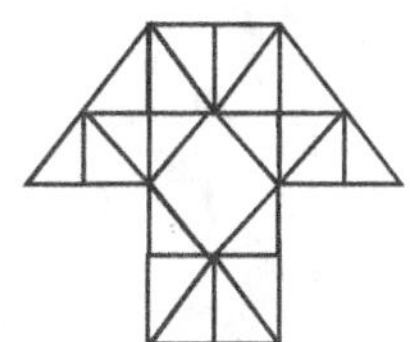

(a) 29   (b) 38
(c) 40   (d) 35

23. How many squares are there in a given figure?

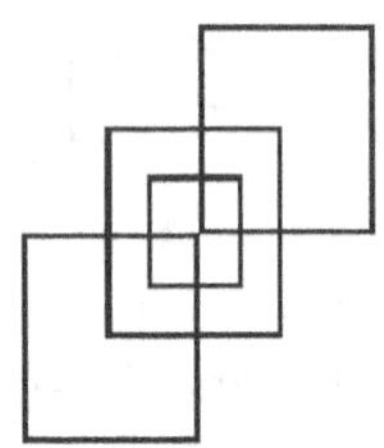

(a) 12   (b) 13
(c) 10   (d) 11

24. How many triangles are there in the figure ABCDEF?

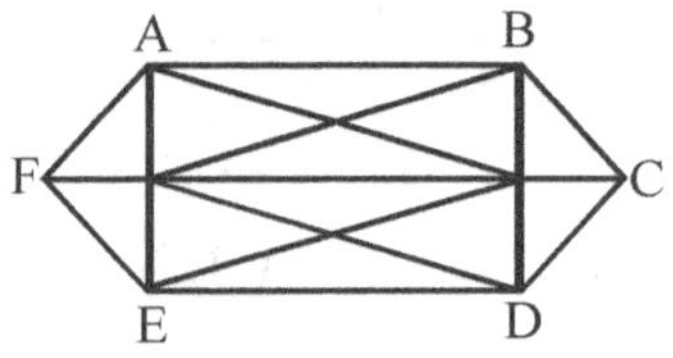

(a) 24   (b) 26
(c) 28   (d) 30

25. How many parallelograms are there in the figure ?

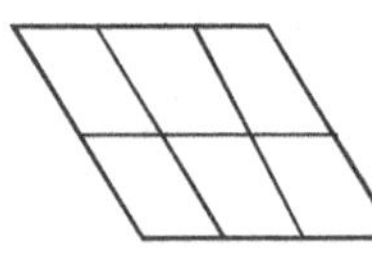

(a) 14   (b) 15
(c) 16   (d) 18

26. How many cubes are there in the following figure?

(a) 6   (b) 10
(c) 12   (d) 8

27. What is the number of squares in figure?

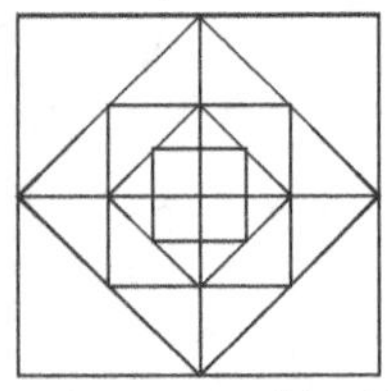

(a) 12   (b) 13
(c) 15   (d) 17

28. What is the number of triangles in figure?

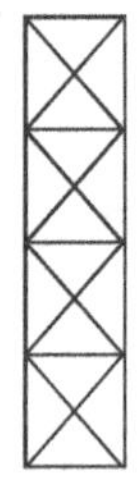

(a) 16   (b) 28
(c) 32   (d) 38

29.

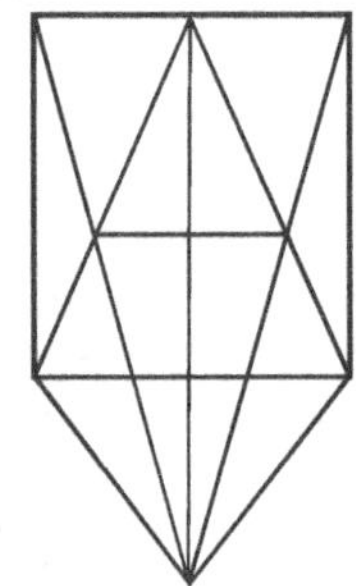

How many triangles are there ?
(a) 20   (b) 21
(c) 26   (d) 28

30. How many Rectangles are there in the given figure?

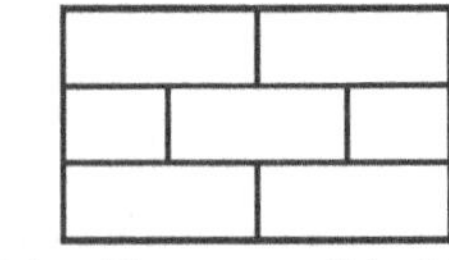

(a) 13   (b) 14
(c) 15   (d) 17

31. How many Semicircles are there in the given figure?

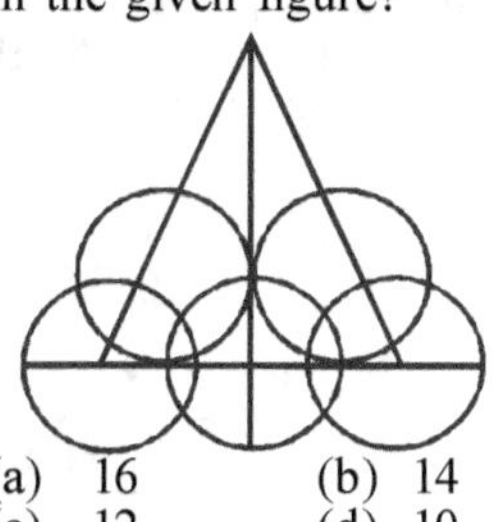

  (a) 16   (b) 14
  (c) 12   (d) 10

32. Count the number of squares in the given figure.

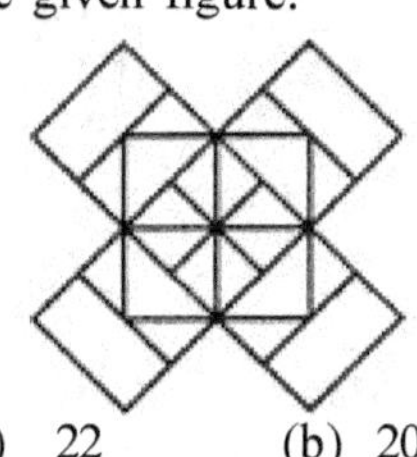

  (a) 22   (b) 20
  (c) 18   (d) 14

33. How many circles are there in the adjoining figure.

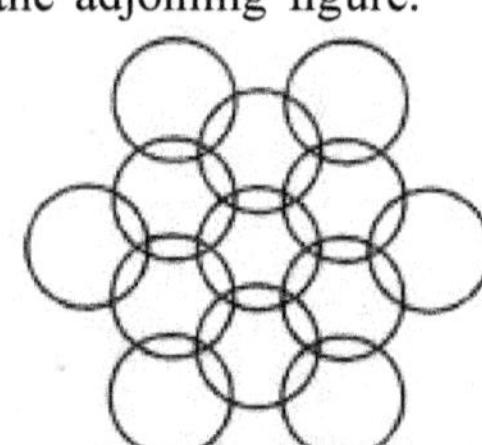

  (a) 11   (b) 12
  (c) 13   (d) 14

34. What is the number of triangles in figure ?

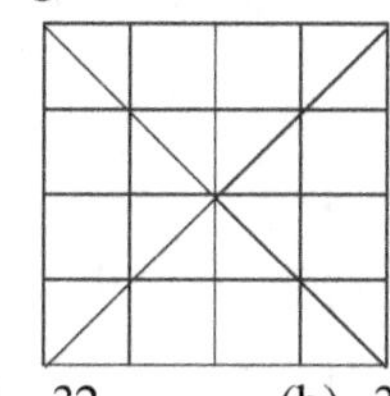

  (a) 32   (b) 36
  (c) 40   (d) 56

35. What is the number of triangles in figure ?

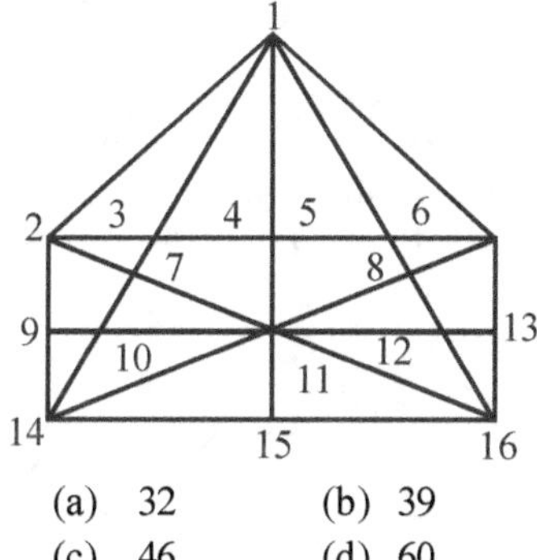

  (a) 32   (b) 39
  (c) 46   (d) 60

SOLUTIONS

1. (b)	**2.** (d)	**3.** (c)	
4. (b)	**5.** (a)	**6.** (d)	
7. (b)	**8.** (c)	**9.** (c)	
10. (b)	**11.** (c)	**12.** (b)	
13. (b)	**14.** (c)	**15.** (c)	
16. (a)			

17. (c) All of the components of figure (X) are present in the figure (c)

18. (c) All of the components of figure (X) are present in the figure (c)

19. (a)

20. (b)

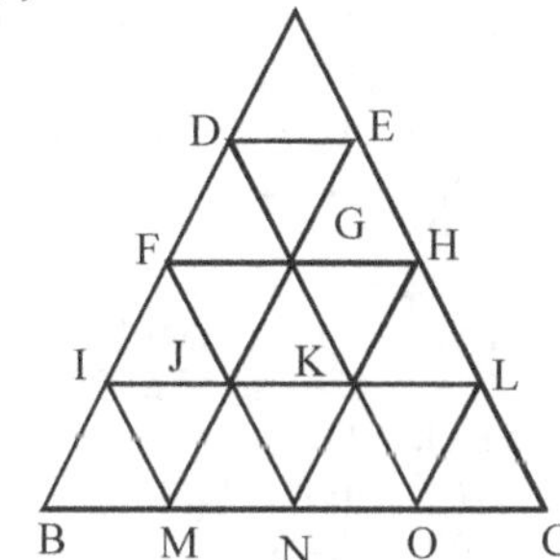

The triangles are:
ΔABC; ΔADE; ΔAFH; ΔAIL;
ΔDFG; ΔDIK; ΔDBO; ΔGDE;
ΔEGH; ΔEJL; ΔEMC; ΔFIJ;
ΔFBN; ΔJFG; ΔGJK; ΔKGH;
ΔHKL; ΔHNC; ΔNFH; ΔGMO;
ΔIBM; ΔMIJ; ΔJMN; ΔNJK;
ΔKNO; ΔOKL; ΔLOC;

21. **(a)**

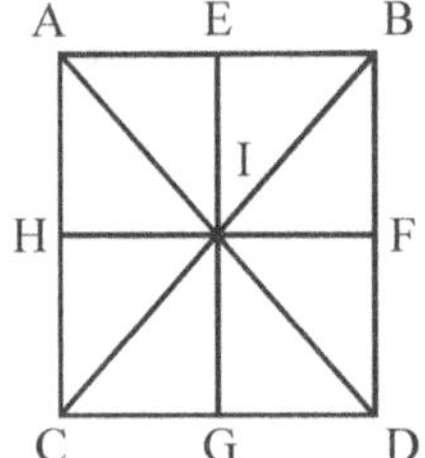

The triangles are:
ΔAIH; ΔAIE; ΔEIB; ΔBFI;
ΔIHC; ΔIGC; ΔIGD; ΔDFI;
ΔIAB; ΔIBD; ΔICD; ΔIAC;
ΔBAC; ΔACD; ΔBDC; ΔBDA;

22. **(c)**

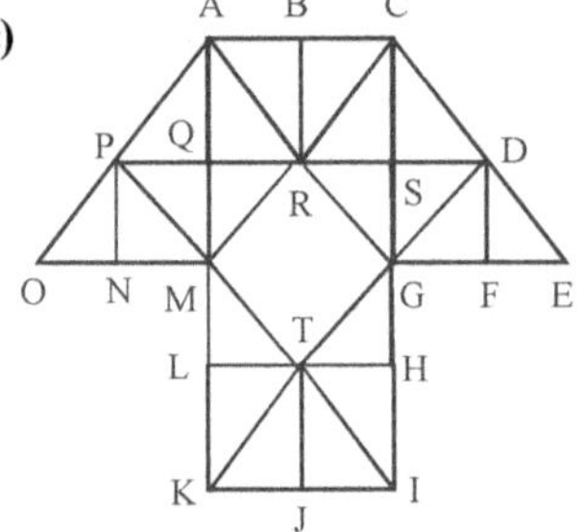

The simplest triangles are:
ΔPNO; ΔPNM; ΔMPQ;
ΔMQR; ΔAQP; ΔAQR;
ΔBRA; ΔBRC; ΔSRC;
ΔSCD; ΔSGR; ΔSGD;
ΔDFG; ΔDFE; ΔTLM;
ΔTJK; ΔTLK; ΔTIH;
The triangles composed of two
components are:
ΔPON; ΔPMA; ΔAPR;
ΔRAM; ΔRAC; ΔRGC;
ΔDGC; ΔDGE; ΔMPR;
ΔGRD; ΔDGE; ΔTMK;
ΔTKI; ΔTIG
The triangles composed of four
components are:

ΔAMO; ΔAMC; ΔCAG;
ΔCGE; ΔMKI; ΔGIK;
Other triangles are :ΔSPI; ΔDQK
Total number of triangles
18 + 14 + 6 + 2 = 40

23. **(a)**

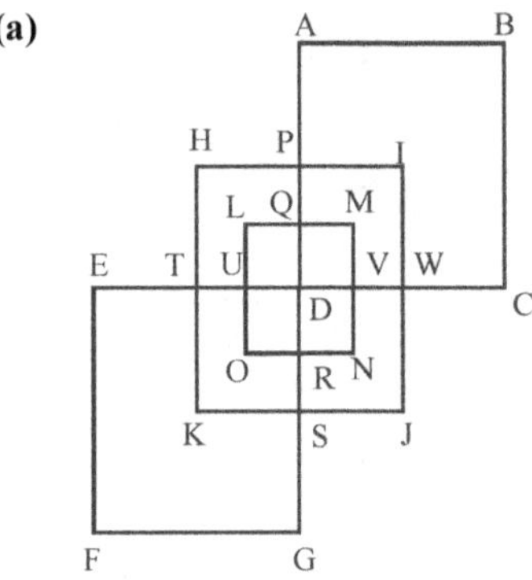

Squares are:
ABCD, DEFG, HIJK, LMNO,
HPDT, TDSK, PIWD, DWJS,
LQDU, UDRO, QMVD, DVNR.

24. **(c)**

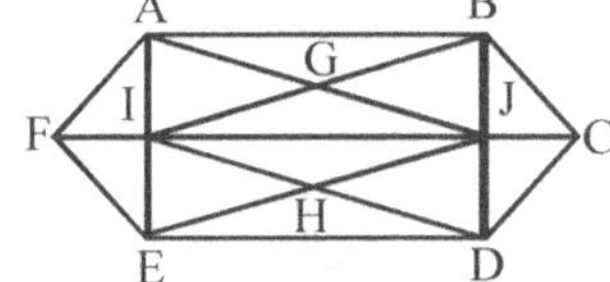

The triangles are:
ΔFAE; ΔFAI; ΔFIE; ΔCBD;
ΔCBJ; ΔCJD; ΔAIJ; ΔBJI;
ΔBJA; ΔAIB; ΔIED; ΔJDE;
ΔJDI; ΔIEJ; ΔGAB; ΔGAI;
ΔGJI; ΔGJB; ΔHJI; ΔHDE;
ΔHEI; ΔHJD; ΔAJF; ΔEFJ;
ΔBCI; ΔCDI; ΔIBD; ΔJEA;

25. **(c)** We can label the figure as
shown.

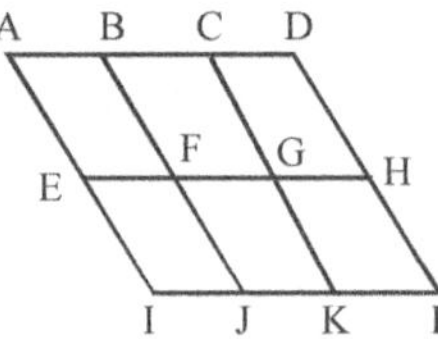

The simplest parallelogram are
ABFE, BCGF, CDHG, EFJI,
FGKJ and GHLK. These are 6 in
number.

The parallelograms composed of two components each, are ACGE, BDHF, EGKI, FHLJ, ABJI, BCKJ and CDLK. Thus, there are 7 such parallelograms. The parallelogram composed of four components each are ACKI and BDLJ i.e. 2 in number. There is only one parallelogram composed of six components, namely, ADLI. Thus, there are 6 + 7 + 2 + 1 = 16 parallelograms in the figure.

26.   **(b)**   There are 10 cubes.

27.   **(d)**   We have three squares with vertical and horizontal sides. Each such square has $1^2 + 2^2 = 5$ squares in it. Thus there are 15 such squares. In addition, we have two obliquely placed squares.

Hence total no. of squares = 17

28.   **(d)**

29.   **(d)**

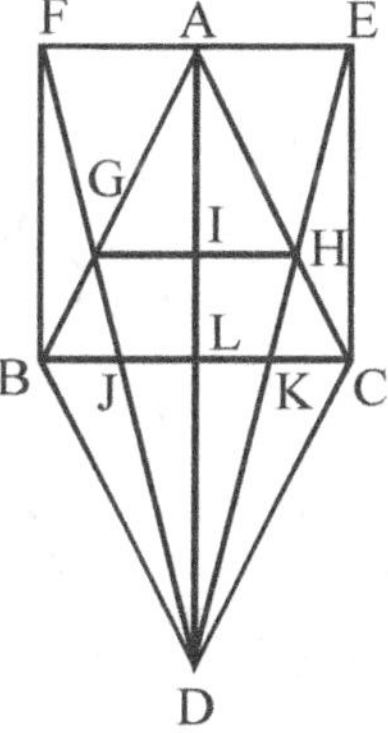

ΔFDE, ΔACD, ΔABD,
ΔFBD, ΔABC, ΔBCD,
ΔBKD, ΔBLD, ΔBJD,
ΔJCD, ΔJKD, ΔLDJ, ΔLCD,
ΔLKD, ΔHDC, ΔKDC, ΔEDC,
ΔHKC, ΔEKC, ΔAEC, ΔEHC,
ΔAEH, ΔAGH, ΔAIH, ΔAGI.
ΔAFB, ΔAGF, ΔFBG.

∴ Total 28 triangles.

30.   **(a)**   The rectangles are —
ABKJ, BCDK, JLPI, LMNP, MDEN, IOGH, OEFG, ACDJ, JMNI, LDEP, JDEI,   IERH, ACFH

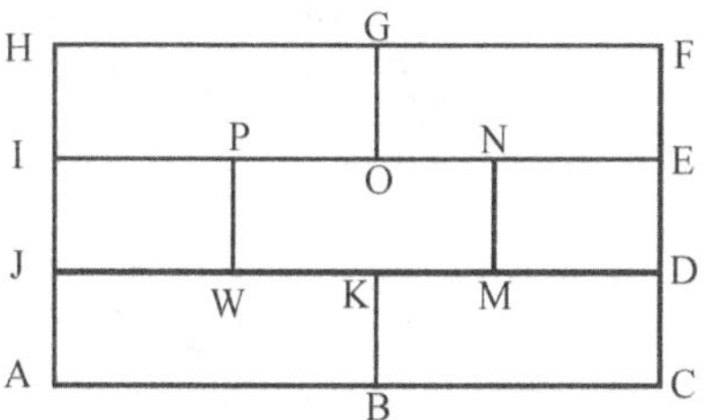

31.   **(c)**   According to the figure there are 12 semicircles.

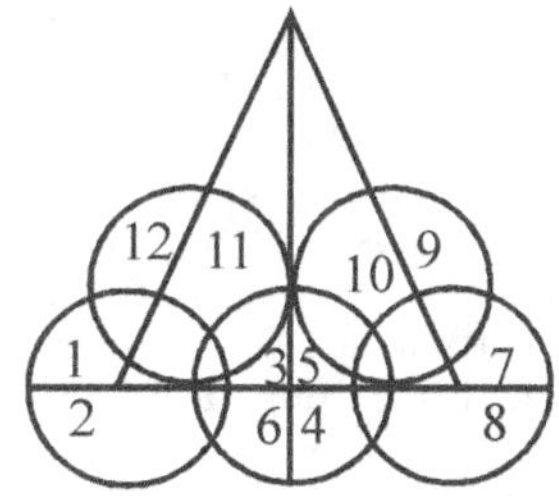

32.   **(c)**   The figure may be labelled as shown.

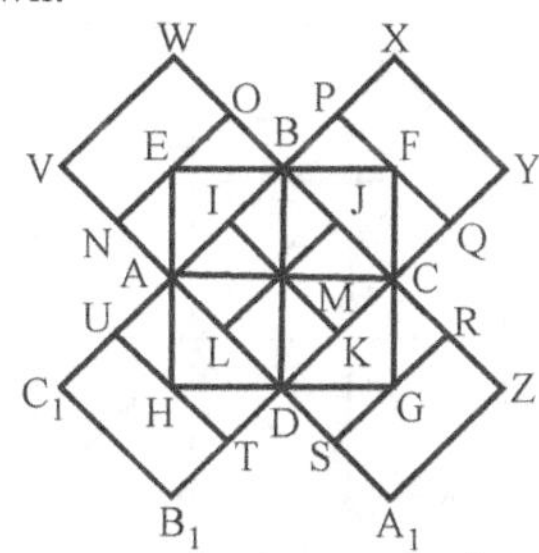

The squares composed of two components each are BJMI, CKMJ, DLMK and AIML i.e. 4 in number.

The squares composed of three components each are EBMA, BFCM, MCGD and AMDH i.e. 4 in number.

The squares composed of four components each are VWBA, XYCB, ZA1DC and B1C1AD i.e. 4 in number.

The squares composed of seven components each are NOJL, PQKI, RSLJ and TUIK i.e. 4 in number.

There is only one square i.e. ABCD

composed of eight components. There is only one square i.e. EFGH composed of twelve components. Total number of squares in the figure = 4 + 4 + 4 + 4 + 1 + 1 = 18.

33.   (c)   The figure may be labelled as shown.

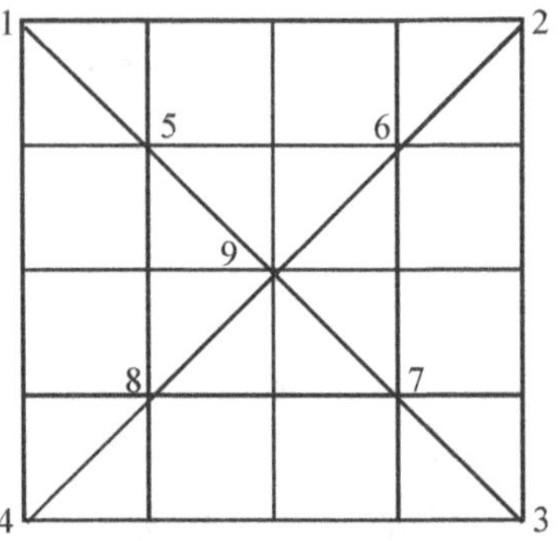

There are 13 circles in the given figure. This is clear from the adjoining figure in which the centres of all the circles in the given figure have been numbered from 1 to 13.

34.   (d)   With vertex no. 1 we have four triangles on one side of the diagonal and four triangles on the other side.

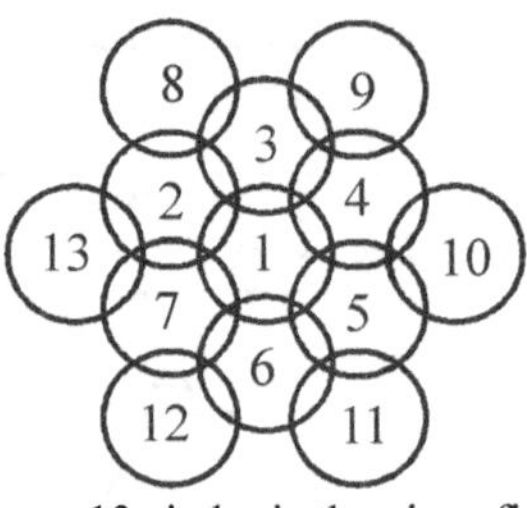

Thus from four vertices. We have in all 4 × 8 = 32 triangles.

Next consider square (5 – 6 – 7 – 8). There are four triangles from each vertex.

Thus we have another 4 × 4 = 16 triangles.

Lastly, we have oblique triangles with vertex 9 such as (9 – 6 – 7), (9 – 2 – 3) and so on. There are 8 such triangles.

Hence, total no. of triangles = 32 + 16 + 8 = 56

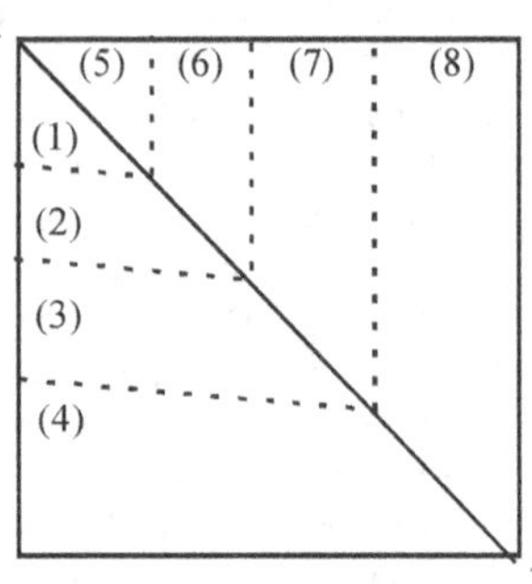

35.   (d)   Within the triangle with vertices 1, 2, 6, there are 4 + 3 + 2 + 1 = 10 triangles. In the triangle with vertices 1, 2, 14 there are 6 triangles.

In the triangle with vertices 1, 14, 15 there are 8 triangles.

This pattern is repeated for triangle 1, 6, 16 and for triangle 1, 15, 16.

In the triangle with vertices 1, 6, 14 there are 3 triangles and the pattern is repeated for the triangle with vertices 1, 2, 16.

In the parallelogram, there are 4 triangles each half the size, 4 triangles of quarter size and 6 triangles each made up of two small triangles.

Finally, there two triangles with vertices 1, 10, 12 and 1, 14, 16 respectively

Hence total no. of triangles.
= 10 + 2 (6 + 8) + 2 × 3 + (4 + 4 + 6) + 2 = 60

MOCK TEST-I

Max. Marks : 20   **Time : 20 mins.**

Logic & Quantitative Reasoning

1. Arrange the following words as per order in the dictionary.
   1. Manifest
   2. Meticulous
   3. Meridian
   4. Merchant
   (a) 1,4,3,2   (b) 2,1,4,3
   (c) 1,3,2,4   (d) 2,3,4,1

2. A series is given, with one term missing. Choose the correct alternative from the given ones that will complete the series.
   T Q N K H E B Y V S P ? ? ?
   (a) NKG   (b) NKI
   (c) MJG   (d) MJH

3. Sonam starts from a point walks 20 m towards East, turns towards her right and walks 10 m, then turns left walks 5m. Then turns towards her right and walks 5m more. In which direction is she now from the starting point?
   (a) North
   (b) South-East
   (c) South
   (d) West

4. A, B, C, D, E, F and G are members of a family consisting of 4 adults and 3 children, two of whom, F and G are girls. A and D are brothers and A is a doctor. E is an engineer married to one of the brothers and has two children. B is married to D and G is their child. Who is C?
   (a) G's brother
   (b) F's father
   (c) E's father
   (d) Can't determine

DIRECTIONS (Qs. 5 & 6): The following questions are based upon the alphabetical series given below:

S L U A Y J V E I O N Q G Z B D R H

5. What will come in place of question (?) mark in the following series?
   LAJEOQ?
   (a) ZH   (b) IB
   (c) ZD   (d) QR

6. If 'SU' is related 'HD' and 'UY' is related to 'DZ' in a certain way, to which of the following is YV related to following the same pattern?
   (a) ZQ   (b) IN
   (c) BG   (d) QO

7. Pointing to a man in a photograph, a woman said, "His brother's father is the only son of my grandfather." How is the woman related to the man in the photograph?
   (a) Mother   (b) Aunt
   (c) Sister   (d) Daughter

DIRECTIONS (Q. 8): In the following question, a letter-number series is given with one term missing as shown by (?). Choose the missing term out of the given alternatives.

8. 2B, 4C, 8E, 14H, ?
   (a) 16K   (b) 22L
   (c) 20L   (d) 20I

9. How many such pairs of letters are there in the word CONTRACT each of which has as many letters between them in the word as in the English alphabet?
   (a) Three   (b) One
   (c) Two   (d) None

10. In every 30 minutes, the time of a watch increases by 3 minutes. What time will the watch show after 6 hours when the current time is 12:30 pm?
    (a) $7:06$ pm   (b) 7 pm
    (c) $6:56$ pm   (d) $6:45$ pm

English Proficiency

DIRECTIONS (Qs. 11 & 12) : In the following questions, out of the four alternatives choose the one that can be substituted for the given words/phrase:

11. One who feels at home in every country
    (a) metropolitan
    (b) cosmopolitan
    (c) citizen
    (d) denizen

12. A statement that is absolutely clear
    (a) cliché
    (b) confused
    (c) ambiguous
    (d) unequivocal

DIRECTIONS (Qs. 13 & 14) : Find out the correct meaning of the idiomatic expression and mark the correct options.

13. Let the grass grow under one's feet
    (a) to accept responsibility
    (b) to engage in useless talk
    (c) to be trifled with
    (d) to remain idle

14. Fights shy of
    (a) afraid of
    (b) frightened
    (c) avoids from a feeling of mistrust
    (d) quarrels bitterly with

DIRECTIONS (Qs. 15 & 16) : The sentences are given in different parts. Read each sentence to find out whether there is an error in any part. No sentence has more than one error.

15. Education helps us understand and tolerate differences and so holds out the promise that we can live together harmoniously.
    (a) Education helps us understand and tolerate differences
    (b) and so holds out the promise
    (c) that we can live together harmoniously.
    (d) No error

16. He refused to disclose to his friends whether he will leave for England immediately after finishing his studies.
    (a) He refused to disclose to his friends
    (b) whether he will leave for England
    (c) immediately after finishing his studies.
    (d) No error

DIRECTIONS (Qs. 17 & 18): In the following questions, out of the four alternatives, choose the one which best expresses the meaning of the given word.

17. Cajole
    (a) Insist
    (b) Persuade

   (c)   Permit
   (d)   Recommend

18. Fragrance
   (a)   Taste   (b)   Aroma
   (c)   Sight   (d)   Touch

DIRECTIONS (Qs. 19 & 20): In the following questions, select the appropriate word from the given options to complete the sentence

19. There are always problems to overcome at the _________ of a new policy, but those should be dealt with in a few months.

   (a)   inception   (b)   exhume
   (c)   eschew   (d)   escapade

20. There wasn't a _________ of cheesecake left by the time I got home.

   (a)   trace   (b)   proletariat
   (c)   totalitarian   (d)   faux pas

SOLUTIONS

1. (a) Sol. Order according to dictionary:
1. Manifest , 4. Merchant , 3. Meridian , 2. Meticulous

2. (c) T -3 Q -3 N -3 K -3 H -3 E -3 B -3 Y -3 V -3 S -3 P -3 M -3 J -3 G

3. (b) Sonam's direction shown in figure below:

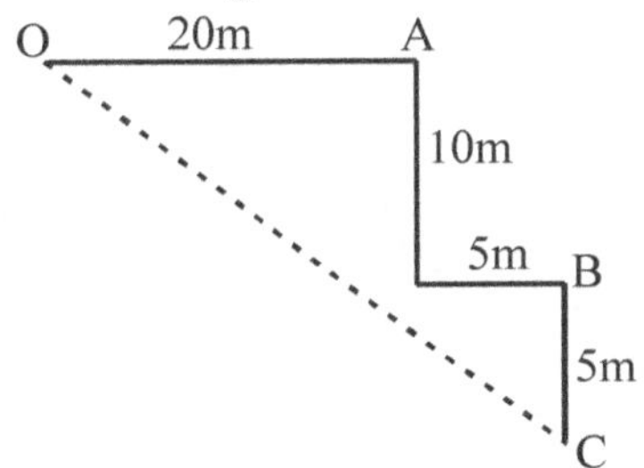

Now, it is obvious that Sonam is in South-East direction.

4. (d)

Members	Profession
A+ (Male)	Doctor
B– (Female)	
C	
D+ (Male)	
E	Engineer
F– (Female)	
G– (Female)	

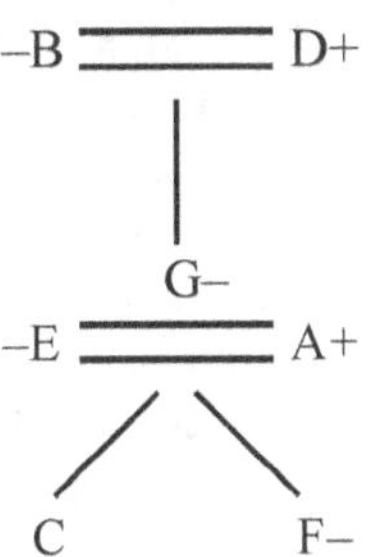

C's gender is not specified, So we can't determine.

5. (c) Difference between letter is +2.

6. (a) The corresponding letters from the right end

7. (c) Only son of woman's grandfather - Woman's father;

Man's brother's father - Man's father.

So, the woman is man's sister

8. (b)

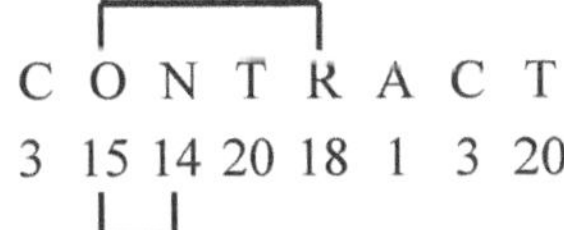

9. (c)

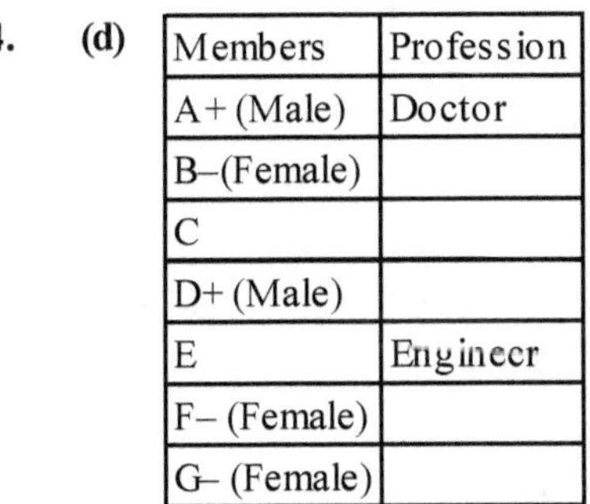

10. **(a)** Total increase in 6 hours =
$6 \times 2 \times 3 = 36$ minutes
Hence, after 6 hours from 12:30 pm,
Actual time will be 6:30 pm + 36 minutes = 7:06 pm

11. **(b)** cosmopolitan-familiar with and at ease in many different countries and cultures.

12. **(d)** unequivocal -leaving no doubt; unambiguous.

13. **(d)** let the grass grow under one's feet-to wait before doing something or to do something slowly.

14. **(c)** fight shy of something/ doing something-to try to avoid something.

15. **(d)** If you 'hold out' hope of something happening, you hope that in the future something will happen as you want it to. Hence the given question is correct.

16. **(b)** Substitute 'would' for 'will' because 'refused' is in the past tense.

17. **(b)** cajole: persuade (someone) to do something by sustained coaxing or flattery.

18. **(b)** fragrance: a pleasant, sweet smell.

19. **(a)** inception: the establishment or starting point of an institution or activity.

20. **(a)** trace: a very small quantity, especially one too small to be accurately measured.

MOCK TEST-2

Max. Marks : 20

Time : 20 mins.

DIRECTIONS (1&2): Read the following information and answer the questions given below it:

A is the father of C. But C is not son. E is the daughter of C. F is the spouse of A.

B is the brother of C. D is the son of B. G is the spouse of B. H is the father of G.

1. Who is the grandmother of D?
   - (a) A
   - (b) C
   - (c) F
   - (d) H

2. Who is the son of F?
   - (a) B
   - (b) C
   - (c) D
   - (d) E

3. Shubham walks three km towards East and takes a left turn and walks for one km before he turns left and walks two km to take another left turn to walk for another one km. How many km is he away from his starting point?
   - (a) 4kms
   - (b) 3kms
   - (c) 2kms
   - (d) 1km

4. In a certain code, DANCE is written as CCKGZ. How is MUSIC written in that code?
   - (a) KWPMX
   - (b) LVPMX
   - (c) LWPNX
   - (d) LWPMX

5. Select the related letters from the given alternatives:
   ZXVT:YWUS::RPNL:?
   - (a) QVTS
   - (b) TSQP
   - (c) SQPM
   - (d) QOMK

6. A,B,C,D,E,F are sitting on the round table with equal distances and facing center. F is sitting opposite to E and between A and D. C is sitting right side of E and opposite to A. Who are the neighbours of A?
   - (a) F and D
   - (b) E and F
   - (c) E and C
   - (d) B and F

DIRECTIONS (Q. 7): Choose the pair that best illustrate a similar relationship.

7. Pakistan : Moon-star : : America : ?
   - (a) Rose
   - (b) White Lily
   - (c) Golden rod
   - (d) None of these

8. How many even numbers are there in the following sequence of numbers each of which is immediately followed by an odd number as well as immediately preceded by an even number?
   8 6 7 6 8 9 3 2 7 5 3 4 2 2 3 5 5 2 2 8 1 1 9
   - (a) One
   - (b) Three
   - (c) Five
   - (d) None of these

9. A number is greater than 3 but less than 8. Also, it is greater than 6 but less than 10. The number is:
   - (a) 5
   - (b) 7
   - (c) 6
   - (d) 8

10. The positions of how many alphabets in the word ECCEDENTESIAST will remain same when the digits are arranged in alphabetical order?
    (a) Three   (b) One
    (c) Two   (d) None

English Proficiency

DIRECTIONS (Qs. 11 & 12) : In the following questions, select the appropriate word from the given options to complete the sentence.

11. The Website guaranteed that it would __________ my personal information, so I decided to use my credit card to buy new clothes.
    (a) humanoid
    (b) embellish
    (c) encrypt
    (d) inference

12. The western film took advantage of the landscape to show the wagons crossing the valley with the impressive __________ rising in the background.
    (a) virulent   (b) plateaus
    (c) void   (d) salient

DIRECTIONS (13&14): Choose the alternative which best expresses the meaning of the Idiom/Phrase .

13. The captors of the kidnapped kept his family on tenterhooks.
    (a) an anxious suspense
    (b) on constant move
    (c) in seething anger
    (d) in excited state

14. I have come to know of your hole-and-corner methods of dealing with people.
    (a) suspicious
    (b) secret
    (c) servile
    (d) strict

DIRECTIONS (15 & 16): In the following questions a word is given and followed by four alternatives. Select the alternative that conveys the same meaning as the word/phrase given.

15. Prelapsarian
    (a) noting or pertaining to an era occurring between 230 and 65 million years ago.
    (b) a person or thing that repeats.
    (c) a person who has been convicted and sentenced for one crime, and later for another; recidivist.
    (d) characteristic of or pertaining to any innocent or carefree period.

16. Aegis
    (a) protection; support.
    (b) anything serving to catch or ensnare.
    (c) affectionate concern for the well-being of others.
    (d) highly unusual or unconventional;extravagant; remarkable.

DIRECTIONS (Qs. 17 & 18): A sentence has been given in Direct/Indirect form. Out of the four alternatives suggested, select the one which best expresses the same sentence in Indirect/Direct form

17. She exclaimed, "I'm afraid we are rather late"
    (a) She exclaimed that they were frightened of being late.
    (b) She exclaimed that she was afraid that they were rather late.

(c) She shouted that they were scared that they would be late.

(d) She screamed that she was worried that they would all be late.

18. She said to me, "What can I do for you?"

  (a) She asked me what she could do for me.

  (b) She asked me what can she do for me.

  (c) She asked me what she can do for me.

  (d) She asked me whether she can do anything for me.

DIRECTIONS (Qs. 19 & 20):
Look at the bold part of each sentence. Below each sentence are three possible alternatives for the bold part. If one of them is better than the bold part, indicate your response on the answer sheet against the corresponding letter. If none of the alternatives improve the sentence, indicate (d) as your response.

19. **When** he left the house, it has not ceased raining.

  (a) Even before

  (b) Ever since

  (c) Until

  (d) no improvement

20. While campaigning against child-labour the leader said that he **was feeling strongly** about children being made to work when they should be going to school.

  (a) was feeling strong

  (b) felt strong

  (c) felt strongly

  (d) no improvement

SOLUTIONS

1. **(c)**

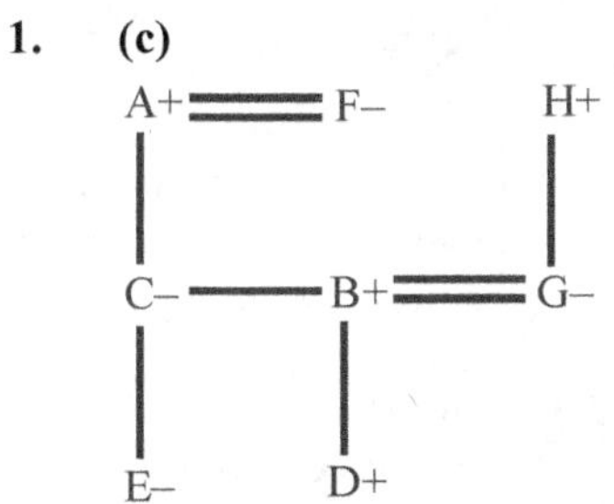

So F is the grandmother of D.

2. **(a)**

3. **(d)**

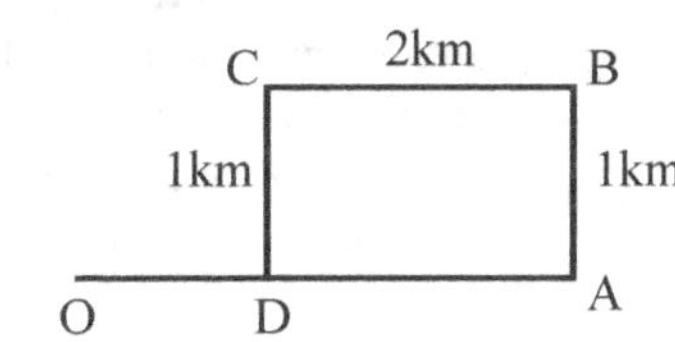

$OD = OA - AD = 3 - 2 = 1$ km

4. **(d)**

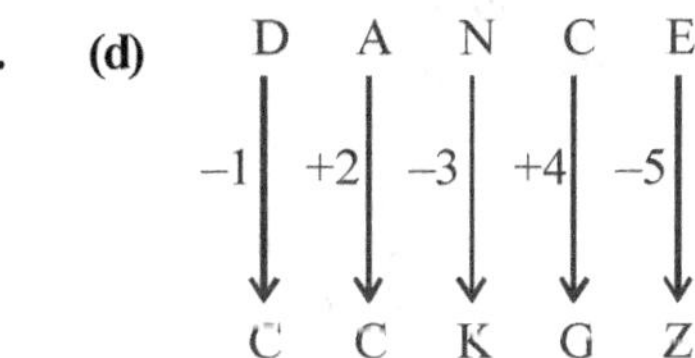

Same pattern follow by Music
→ LWPMX

5. **(d)**

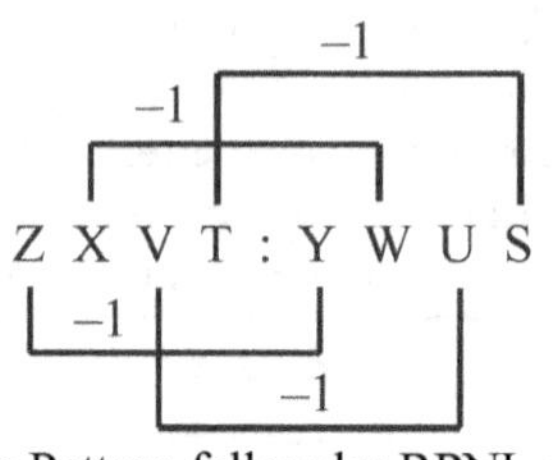

Same Pattern follow by RPNL : QOMK

6. **(d)**

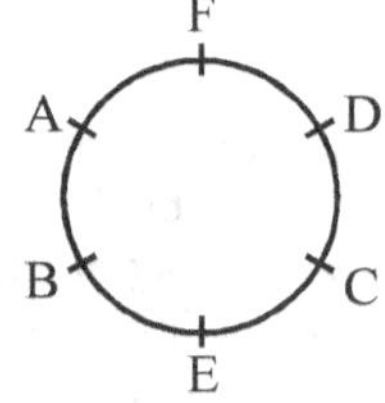

7. **(c)** As the 'moon-star' is the 'national emblem' of 'Pakistan' similarly 'Golden Rod' is the 'national emblem of America.

8. **(d)** As the correct answer is four, which is not given in any option so 'None of these' will be the correct answer.

8$\boxed{6}$76$\boxed{8}$93275342$\boxed{2}$35522$\boxed{8}$119

9. **(b)** According to first condition, the number is greater than 3 but less than 8. Such numbers are 4, 5, 6, 7. According to the second condition, the number is greater than 6 but less than 10. Such numbers are 7, 8, 9.

Hence, that number is 7.

10. **(d)**

Word	E C C E D E N T E S I A S T
Letters in alphabetical order	A C C D E E E I N S S T T

11. **(c)** encrypt: convert (information or data) into a code, especially to prevent unauthorized access.

12. **(b)** plateau- an area of fairly level high ground

13. **(a)** On tenterhooks-in a state of suspense or agitation because of uncertainty about a future event., anxiously waiting for news about someone or something

14. **(b)** Hole-and-corner: hole-and-corner activities are kept secret, usually because they are dishonest

15. **(d)** Prelapsarian: characteristic of or pertaining to any innocent or carefree period.

16. **(a)** Aegis: protection; support

17. **(b)** Change 'I' into 'She', change 'we' into 'they', change tense into past tense.

18. **(a)** Change 'said to' into 'asked', change "I' into 'she', You' into 'me. Change the interrogative into statement sentence.

19. **(b)** Ever since- is correct usage.

20. **(c)** 'felt strongly' is correct verb form and adverb.

MOCK TEST-3

Max. Marks : 20 **Time : 20 mins.**

DIRECTIONS (Q.1): In the following question, four words have been given, out of which three are alike in some manner and the fourth one is different. Choose out the odd one.

1.   (a) Illusion
  (b) Delusion
  (c) Identification
  (d) Hallucination

DIRECTION (Q.2): In the following question, choose that set of numbers/letter-groups from the four alternative sets, that is similar to the given set.

2.   Given set - (81, 77, 69)
  (a) (75, 71, 60)
  (b) (64, 61, 53)
  (c) (56, 52, 44)
  (d) (92, 88, 79)

DIRECTIONS (Q.3): Read the given infromation carefully and answer the question.

3.   I.   Kamal is the brother of Mallika,
  II. Anshika is the daughter of Mallika,
  III. Kumud is the sister of kamal,
  IV. Rahul is the brother of Anshika.
Who is the aunt of Rahul?
  (a) Mallika   (b) Anshika
  (c) kamal   (d) Kumud

4.   Count each 2 in the following sequence of numbers that is immediately followed by 1, if 1 is not immediately followed by 2. How many such 2s are there?
1 2 1 3 4 5 1 2 3 5 2 1 2 6 1 4 5 1 1 2 4 1 2 3 2 1 7 5 2 1 2 5
  (a) 2   (b) 5
  (c) 4   (d) 7

5.   Which of the following comes in place of '?'
64   4   40
42   3   18
91   2   ?
  (a) 10   (b) 14
  (c) 16   (d) 20

6.   If with the third, fourth, fifth, seventh and tenth letters of the word PERSONALITY, a meaningful word is formed, then first letter of the word is the answer. If no word is possible, then 'X' is the answer.
  (a) O   (b) T
  (c) R   (d) X

7.   A pineapple costs ₹ 7 each. A watermelon costs ₹ 5 each. X spends ₹ 38 on these fruits. The number of pineapples purchased is
  (a) 2
  (b) 3
  (c) 4
  (d) Data inadequate

8.   Nisha moved a distance of 75 metres towards the north. She then turned to the left and walking for about 25 metres, turned left again and walked 80 metres. Finally, she turned to the right at an angle of 45°. In which direction was she moving finally?
  (a) North-east (b) North-west
  (c) South-west (d) South-east

9. In the adjoining figure, if the centres of all the circles are joined by horizontal and vertical lines, then find the number of squares that can be formed.
   (a) 6   (b) 7
   (c) 8   (d) 1

10. In a certain code language, ROUTINE is written as VMRGFLI. How will CRUELTY be written in that code language?
    (a) VOCVZRL
    (b) VPCVZRL
    (c) V PVCZRL
    (d) None of these

English Proficiency

DIRECTIONS (Qs. 11 & 12) : Find out the correct meaning of the idiomatic expression and choose the correct option.

11. Far from cry
    (a) to come from far
    (b) to leave silently
    (c) very different from
    (d) to approach silently

12. Feel a bit under the weather
    (a) showing signs of torture
    (b) traumatized
    (c) feeling ignored or unattended
    (d) feeling slightly ill

DIRECTIONS (Qs. 13 & 14): Read each sentence to find out whether there is any grammatical error in it. The error, if any, will be one part of the sentence. The number of that part is the answer. If there is no error, the answer is (d).

13. (a) Despite for her protests,
    (b) I decided to buy
    (c) the saree which she did not like.
    (d) No error

14. (a) The government warned the shopkeepers
    (b) that if they persist in charging unfair prices
    (c) their licences would be cancelled.
    (d) No error

DIRECTIONS (Qs. 15-17): In this section, you have one short passage. After this passage, you will find several questions based on the passage. First, read Passage, and answer the questions based on it.

PASSAGE

Our home stood behind the railroad tracks. Its skimpy yard was paved with black cinders. The only touch of green we could see was far away, beyond the tracks over where the white folks lived. But cinders were fine weapons. All you had to do was crouch behind the brick pillars of a house with your hands full of gritty ammunition, and the first wooly black head you saw from behind another row of pillars was your target. It was fun. One day, the gang to which I belonged found itself engaged in a war with the white boys who lived beyond the tracks. As usual, we laid down our cinder barrage thinking this would wipe the white boys out. But they replied with a steady bombardment of broken bottles. We retreated. During the retreat, a broken milk bottle caught me behind the ear, opening a deep gash. The sight of blood pouring over my face completely demoralized our ranks. My fellow combatants left me standing paralyzed in the center of the yard and scurried for their houses. A kind neighbor saw me and rushed me to a doctor.

15. The locality, where the author lived, was
    (a) behind a brick quarry
    (b) near a coal mine
    (c) far away from where the whites lived
    (d) close to where
16. The weapons used by the whites in the gang fight were
    (a) as effective as the author's
    (b) less effective than the author's
    (c) more dangerous than the author's
    (d) as harmless as the author's
17. The author was hit by a broken bottle
    (a) as soon as the fight began
    (b) during a lull in the fight
    (c) after the fight was over
    (d) when the author's gang was withdrawing

18. In the following question, out of the four alternatives, choose the word which best expresses the meaning of the given word.
    REVILE
    (a) REVIVE (b) REVIEW
    (c) ABUSE   (d) REVEAL

DIRECTIONS (Qs. 19 & 20): In the following question, out of the four alternatives, choose the word which is opposite in meaning to the given word.

19. SQUANDER
    (a) SPEND   (b) REDUCE
    (c) SLANDER (d) SKIMP
20. DISAVOWAL
    (a) REBUTTAL
    (b) REPEAL
    (c) APPROVAL
    (d) APPEAL

SOLUTIONS

1. **(c)** All except Identification are synonyms
2. **(c)** In each set, 2nd number = (1st number - 4) and 3rd number = (2nd number - 8)
3. **(d)** Kumud→Kamal→Mallika
                         ↓
       Rahul ← Anishka
       Kumud is the aunt of Rahul.
4. **(a)** 1 $\boxed{2\,1\,3}$ 4 5 1 2 3 5 2 1 2 6 1

    4 5 1 1 2 4 1 2 3 $\boxed{2\,1\,7}$ 5 2 1 2 5
5. **(d)** (4 +6) 4 40 [10 × 4 = 40]
    Similarly,
    (9+1) 2 20[10 × 2 = 20]
6. **(c)** The third, fourth, fifth, seventh and tenth letters of the word PERSONALITY and R, S, O, A and T respectively. The word formed is ROAST. So, the first letter is R.
7. **(c)** Let the number of pineapples and watermelons be x and y respectively.
    Then, $7x + 5y = 38$ or $5y = (38 - 7x)$ or $y = \dfrac{38 - 7x}{5}$.

    Clearly, y is a whole number, only when $(38 - 7x)$ is divisible by 5.
    This happens when $x = 4$.

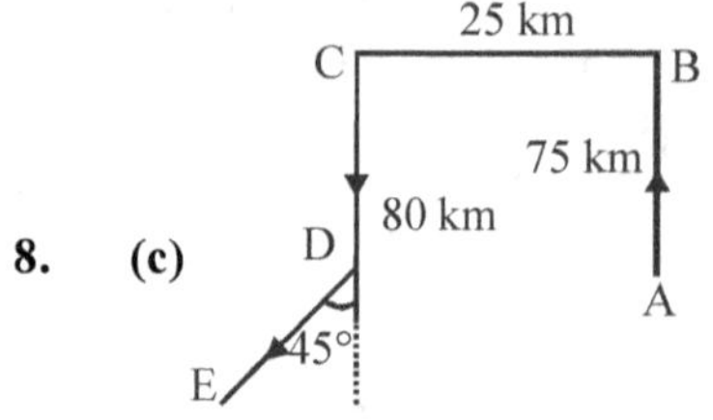

8.   (c)

Finally she was moving in the direction DE i.e. south-west.

9.   (c)   The figure my be labelled as shown.

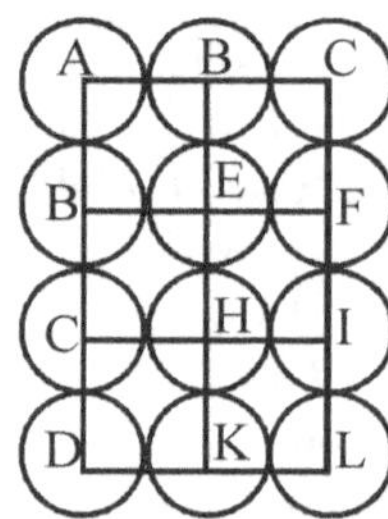

We shall join the centres of all the circles by horizontal and vertical lines and then label the resulting figure as shown. The simplest squares are ABED, BCFE, DEHG, EFIH, GHKJ and HILK i.e. 6 in number.

The squares composed of four simple squares are ACIG and DFLJ i.e. 2 in number.

Thus, $6 + 2 = 8$ squares will be formed.

10.   (d)   Each letter in the word is replaced by the letter which occupies the same position from the other end of the English alphabet, and the group of letters so obtained is then written in the reverse order to get the code. Thus, we have:

CRUELTY → XIFVOGB → BGOVFIX

11.   (c)   The expression far cry means "very different from."

12.   (d)   be/feel under the weather: to feel ill

13.   (a)   Delete 'for', 'Despite' is followed by an object.

14.   (b)   use 'persisted' because 'warned' is in the past tense the whites lived

15.   (b)   The locality, where the author lived, was near a coal mine.

16.   (c)   The weapons used by the whites in the gang fight were more dangerous than the author's.

17.   (d)   The author was hit by a broken bottle when the author's gang was withdrawing.

18.   (c)   REVILE meaning: criticize in an abusive or angrily insulting manner. Hence, abuse is correct.

19.   (d)   SLANDER-the action or crime of making a false spoken statement damaging to a person's reputation.
SQUANDER-waste (something, especially money or time) in a reckless and foolish manner.
SKIMP-expend or use less time, money, or material on something than is necessary in an attempt to economize.   Hence, squander and skimp is antonyms to each other in meaning.

20.   (c)   DISAVOWAL-the denial of any responsibility or support for something; repudiation.

MOCK TEST-4

Max. Marks : 20　　　　　　　　　　**Time : 20 mins.**

1. In the following list of letters, how many Q's are preceded by O's and followed by D's?

   D O Q O D Q O D O D Q D O Q
   D S D Q P
   O Q D S S S D O Q O Q D O Q D
   D D O Q

   (a) 1　　　　　(b) 2
   (c) 3　　　　　(d) 4

2. Five children take part in a tournament. Everyone has to play with one another. How many games must they play?

   (a) 8　　　　　(b) 10
   (c) 24　　　　(d) 30

3. In this letter series, some of the letters are missing which are given in that order as one of the alternatives below it. Choose the correct alternative.

   c _ b a a _ a c a _ c a c a b _ a c
   a c _ b c a

   (a) bccab　　　(b) bbcaa
   (c) acbaa　　　(d) cbaac

DIRECTIONS (Q. 4): Read the information given below and answer the questions that follow:

(i)　In a family of six persons X, Y, Z, L, M and N, there are two married couples.

(ii)　L is grandmother of X and mother of Y.

(iii)　Z is wife of Y and mother of N.

(iv)　N is the grand-daughter of M.

4. How many male members are there in the family?

   (a) Two
   (b) Three
   (c) Four
   (d) Cannot be determined

DIRECTIONS (Qs. 5 & 6): Read the following information carefully and answer the questions that follow:

Six lectures A, B, C, D, E and F are to be organized in a span of seven days - from Sunday to Saturday, only one lecture on each day in accordance with the following:

(i)　A should not be organized on Thursday.

(ii)　C should be organized immediately after F.

(iii)　There should be a gap of two days between E and D.

(iv)　One day there will be no lecture (Friday is not that day), just before that day D will be organized.

(v)　B should be organized on Tuesday and should not be followed by D.

5. Which day will the lecture E be organized?

   (a) Thursday
   (b) Friday
   (c) Saturday
   (d) Wednesday

6. Which of the following is the first lecture in the series?

   (a) A
   (b) B
   (c) D
   (d) Cannot be determined

7. In this question, select the related word from the given alternatives.
    Tanning : Leather :: Pyrotechnics : ?
    (a) Machinery
    (b) Bombs
    (c) Fireworks
    (d) Wool
8. How many rectangles are there in below figure?

    (a) 20   (b) 21
    (c) 22   (d) 23
9. In each of the letters in the English alphabet is assigned an even numerical value by giving A = 2, B = 4 and so on, what would be the total value of the letters for the word LADY when similarly coded?
    (a) 78   (b) 84
    (c) 58   (d) 62
10. Today is Monday. After 61 days, it will be:
    (a) Wednesday
    (b) Saturday
    (c) Tuesday
    (d) Thursday

English Proficiency

DIRECTIONS (Qs. 11 & 12) : Read the passage carefully and choose the correct option.

PASSAGE

Indian airlines had no positive response to the incident occurred in the failure of an aeroplane engine. It was 1989, Indian airline B059 got crashed in the middle of the Indian ocean, 205 passengers died. There were no clues about the B059, some says that it got crashed but some said it got lost. Passengers relative were worried about their dear ones. The government declared the issue of B059 as a priority, Indian navy were given responsibility to find the B059 but nothing was found. After a year some fishermen found the black box of B059, which confirms about the crash of Indian aeroplane B059 due to engine failure.

11. What was the reason for the crash of B059?
    (a) Engine failure.
    (b) Crashed with a bird.
    (c) B059 catches Fire.
    (d) Pilot failure.
12. Who got the responsibility to find out clues about B059?
    (a) Indian Coastal Guard.
    (b) Indian Army.
    (c) Indian Navy.
    (d) Indian Air Force.
13. What could be assumed from the passage?
    (a) It was an airline mistake.
    (b) The government did not take any step.
    (c) Indian Navy did not work properly.
    (d) None of these.

DIRECTIONS (Qs. 14 & 16): The sentences have been given in Active/Passive voice. From the given alternatives, choose the one which best expresses the given sentence in Passive/Active voice .

14. One cannot gather grapes from thistles.
    (a) Thistles cannot be gathered from grapes.
    (b) Grapes cannot be gathered from thistles.

(c)   Grapes and thistles cannot be gathered by one.

(d)   Grapes cannot be gathered by them.

15. They will have completed the work by the time we get there.

(a)   The work will be completed by the time we get there.

(b)   The work will have been completed by the time we get there.

(c)   The work will have completed by the time we get there.

(d)   The work will have been completed by the time we have got there.

16. You will have to pull down this skyscraper as you have not complied with the town planning regulations.

(a)   This skyscraper will have to be pulled down as the town planning regulations have not been complied with.

(b)   This skyscraper will have to be pulled down by you as the town planning regulations has not been complied by you.

(c)   This skyscraper will be pulled down as the town planning regulations have not been complied with.

(d)   This skyscraper will have to be pulled down as the town planning regulations have not been complied.

DIRECTIONS (Qs. 17&18): In these questions, the 1st and the last parts of the sentences are numbered 1 and 6. The rest is split into four parts and named P, Q, R and S. These four parts are not given in their proper order. Read the sentence and find out which of the four combinations is correct. Then find the correct answer and select your answer accordingly.

17. 1.   The Leeds University
P.   a number
Q.   offers
R.   to international
S.   of scholarships
6.   students
(a)   QRPS   (b)   RPSQ
(c)   QPSR   (d)   PQRS

18. 1.   Academicians
P.   who have been involved in the debate
Q.   including former Vice-Chancellors
R.   that the legislation can help providing a uniform character
S.   on a common university law, think
6.   to the university bodies such as senate, syndicate etc.
(a)   RQPS   (b)   SRQP
(c)   PSRQ   (d)   QPSR

DIRECTIONS (Qs. 19 & 20): In each question, a part of the sentence is printed in bold. Below each sentence, some phrases are given which can substitute the bold part of the sentence. Find out the phrase which can correctly substitute that part of the sentence. If the sentence is correct as it is, the answer is 'No correction required' or 'No improvement'.

19. The poor villagers **have waited** in the bitter cold for more than four hours now.
(a)   has been waiting
(b)   had waited
(c)   have been waiting
(d)   No improvement

20. As John dived off the springboard, he was horrified to see that the water **was drained from** the pool the night before.
(a)   was drained away
(b)   was drained
(c)   had been drained off
(d)   No improvement

SOLUTIONS

1. **(d)** D O Q O D Q O D O D Q D
    O **Q** D S D Q P
    O **Q** D S S S D O **Q** O Q D O **Q** D
    D D O Q

2. **(b)** Number of games = (n(n-1))/2 = (5(5-1))/2 = 10

3. **(c)** The series is cab/aa/cacab/cacab/aa/cacab/ca.
    Thus, the pattern 'cacab/cacab/aa' is repeated.

4. **(d)**

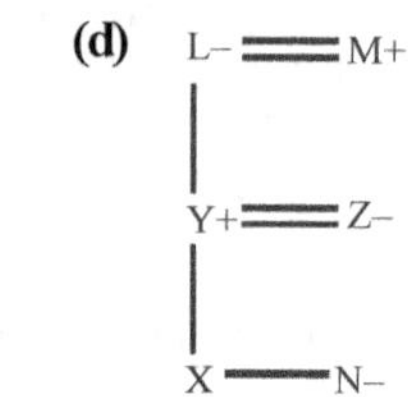

Clearly, the gender of X cannot be determined.

Sol. (5-6)

Sunday	Monday	Tuesday	Wednesday	Thursday	Friday	Saturday
D	×	B	E	F	C	A

5. **(d)** E is organized on Wednesday.

6. (c) D is the first lecture.

7. **(c)** Tanning is the process of manufacturing leather. Similarly, Pyrotechnics is the process of manufacturing fireworks.

8. **(b)** The number of rectangles = 21

9. **(b)**
$$L \Rightarrow 12 \times 2 = 24$$
$$A \Rightarrow 01 \times 2 = 02$$
$$D \Rightarrow 04 \times 2 = 08$$
$$Y \Rightarrow 25 \times 2 = 50$$
$$\overline{84}$$

10. (b) Each day of the week is repeated after 7 days.
    So, after 63 days, it will be Monday.
    After 61 days, it will be Saturday.

11. **(a)** It's is mentioned in the paragraph about 'Engine failure.'

12. **(c)** Sol. It's is mentioned in the paragraph about 'Indian Navy.'

13. **(d)** None of the statement is true.

14. **(b)** 'Grapes cannot be gathered from thistles.' Option B is correct passive form of the sentence.

15. **(b)** 'The work will have been completed by the time we get there.' Write 'the work' as subject of the passive voice, (been + past participle) form of the verb.

16. **(a)** This skyscraper will have to be pulled down as the town planning regulations have not been complied with.

17. **(c)** The correct logical order of the sentences of the given paragraph will be: QPSR

18. **(d)** The correct logical order of the sentences of the given paragraph will be :QPSR

19. **(c)** The phrase 'for more than four hours now' suggests that the sentence should be written in Present Perfect Continuous Tense. Therefore 'have 'waited' should be replaced with 'have been waiting'.

20. **(c)** The appropriate phrasal verb is 'drain off'. Therefore 'was drained from' should be replaced with 'had been drained off'.

MOCK TEST-5

Max. Marks : 20 **Time : 20 mins.**

1. If ASSIGN is coded as SASING, then KIDNAP is coded as
   - (a) IKNDPA
   - (b) IKDNPA
   - (c) IKDNAP
   - (d) IKAPDN

2. Which number will complete the series?
   63, 72, 81, 90, ____, 108
   - (a) 80
   - (b) 99
   - (c) 100
   - (d) 117

3. Rajiv is the brother of Sonia. Sunil is the son of Sonia Gandhi's sister Hakarun. Rajiv's relationship with Sunil?
   - (a) uncle
   - (b) son
   - (c) brother
   - (d) Father

4. A mother is five times older than her daughter. After 5 years her age will be 3 times of her daughter's age. Find the mother's present age.
   - (a) 20 years
   - (b) 22 years
   - (c) 25 years
   - (d) 29 years

5. Find the number of triangles in the figure ?

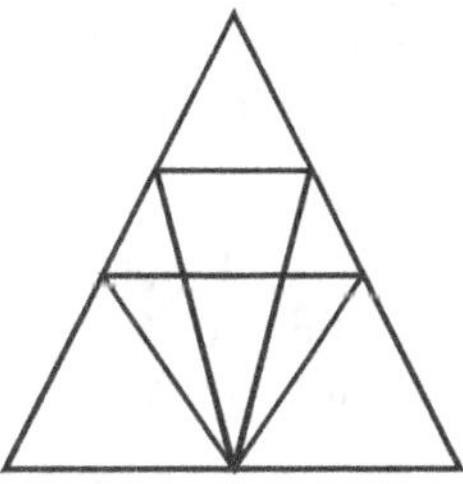

   - (a) Eighteen
   - (b) Nineteen
   - (c) Twenty-six
   - (d) Twenty-two

6. If 1st and 26th, 2nd and 25th, 3rd and 24th, and so on, letters of the English alphabet are paired, then which of the following pairs is correct?
   - (a) GR
   - (b) CW
   - (c) IP
   - (d) EV

7. A series is given, with one term missing. Choose the correct alternative from the given ones that will complete the series.
   8, 15, 28, 53, ?
   - (a) 106
   - (b) 100
   - (c) 108
   - (d) 102

8. Six friends are playing cards in a circular enclosure facing the centre. Shubhash is on the right of Pramod. There is one person in between Umesh and Suresh. Praveen is in between Shubhash and Umesh and Praveen is second to the left of Alok. If Alok and Shubhash mutually change their places, then who will be second to the right of Praveen?
   - (a) Suresh
   - (b) Umesh
   - (c) Shubhash
   - (d) Pramod

9. Select the missing number from the given responses:

3	5	9
4	6	?
3	7	2
36	210	36

    (a) 4   (b) 3
    (c) 2   (d) 1

10. If the words in the sentence, "She sells sea shells on the sea shore" are rearranged in the alphabetical order, which will be the middle word?

    (a) shells   (b) she
    (c) sea   (d) shore

English Proficiency

DIRECTIONS (Qs. 11 & 12) : In the following passages, some of the words have been left out. First read the passage over and try to understand what it is about. Then fill in the blanks with the help of the alternatives given.

The temple was (11) as a massive chariot (12) on an east-west axis, in which the Sun god, Surya, was pulled across the sky. Each day his (13) brought life and light back to earth and his procession was a continual rejoicing. The chariot had twenty-four wheels, and was (14) by seven horses, (15) the seven days of the week and the seven sages who govern the constellations.

11. (a) Conceived
    (b) Celebrated
    (c) Bases
    (d) Viewed

12. (a) Found
    (b) Originated
    (c) Lying
    (d) Lifted

13. (a) Experience
    (b) Scheduled
    (c) Journey
    (d) Trial

14. (a) Pulled
    (b) Brought
    (c) Dominated
    (d) Carried

15. (a) Overseeing
    (b) Managing
    (c) Representing
    (d) Showing

DIRECTIONS (Qs. 16 & 17): Some parts of the sentences have errors and some are correct. Find out which part of a sentence has an is free from error marked (d).

16. Reading is no longer popular among the youthful of today, as the influence of the internet has taken over a very important and active hobby.
    (a) Very Important and active Hobby
    (b) Influence of the internet
    (c) among the youthful of today
    (d) No Error

17. Mobile phones are so importance these days that they are no longer luxury items but have become a necessity.
    (a) No longer
    (b) So Importance these days
    (c) A necessity
    (d) No Error

DIRECTIONS (Qs. 18 - 20): A sentence has been given in Direct/Indirect form. Out of the four alternatives suggested, select the one which best expresses the same sentence in Indirect/Direct form.

18. The Colonel said to the soldier, "Next month' you will be promoted."
    (a) The Colonel commanded the soldier that he must be promoted.
    (b) The Colonel told the soldier he would be promoted the following month.

    (c) The Colonel promised the soldier that he would promote him next month.

    (d) The Colonel said the soldier will be promoted the following month.

19. "It is a pleasure to do business with you", He said

    (a) He said that it was a pleasure to do business with me.

    (b) He said that it is a pleasure to do business with you.

    (c) He conveyed the pleasure to do business with you.

    (d) He wondered at the pleasure to do business with you.

20. Rahim said, "I will watch a horror movie tonight".

    (a) Rahim said that he will watch a horror movie tonight.

    (b) Rahim said that he would watch a horror movie tonight.

    (c) Rahim said that he would watch a horror movie that night.

    (d) Rahim said that he should watch a horror movie tonight.

SOLUTIONS

1. **(b)**

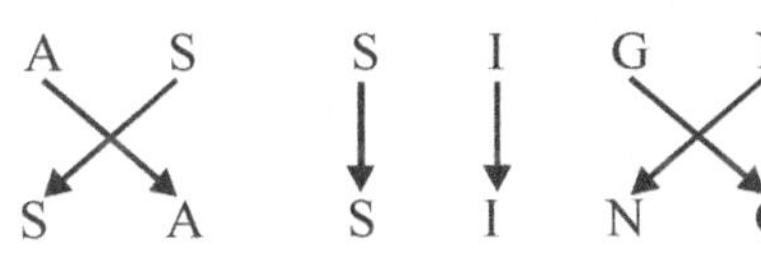

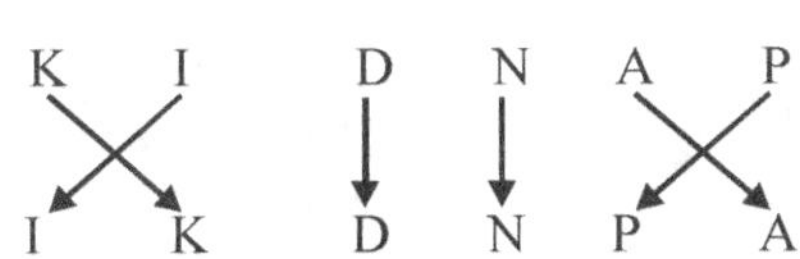

2. **(b)** Pattern of series:
$$63 + 9 = 72$$
$$72 + 9 = 81$$
$$81 + 9 = 90$$
$$90 + 9 = 99$$

3. **(a)**

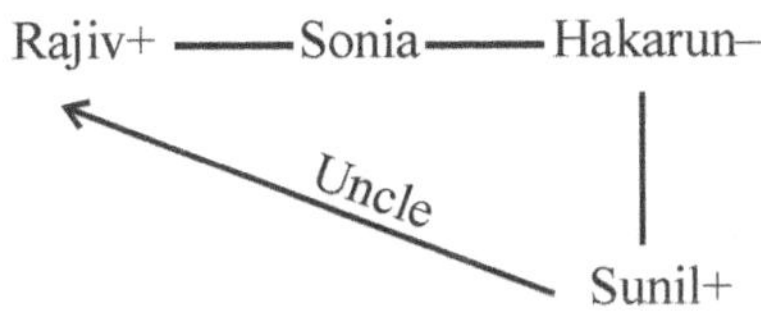

4. **(c)** Let daughter's present age $= x$

Mother's present age $= 5x$

After 5 years:

$5x + 5 = 3(x+5)$ $x = 5$

So, Mother's present age $= 5 \times 5 = 25$ years

5. **(b)** The number of triangles = 18

6. **(d)** The paring up of letters may be done as shown below.

AZ, BY, CX, DW, EV, FU, GT, HS, IR, JQ, KP, LO, MN.

7. **(d)** $8 \times 2 - 1 = 15$
$$15 \times 2 - 2 = 28$$
$$28 \times 2 - 3 = 53$$
$$53 \times 2 - 4 = 102$$

8. **(c)**

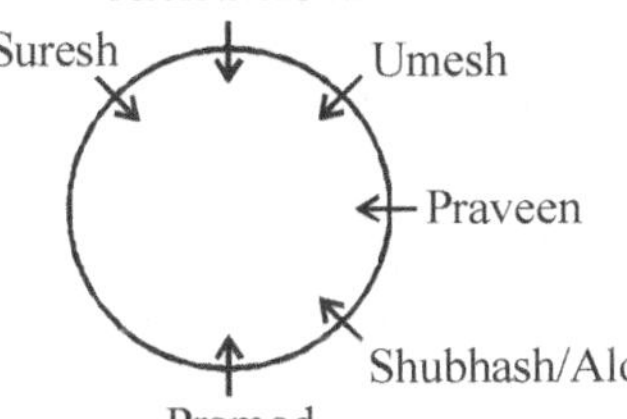

9. **(c)** In 1st column:
$3 \times 4 \times 3 = 36$
In 2nd column:
$5 \times 6 \times 7 = 210$
So, in 3rd column:
$9 \times ? \times 2 = 36$

10. **(b)** The correct alphabetical order is: on, sea, sells, she, shells, shore, the

11. **(a)** Conceived- fits in the context of the sentence correctly.

12. **(c)** Lying- fits in the context of the sentence correctly.

13. **(c)** Journey- fits in the context of the sentence correctly.

14. **(a)** Pulled- fits in the context of the sentence correctly.

15. **(c)** Representing- fits in the context of the sentence correctly.

16. **(c)** change "Youthful" into "youths"

17. **(b)** Change 'importance' into 'important'

18. **(b)** Change 'said to' into 'told, you into 'he', 'next month' into 'the following month'.

19. **(a)** Use simple past tense, and change 'you' into 'me'.

20. **(c)** Use conjunction 'that', change pronoun 'I' into 'he', and 'tonight' into 'that night'.

MOCK TEST-6

Max. Marks : 20   **Time : 20 mins.**

1. Find the missing term in the series

EJO, TYD, INS, XCH, ?

   (a) NRW   (b) MRW

   (c) MSX   (d) NSX

2. If the first three letters of the word COMPRE HENSION are reversed, then the last three letters are added and then the remaining letters are reversed and added, then which letter will be exactly in the middle ?

   (a) H   (b) N

   (c) R   (d) S

3. Choose the odd one out

   (a) Metre   (b) Furlong

   (c) Acre   (d) Mile

DIRECTIONS (Qs. 4) : Find out the correct alternatives.

4. Filter : water : : censor

   (a) Book   (b) Text

   (c) Play   (d) Activity

5. In a certain code, ELEPHANT is written as TNPEAHLE, the CROCODILE will be written as ?

   (a) RCCOOIDEL

   (b) ELCOOIDRC

   (c) ELCIOODRC

   (d) ELCOIODRC

6. Roshan ranked 11 th from the top and thirty one from the bottom in a class. How many students are there in the class?

   (a) 42   (b) 43

   (c) 41   (d) 40

7. Introducing a boy, a girl said, "He is the son of the daughter of the father of my uncle." How is the boy related to the girl?

   (a) Brother

   (b) Nephew

   (c) Uncle

   (d) Son-in-low

8. If P denotes ÷, Q denotes ×, R denotes + and S denotes –, then the value of 18 Q 12 P 4 R 5 S 6 when simplified gives

   (a) 36   (b) 53

   (c) 59   (d) 65

9. Divya journeys 10 km to east then 10 km to south-west. He turns again and journeys 10 km to North-West. Which direction is he in from the starting point ?

   (a) South   (b) North

   (c) West   (d) East

10. The first republic day of India was celebrated on 26th January, 1950. It was –

   (a) Monday   (b) Tuesday

   (c) Thursday   (d) Friday

DIRECTIONS (Qs. 11 & 12) : Choose the correct meaning of an idiom/ phrase.

11. To turn over a new leaf :

   (a) To change completely one's course of action

   (b) To shift attention to new problems

   (c) To cover up one's faults by wearing new marks

   (d) To change the old habits and adopt new ones

12. To wrangle over an ass's shadow :
    - (a) To act in a foolish way
    - (b) To quarrel over trifles
    - (c) To waste time on petty things
    - (d) To do something funny
13. Choose the correct spelling of the given word.
    - (a) Efflorascence
    - (b) Efflorescence
    - (c) Efllorescence
    - (d) Eflorescence

DIRECTIONS (Qs. 14 & 15): In each of the following sentences four words or phrases have been underlined. Find out which part of a sentence has an error.

14. I have seen $\underset{a}{\underline{\text{as bad or}}}$ worse scenes of $\underset{b}{\underline{\text{disorder}}}$ at the English fair $\underset{c}{\underline{\text{than}}}$ in $\underset{d}{\underline{\text{any other}}}$ Australian mining town.

15. The officers are $\underset{a}{\underline{\text{now}}}$ $\underset{b}{\underline{\text{perfectly}}}$ happy fishing, boating, shooting, $\underset{c}{\underline{\text{playing cricket}}}$ and $\underset{d}{\underline{\text{other sports}}}$.

DIRECTIONS (Qs. 16 & 17): In each of these questions, in the given sentences, a part of the sentence is underlined. Beneath each sentence, four different ways of phrasing the underlined part are indicated. Choose the best alternative. In case no improvement is needed, your answer would be 'No improvement'.

16. <u>Expect for you and I, everyone brought</u> a present to the party.
    - (a) With the exception of you and I, everyone brought
    - (b) Except for you and I, everyone had brought
    - (c) Except for you and me, everyone brought
    - (d) Except for you and me, everyone had brought
17. <u>Although I calculate that he will be here</u> any minute, I cannot wait much longer for him.
    - (a) Although I reckon that he will be here
    - (b) Although I think that he will be here
    - (c) Because I am confidant that he will be here
    - (d) Because I calculate that he will be here

DIRECTIONS (Qs. 18 - 20): Read the passage carefully to answer the questions.

In a disarmingly frank talk at the Indian Merchants Chamber in Mumbai, the Japanese Ambassador in India dwelt at length on issues that exercise the minds of Japanese investors when they consider investment proposals in India.

Raising the question "What comparative advantages does India offer as an investment market ?", he said though labour in India is expensive, wage-levels are offset by productivity level to a large extent.

Acknowledging that the vastness of the Indian market is a great inducement for investment in manufacturing industry, he wondered if it was justifiable to provide that overseas termittance of profit in foreign exchange be fully covered by exchange earnings as had been done. Significantly, on the eve of the Prime Minister's visit to Japan, the government delinked profits repatriation from exports, meeting this demand.

The Ambassador said foreign investors needed to be assured of the continuity and consistency of the liberalisation policy and the fact that new measures had been put into force by means of administrative notifications without amending government laws acted as a damper.

The Ambassador pleaded for speedy formulation of the exit policy and pointed to the highly restrictive control by the government on disinvestment by foreign partner in joint ventures in India.

While it is all too easy to dismiss critical comment on conditions in India contemptuously, there can be little doubt that if foreign investment is to be wooed assiduously, we will have to meet exacting international standards and cater at least partially to what we may consider the idiosyncrasies of our foreign collaborators. The Japanese too have passed through a stage in the fifties when their products were derided as sub-standard and shoddy. That they have come out of that ordeal of fire to emerge as an economic superpower speaks a much of their doggedness to pursue goals against all odds acceptable standards.

There is no gainsaying that the paste record of Japanese investment is a poor benchmark for future expectations.

18. According to the Japanese Ambassador, which of the following motivates the foreign investors to invest in Indian manufacturing industry?
   (a) very large scope of Indian market
   (b) overseas remittance of profit in foreign exchange
   (c) assurance of continuity of the liberalisation policy
   (d) high productivity levels

19. The purpose of the author in writing this passage seems to be to:
   (a) discourage foreign investment in India.
   (b) critically examine Indian investment environment.
   (c) paint a rosy picture of India's trade and commerce.
   (d) criticize government's liberalization policy.

20. Choose the word which is most OPPOSITE in meaning of the word printed in capital as used in the passage.
   INDUCEMENT
   (a) incentive
   (b) motive
   (c) impediment
   (d) temptation

SOLUTIONS

1. **(b)** There is a gap of four letters between first and second, second and third letter of each term. Also there is a gap of 4 letters between the last letter of a term and the first letter of the next term.

2. **(d)** Clearly, we have :
C O M P R E H E N S I O N →
(COM) (PREHENS) (ION)
→ MOCIONSNEHERP
The middle letter is the seventh letter, which is S.

3. **(c)** All except Acre are units of measuring distance, while acre is a unit of area.

4. **(c)** A filter removes the objectionable impurities from water, similarly, censor removes the objectionable scenes from a play.

5. **(b)** Type – Simple Arrangement (Swap Coding)
Positions of T and E and L and N are swapped.
Also, positions of second E and P and H and A are swapped.
Therefore, for CROCODILE the code after swapping in the same pattern is ELOCIDRC.

6. **(c)** $T_r = 11$, $B_r = 31$
⇒ No. of students $= T_r + B_r - 1 = 11 + 31 - 1 = 41$

7. **(a)** The father of the boy's uncle → the grandfather of the boy and daughter of the grandfather → sister of father.

8. **(b)** Using correct symbols, we have
Given expression $= 18 \times 12 \div 4 + 5 - 6$
$= 18 \times 3 + 5 - 6 = 54 + 5 - 6 = 53$

9. **(c)**

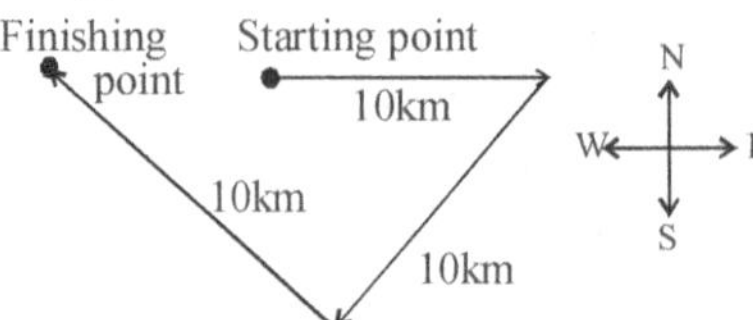

10. **(c)** 1600 years have 0 odd day and 300 years have 1 odd day.
49 years contain 12 leap years and 37 ordinary years and therefore (24 + 37) odd days i.e., 5 odd days
i.e., 1949 years contain (0 + 1 + 5) or 6 odd days.
26 days of January contain 5 odd days.
Total odd days $= (6 + 5) = 11$ or 4 odd days.
So, the day was Thursday.

11. **(d)**   12. **(b)**   13. **(b)**

14. **(c)** In place of 'than' it will be 'as'

15. **(d)** and indulging in other sports.

16. **(c)** When the word 'except' is used 'me' is used with it instead of I, so the most appropriate form of this phrase will be except for you and me.

17. **(a)** 'Calculate' is not an appropriate word for this sentence, calculation is done on the basis of available facts with certain fixed rules, whereas according to the sense of the sentence the person is only making a guess or a supposition, thus reckon is the most appropriate word that can be used to replace calculate.

18. **(a)** The Japanese ambassador acknowledges that the vastness of the Indian market is a great inducement for investment in the manufacturing industry.

19. **(b)** The author describes the Indian investment scenario in toto. He presents a comparative analysis regarding foreign investment in India.

20. **(c)**

MOCK TEST-7

Max. Marks : 20   **Time : 20 mins.**

DIRECTIONS (Qs. 1 & 2) : Choose the missing term out of the given alternatives.

1. 3, 8, 35, 48, ?, 120
   (a) 64   (b) 72
   (c) 80   (d) 99

2. a a b – a a a – b b a –
   (a) b b a   (b) a b b
   (c) b a b   (d) b b b

3. In a certain code if FRIEND is written as DNEIRF. Then, what will be the code for DESERT ?
   (a) TRESED   (b) DSERET
   (c) TRSEED   (d) TESERD

4. Pointing out to a lady, a girl said " she is the daughter-in-law of the grandmother of my father's only son." How is the lady related to the girl ?
   (a) Sister-in-law
   (b) Mother
   (c) Aunt
   (d) Mother-in-law

5. Jatin leaves his house and walks 12 km towards North. He turns right and walks another 12 km. He turns right again, walks 12 km more and turns left to walk 5 km. How far is he from his home and in which direction ?
   (a) 7 km East
   (b) 10 km East
   (c) 17 km East
   (d) 24 km East

6. Find the missing number

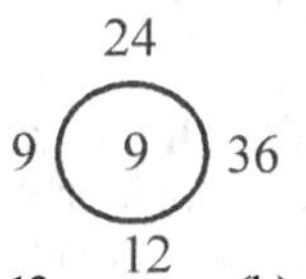

   (a) 12   (b) 15
   (c) 17   (d) 18

7. Choose the odd one out.
   (a) Atom : Electron
   (b) Train : Engine
   (c) House : Room
   (d) Curd : Milk

8. If the seventh day of a month is three days earlier than Friday, what day will it be on the nineteenth day of the month?
   (a) Sunday
   (b) Monday
   (c) Wednesday
   (d) Friday

9. If + means ÷ , – means ×, ÷ means + and × means – , then
   $36 \times 8 + 4 \div 6 + 2 - 3 = ?$
   (a) 2   (b) 18
   (c) 43   (d) $6\dfrac{1}{2}$

10. What is the number of squares in fig (X) ?

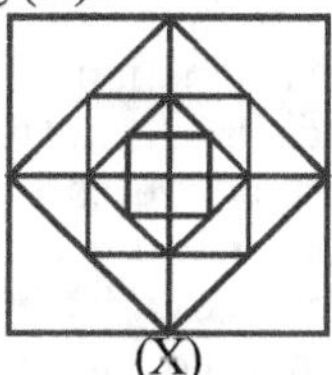

   (a) 12   (b) 13
   (c) 15   (d) 17

DIRECTIONS (Qs. 11 - 13): Read the passage carefully to answer the questions.

Since July 1991, the government of India has effectively put the liberalisation policy into practice. The drastic steps even include some administrative reforms for pruning the government agencies. Last year the Japanese business circles represented by the Ishikawa Mission called attention of their Indian counterparts to what they considered to be the major impediments in India. However, thanks to the almost revolutionary reforms put into effect by the Indian government, those impediments either have been removed or now are on their way out. This development gives a new hope for the future of economic co-operation between the two countries. At the same time, it should be borne in mind that there is a stiff competition with other countries, notably China and South-East Asian countries, in this regard. The success stories of ASEAN countries welcoming Japanese investments with adequate infrastructure are already known in India but it may be useful if further studies of Japanese joint ventures in ASEAN countries be made by Indian business circles. The coastal areas of China have initiated a very active campaign to welcome foreign economic participation.

Beyond our bilateral relationship, India's more active participation in global economy is needed. India certainly deserves a far bigger share of world trade considering its vast resources. It is strongly hoped that the Indian government's recently initiated effort of enlarging its export market would bear fruit.

India has steadfastly maintained its parliamentary democracy since independence. Considering its size, its population and its internal complexity, the overall maintenance of national integrity and political stability under parliamentary democracy is remarkable and admirable indeed. Here lies the base for the status of India in the world. By effectively implementing its economic reform with the support of public opinion, this democratic polity of India has again demonstrated its viability and resilience. At the same time, it gives hope and inspiration to the whole world which faces the difficult problem of North-South confromation.

11. The Ishikawa Mission during its visit to India emphasized on:
    (a) future economic co-operation between Japan and India.
    (b) need for removing policy and/or implementation hurdles.
    (c) need for a stiff competition.
    (d) striking down revolutionary reforms.

12. Which of the following is TRUE about the author's view regarding India's participation in world trade?
    (a) India should actively contribute in a big way as it had tremendous resources.
    (b) India's sharing in global economy has already been very fast and beyond its resources.
    (c) India should refrain from making efforts in enlarging its export market.
    (d) India needs to first strengthen its democracy.

DIRECTION (Q. 13) : Choose the word which is most nearly the SAME in meaning as the word printed in bold as used in the passage.

13. RESILIENCE
 (a) quietening (b) amplifying
 (c) existence (d) adaptability

DIRECTIONS (Qs. 14 & 15): In the following questions, sentences are given with blanks to be filled with appropriate word(s). Choose the correct alternative form the given options and indicate it.

14. She expects me to type the letter in five minutes _______ is impossible.
 (a) that (b) which
 (c) what (d) but

15. It is not time for the cinema to begin ....?
 (a) so far, is it?
 (b) yet, isn't it?
 (c) already, is it?
 (d) before, isn't it?

DIRECTIONS (Qs. 16 & 17): In each of these questions, in the given sentences, a part of the sentence is underlined. Beneath each sentence, four different ways of phrasing the underlined part are indicated. Choose the best alternative. In case no improvement is needed, your answer would be 'No improvement'.

16. We want the teacher to be him who has the best rapport with the students.
 (a) We want the teacher to be he
 (b) We want him to be the teacher
 (c) We desire the teacher to be him
 (d) We anticipate the teacher to be him

17. Today this is a totally different world than we have seen in the last decade.
 (a) than what we seen
 (b) then we have seen
 (c) from what we seen
 (d) from what we have seen

DIRECTIONS (Qs. 18 & 19): In each of the following sentences four words or phrases have been underlined. Only one underlined part in each sentence has error. Find out which part of a sentence has an error.

18. While in conversation $\underset{a}{\underline{\text{with a}}}$ high military officer $\underset{b}{\underline{\text{he told me}}}$ that $\underset{c}{\underline{\text{at the headquarters}}}$ noth-ing $\underset{d}{\underline{\text{was known}}}$.

19. $\underset{a}{\underline{\text{The fear}}}$ of an $\underset{b}{\underline{\text{impending invasion}}}$ has more to do than even $\underset{c}{\underline{\text{the debasing of the coinage}}}$ with the $\underset{d}{\underline{\text{financial}}}$ difficulties.

DIRECTION (Q. 20): Choose the correct meaning of an idom/phrase.

20. Hobson's choice :
 (a) Feeling of insecurity
 (b) Accept or leave the other
 (c) Feeling of strength
 (d) Excellent choicepointed to

SOLUTIONS

1. (d) $3 = 2^2 - 1,$
$8 = 3^2 - 1:$
$35 = 6^2 - 1,$
$48 = 7^2 - 1:$
$? = 10^2 - 1,$
$120 = 11^2 - 1.$

2. (a)

3. (a) Type – Simple arrangement (SWAP CODING)
Interchange F and D, R and N and I and E.
Similarly, DESERT is coded as TRESED.

4. (b) Girl's Father's only son—Girl's brother
Grandmother of Girl's brother – Girl's Grandmother; Daughter-in-law of girl's grandmother — Girls' mother.

5. (c)

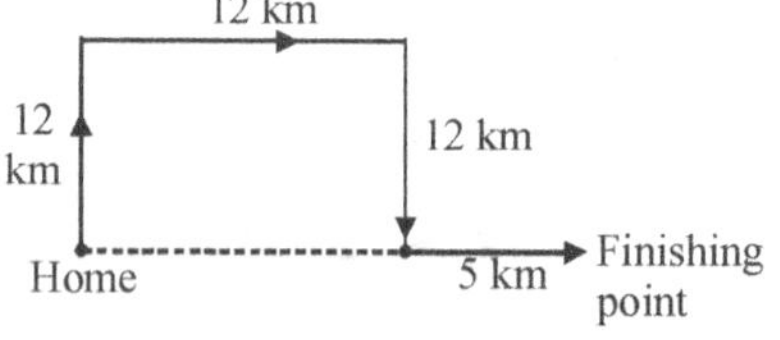

So, 12 km + 5 km = 17 km

6. (a) Add all the four numbers and then take its square root.

7. (d) In all other pairs, second is a part of the first.

8. (a) As mentioned, the seventh day of the month is three days earlier than Friday, which is Tuesday.
So, the fourteenth day is also Tuesday and thus, the nineteenth day is Sunday.

9. (c) Using the proper signs, we get:
$36 - 8\,4 + 6 \div 2 \times 3 = 36 - 2 + 3 \times 3 = 36 - 2 + 9$

$= 45 - 2 = 43$

10. (d) We have three squares with vertical and horizontal sides. Each such square has $1^2 + 2^2 = 5$ squares in it. Thus there are 15 such squares.
In addition, we have two obliquely placed squares. Hence total no. of squares = 17

11. (b) Japanese business circles represented by the Ishikawa Mission called attention of their Indian counterparts in what they considered to be major impediments in India.

12. (a) India deserves a far bigger share of world trade considering its vast resources.

13. (d)   14. (b)   15. (c)

16. (a) 'him' is not the right usage because it is a possessive pronoun, and in the sentence it is followed by who, which is used to refer. So the pronoun he should be used. He, who has the best rapport with the students.

17. (d) Different is used with 'from' e.g. 'you are different from Ritu'. Than is used for comparisons, e.g., The world is more populated than it was in our time.

18. (b) I was told
The subject should come before the verb.

19. (c) with the debasing of the coinage than

20. (b)

MOCK TEST-8

Max. Marks : 20   **Time : 20 mins.**

1. *Wax* is related to *Grease* in the same way as *Milk* is related to ....?
   (a) Drink   (b) Ghee
   (c) Curd   (d) Protein

2. In a certain code, if AFFAIR is FAAFRI, then FERRARIS is coded as ?
   (a) EFRRARIS
   (b) EFRRRASI
   (c) EFRRRAIS
   (d) EFRRARSI

3. In the first and second digits in the sequence 5 9 8 13 2 7 4 3 8 are interchanged. Also the third and fourth digits, the fifth and sixth digits and so on, which digit would be the seventh counting to your left ?
   (a) 1   (b) 4
   (c) 7   (d) 8

4. A and B are brothers. C and D are sisters A's son is D's brother. How is B related to C
   (a) Father
   (b) Brother
   (c) Grand father
   (d) Uncle

5. If the first and second letters in the word DEPRESSION were interchanged, also the third and the fourth letters, the fifth and the sixth letters and so on, which of the following would be the seventh letter from the right ?
   (a) R   (b) O
   (c) S
   (d) None of these

6. If + means × . × means −, ÷ means + and − means ÷, then which of the following gives the result of
   $175 - 25 \div 5 \div 20 \times 3 + 10$?
   (a) 77   (b) 160
   (c) 240   (d) 2370

7. Deepak starts walking straight towards east. After walking 75 metres, he turns to the left and walks 25 metres straight. Again he turns to the left, walks a distance of 40 metres straight, again he turns to the left and walks a distance of 25 metres. How far is he from the starting point ?
   (a) 25 metres
   (b) 50 metres
   (c) 115 metres
   (d) 35 metres

8. If it was Saturday on 17th December, 2002 what was the day on 22nd December, 2004 ?
   (a) Monday
   (b) Tuesday
   (c) Wednesday
   (d) Sunday

9. Find the which of the figures (A), (B), (C) and (D) can be formed from the pieces given in figure (X).

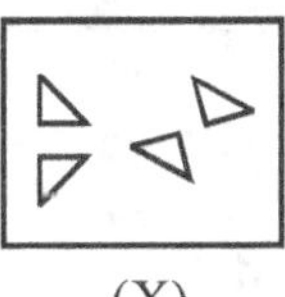

(X)

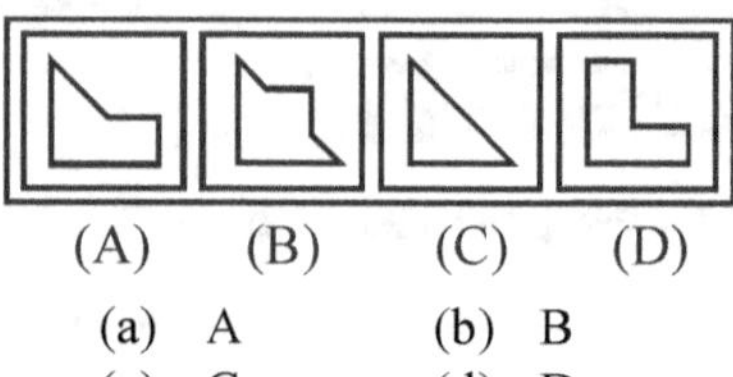

(a) A   (b) B

(c) C   (d) D

10. What number should replace the question mark ?

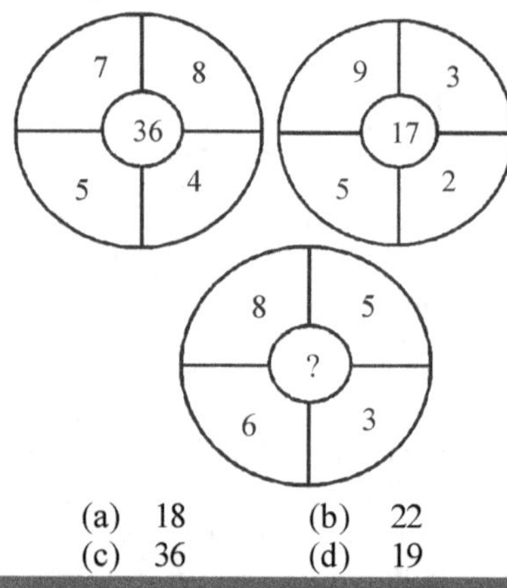

(a) 18   (b) 22

(c) 36   (d) 19

English Proficiency

DIRECTIONS (Qs. 11 & 12) : Pick out the nearest correct meaning or synonym of the words given below:

11. COURAGEOUS

   (a) fickle   (b) insipid

   (c) timorous (d) fearless

12. HARMONY

   (a) cemetery (b) ceremony

   (c) symmetry (d) hierarchy

DIRECTIONS (Qs. 13 & 14) : Pick out the opposite meaning or antonym of the words given below:

13. VACILLATING

   (a) fascinating

   (b) fanaticism

   (c) indolence

   (d) resolute

14. OBSCENE

   (a) decent

   (b) objectionable

   (c) condemnable

   (d) jealousy

DIRECTIONS (Qs. 15 & 16) : Choose the correct meaning of an idom/phrase.

15. To snap one's fingers :

   (a) To speak abruptly

   (b) To accept immediately

   (c) To grasp eagerly

   (d) To become contemptuous of

16. To take the bull by the horns :

   (a) To punish a person severly for his arrogance

   (b) To grapple courageously with difficulty that lies in our way

   (c) To handle it by fierce attack

   (d) To bypass the legal process and take action according to one's own whims

DIRECTION: (Q. 17) Choose the correct spelling of the given word.

17. (a) Aliennate (b) Allienate

   (c) Alienate (d) Alienatte

DIRECTIONS (Qs. 18 & 19) : In each of the following sentences four words or phrases have been underlined. Only one underlined part in each sentence has error. Find out which part of a sentence has an error.

18. His assistants $\underset{a}{\underline{\text{have}}}$ and $\underset{b}{\underline{\text{are still}}}$ doing

excellent / c **work** for the / d orga-
nization.

19. There is something more in the / a **fact** that the / b guns have / c **or** are about / d to be sent abroad.

DIRECTION (Q. 20): In the following question, sentences are given with blanks to be filled with appropriate word(s). Choose the correct alternative form the given options and indicate it.

20. Because of the power cut, many workers were __________.
    (a) laid off
    (b) lay out
    (c) laid of
    (d) would have known

SOLUTIONS

1. **(c)** First is used to prepare the second.

2. **(b)** Type – Simple Arrangement (Swap coding).
    In the word AFFAIR, the positions of first A & first F are interchanged second A & second F are interchanged and I and R are interchanged.
    Similarly, RERRARIS is coded as EFRRRASI.

3. **(d)** The new sequence becomes 9 5 1 8 2 3 4 7 8 3 counting to the left, the seventh number is 8.

4. **(d)** Studying the statements carefully, was find that B is the brother of A and A's son is the brother of D, so D is the daughter of A. Since C and D are sister, so C is also the daughter of A. The B is the uncle of C. The answer is (d)

5. **(d)**

6. **(a)** Using the proper signs in the given expression , we get
    $175 \div 5 \times 20 - 3 \times 10 = 7 + 5$
    $\times 20 - 3 \times 10$
    $= 7 + 100 - 30 = 107 - 30 = 77.$

7. **(d)** The movements of Deepak are as shown in fig.

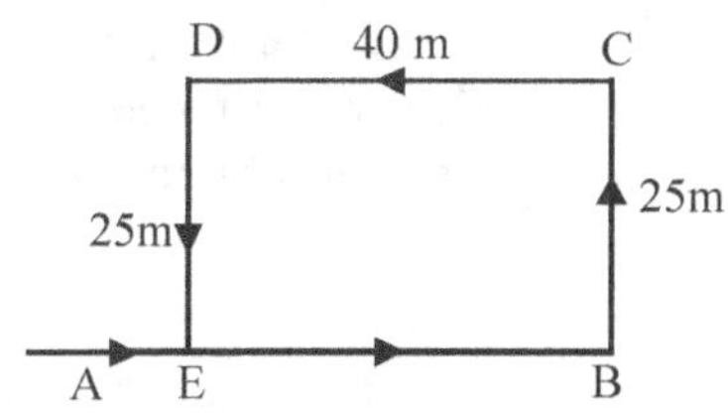

Clearly, $FB = DC = 40\,m$.
∴ Deepak's distance from the starting point A
$= (AB - EB) = (75 - 40)\,m = 35m.$

8. **(d)** Clearly, every day repeats itself on the seventh day. Now, 17th Dec. 2002 - 16th Dec.

2003 is a period of 365 days. Dividing by 7, we get 52 weeks and one day. Thus, the 365th day will be the same as the first day, i.e., 16th Dec. 2003 is also Saturday.

Now, 16th Dec. 2003 - 15th Dec. 2004 is a period of 366 days (because 2004, being a leap year, has 29 days in February). Thus, as shown above, 14th Dec. 2004 will be the same as 16th Dec. 2003, i.e., Saturday. So, 21st Dec. 2004 is also Saturday and thus, 22nd Dec. 2004 is a Sunday.

9. **(b)**

10. **(b)** $(7 \times 8) - (5 \times 4) = 36$
$(9 \times 3) - (5 \times 2) = 36$
$(8 \times 5) - (6 \times 3) = 22$

11. **(d)** fearless means lack of fear, fickle means unstable, often changing, not constant, not faithful, Insipid means tasteless

12. **(c)** cemetery means graveyards, hierarchy means a system of society in which people are graded into different classes according to certain norms, harmony is when many things work together in the same mode.

13. **(d)** Fascinating means charming, fanaticism means madness, especially in religious or political matters, indolence means laziness.

14. **(a)** Obscene means indecent, objectionable and condemnable mean similar to obscene.

15. **(d)**   **16.** **(b)**   **17.** **(c)**

18. **(a)** have done
The present perfect tense is used to denote an action beginning at some time in the past and continuing upto the present moment as the words "are still doing" in the sentence reveal.

19. **(c)** have been
The present perfect tense is used to express past actions whose time is not given and not definite.

20. **(d)**

MOCK TEST-9

Max. Marks : 20 **Time : 20 mins**

1. Find the missing term.

   2, 12, 36, 80, 150, ?

   (a) 194 (b) 210

   (c) 252 (d) 258

2. If × means ÷, − means × , ÷ means + and + means − then

   (3 − 15 ÷ 19) × 8 + 6 = ?

   (a) − 1 (b) 2

   (c) 4 (d) 8

3. If all the directions are rotated, i.e., if North is changed to West and East to North and so on, then what will come in place of North-West ?

   (a) South-West

   (b) North-East

   (c) East-North

   (d) East-West

4. What number should replace the question mark ?

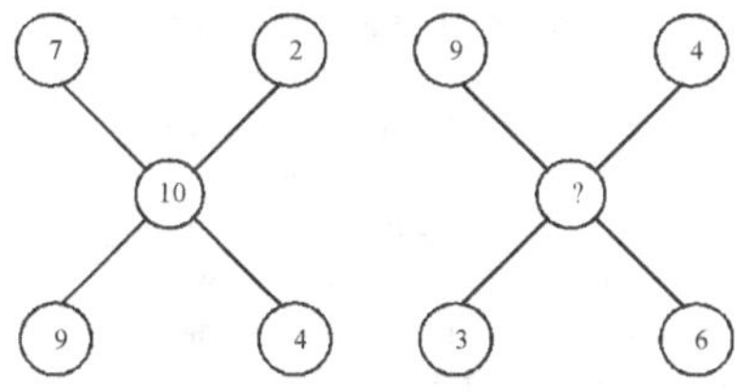

   (a) 2 (b) 9

   (c) 12 (d) 19

5. Pointing out to a photograph, a man tells his friend, " she is the daughter of the only son of my father's wife. How is the girls related to the man in the photograph?

   (a) Daughter (b) Cousin

   (c) Mother (d) Sister

6. Manisha ranked sixteenth from the top and twenty-nineth from the bottom among those who has passed an examination. Six boys did not participate in the examination and five failed in it. How many boys were there in the class.?

   (a) 40 (b) 44

   (c) 50 (d) 55

7. If in a code, ALTERED is written as ZOGVIVW, then in the same code, how is IVOZGVW written as ?

   (a) FEATHER (b) DEARST

   (c) RELATED (d) BELATED

8. Supervisor : Worker ::

   (a) Junior : Senior

   (b) Elder : Younger

   (c) Debtor : Creditor

   (d) Officer : Clerk

9. Select the combination of numbers so that the letters arranged accordingly will form a meaningful word.

   V A R S T E

   (a) 2, 3, 1, 6, 4, 5

   (b) 4, 5, 2, 3, 1, 6

   (c) 6, 3, 4, 5, 2, 1

   (d) 3, 2, 4, 5, 6, 1

10. Find out which of the figures (A), (B), (C) and (D) can be formed from the pieces given in figure (x).

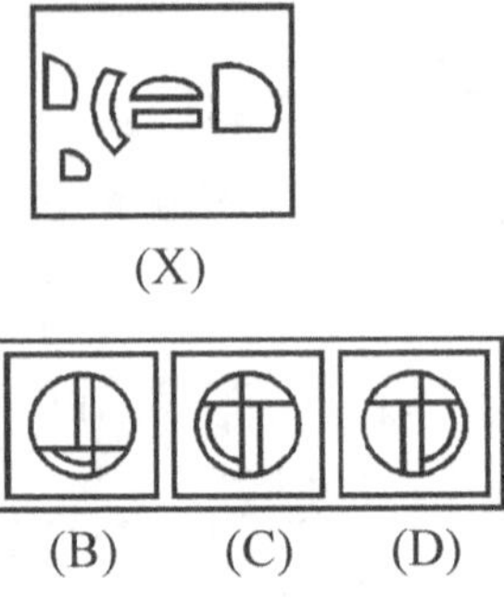

(X)

(A)   (B)   (C)   (D)

(a) A   (b) B
(c) C   (d) D

English Proficiency

DIRECTIONS (Qs. 11 & 12) : In the following questions, sentences are given with blanks to be filled with appropriate word(s). Choose the correct alternative form the given options and indicate it.

11. He is _______ handsome boy that he is very popular with girls.
    (a) such a   (b) a such
    (c) such
    (d) rather than the speed

12. The police arrived _______ the scene half an hour after the accident
    (a) on   (b) to
    (c) into   (d) in

DIRECTIONS (Qs. 13 & 14) : Read the passage carefully to answer the questions.

We have inherited the tradition of secrecy about the budget from Britain where also the system has been strongly attacked by eminent economists and political scientists including Peter Jay. Sir Richard Clarke, who was the originating genius of nearly every important development in the British budgeting techniques during the last two decades, has spoken out about the abuse of budget secrecy:

"The problems of long-term tax policy should surely be debated openly with the facts on the table. In my opinion, all governments should have just the same duty to publish their expenditure policy. Indeed, this obligation to publish taxation policy is really essential for the control of public expenditure in order to get realistic taxation implications." Realising that democracy flourishes best on the principles of open government, more and more democracies are having an open public debate on budget proposals before introducing the appropriate Bill in the legislature. In the United States the budget is conveyed in a message by the President to the Congress, which comes well in advance of the date when the Bill is introduced in the Congress. In Finland the Parliament and the people are already discussing in June the tentative budget proposals which are to be introduced in the Finnish Parliament in September. Every budget contains a cartload of figures in black and white - but the dark figures represent the myriad lights and shades of India's life, the contrasting tones of poverty and wealth, and of bread so dear and flesh and blood so cheap, the deep tints of adventure and enterprise and man's ageless struggle for a brighter morning. The Union budget should not be an annual **scourge** but a part of presentation of annual accounts of a partnership between the Government and the people. That partnership would work much better when the nonsensical secrecy is replaced by openness and public consultations, resulting in fair laws and the people's acceptance of their moral duty to pay.

13. How do the British economists and political scientists react to budget secrecy? They are:
    (a) in favour of having a mix of secrecy and openness.
    (b) indifferent to the budgeting techniques and taxation policies.

   (c) very critical about maintenance of budget secrecy.

   (d) advocates of not disclosing in advance the budget contents.

14. The author thinks that openness in budget is essential as it leads to:

   (a) prevention of tax implications

   (b) people's reluctance to accept their moral duties

   (c) exaggerated revelation of the strengths and weaknesses of economy

   (d) None of these

DIRECTIONS (Qs. 15 & 16) : In each of these questions, in the given sentences, a part of the sentence is underlined. Beneath each sentence, four different ways of phrasing the underlined part are indicated. Choose the best alternative.

15. Although he was the most friendly of all present and <u>different from the others, he hadn't hardly any friends except me.</u>

   (a) different from the others, he hardly had any friends except I

   (b) different than the others, he hardly had any friends except me

   (c) different than the others, he hardly had any friends except I

   (d) different from the others, he hardly had any friends except me

16. <u>Since we are living</u> in Bombay for five years, we are reluctant to move to another city.

   (a) Being that we living

   (b) Since we were living

   (c) Since we have been living

   (d) Being that we have been living

DIRECTIONS (Qs. 17 & 18): In each of the following sentences four words or phrases have been underlined. Only one underlined part in each sentence has error. Find out which part of a sentence has an error.

17. A $\underset{a}{\underline{\text{long}}}$ life is good $\underset{b}{\underline{\text{if one}}}$ $\underset{c}{\underline{\text{be}}}$ happy and $\underset{d}{\underline{\text{has}}}$ friends.

18. $\underset{a}{\underline{\text{The}}}$ deceased Lord $\underset{b}{\underline{\text{along with}}}$ his brother $\underset{c}{\underline{\text{started a}}}$ business $\underset{d}{\underline{\text{in India}}}$.

DIRECTIONS (QS. 19 & 20) : Choose the correct meaning of an idom/ phrase.

19. To cast pearls before a swine :

   (a) To spend recklessly

   (b) To spend a lot of money on the unkeep of domestic hogs

   (c) To waste monkey over trifles

   (d) To offer to a person a thing which he cannot appreciate

20. To take people by storm :

   (a) To put people in utter surprise

   (b) To captivate them unexpectedly

   (c) To exploit people's agitation

   (d) To bring out something sensational attracting people's attention

SOLUTIONS

1. **(c)** $2 = 1^2 + 1^3$
$12 = 2^2 + 2^3$
$36 = 3^2 + 3^3$ and so on.

2. **(b)** Using the correct symbol, we have
Given Expression =
$= (3 \times 15 + 19) \div 8 - 6$
$= 64 \div 8 - 6 \Rightarrow 8 - 6 = 2$

3. **(a)** Original directions

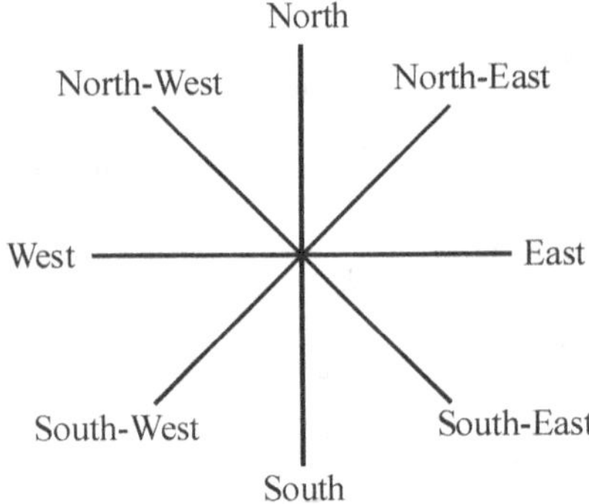

4. **(a)** Subtract the sum of the even numbers from the sum of the odd numbers.
$7 + 9 = 16$ $9 + 3 = 12$
$2 + 4 = 6$ $4 + 6 = 10$
$16 - 6 = 10$ $12 - 10 = 2$

5. **(a)** Father's wife means mother ; mother's only son means himself and thus the girls is the daughter of the man.

6. **(d)** Number of boys who passed $= 16 + 29 - 1 = 44$
∴ Total number of boys in the class $= 44 + 6 + 5$
$= 55$.

7. **(c)**

8. **(d)** As supervisor supervises the worker, in the same way, officer supervises the clerk.

9. **(b)** Clearly the given letters, when arranged in the order
4, 5, 2, 3, 1, 6 form the word 'STRAVE'.

10. **(a)**   11. **(a)**   12. **(a)**

13. **(c)** Eminent British economists and political scientists have strongly attacked the tradition of budget secrecy.

14. **(d)** It leads to the control of public expenditure in order to set realistic taxation implications.

15. **(d)** When we use the word 'hardly', it implies a negative meaning, there is then no need to use not, so the most suitable use is 'he hardly had any friends'.

16. **(c)** The tense in this sentence should be the present perfect continuous because it refers to an action that started at some time in past and continues till the present time so right use is 'have been living in Mumbai.'

17. **(c)** The simplest present is used to express general truths.

18. **(c)** had started
The past perfect tense helps in telling us which action happened earlier than the other when both the actions referred to happen in the past. The simple past is used in one clause and the past perfect in the other.

19. **(d)** 20. **(b)**

MOCK TEST-10

Max. Marks : 20 **Time : 20 mins.**

1. If HELMET is written as IFMNFU. Then how will CHOCOLATE be written as ?
   (a) DIDPMPBUF
   (b) EIDPMPBUF
   (c) DIPDPMBFU
   (d) DIPDPMBUF

DIRECTIONS (Qs. 2 & 3) : Read the following information carefully and answer the questions that follow :

A, B, C, D, E and F are seated in a circle facing the centre D is between F and B. A is second to the left of D and second to the right of E.

2. Who is facing A?
   (a) B (b) D
   (c) F
   (d) Either F or B

3. Who among the following is facing D?
   (a) A
   (b) C
   (c) E
   (d) Cannot be determined

4. Ajay is the brother of Vijay. Mili is the sister of Ajay. Sanjay is the brother of Rahul and Mehul is the daughter of Vijay. Who is Sanjay's Uncle ?
   (a) Rahul
   (b) Ajay
   (c) Mehul
   (d) Data inadequate

5. If the given interchanges namely : signs + and ÷ and numbers 2 and 4 are made in signs and numbers, which one of the following four equations would be correct ?
   (a) $2 + 4 \div 3 = 3$
   (b) $4 + 2 \div 6 = 1.5$
   (c) $4 \div 2 + 3 = 4$
   (d) $2 + 4 \div 6 = 8.$

6. Raj travelled from a point X straight to Y at a distance of 80 metres. He turned right and walked 50 metres, then again turned right and walked 70 metres. Finally, he turned right and walked 50 metres. How far is he from the starting point
   (a) 10 metres (b) 20 metres
   (c) 50 metres (d) 70 metres

7. Find the missing number.

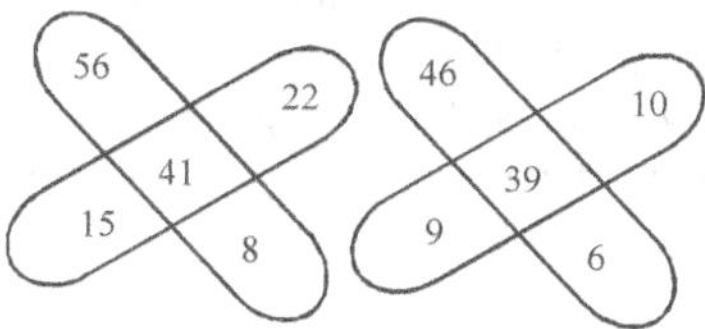

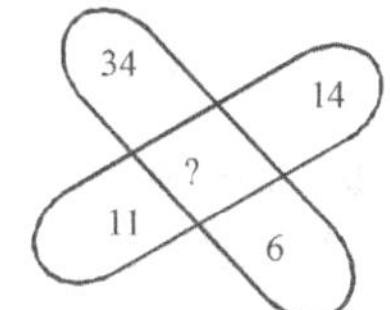

   (a) 12 (b) 25
   (c) 48 (d) 52

8. Find out which of the figures (A), (B), (C) and (D) can be formed from the pieces given in figures (X).

(X)

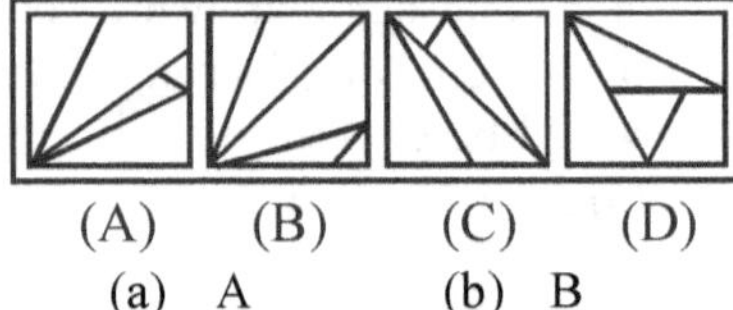

(A)   (B)   (C)   (D)

(a) A   (b) B
(c) C   (d) D

9. Arrange the given words in alphabetical order and tick the one that comes in the 2nd position.

(a) Restrict   (b) Rocket
(c) Robber   (d) Radom

DIRECTION (Q. 10): In the following question, a group of letters is given which are numbered 1, 2, 3, 4, 5 and 6. Below a re given four alternatives containing combinations of these numbers. Select that combination of numbers so that letters arranged accordingly form a meaningful word.

10. T L P N A E
1 2 3 4 5 6
(a) 3, 2, 5, 4, 6, 1
(b) 3, 2, 5, 4, 1, 6
(c) 4, 5, 3, 6, 2, 1
(d) 4, 6, 1, 3, 5, 2

English Proficiency

DIRECTIONS (Q. 11): Pick out the nearest correct meaning or synonym of the words given below:

11. PATRONAGE
(a) donation   (b) support
(c) espionage (d) beneficiary

DIRECTIONS (Q. 12): Pick out the opposite meaning or antonym of the words given below:

12. LEGITIMATE
(a) valid
(b) extend
(c) unlawful
(d) distinguished

DIRECTIONS (Qs. 13 & 14): Choose the correct meaning of an idom/phrase.

13. To split hours :
(a) To sidetrack the issue
(b) To quarrel over trifles
(c) To indulge in over-refined arguments
(d) To find faults with other

14. Will o' the wisp :
(a) Anything which eludes or deceives
(b) To act in a childish way
(c) To act in a foolish way
(d) To have desires unbacked by efforts

DIRECTIONS: (Qs. 15 & 16) Choose the correct spelling of the given word.

15. (a) Comemorate
(b) Commemmorate
(c) Momemmorate
(d) Commemorate

16. (a) Psychology
(b) Sycology
(c) Psykology
(d) Sychology

DIRECTIONS (Qs. 17 & 18): In each of the following sentences four words or phrases have been underlined. Only one underlined part in each sentence has error. Find out which part of a sentence has an error.

17. You $\dfrac{\text{have been}}{a}$ more able to $\dfrac{\text{withstand}}{b}$ $\dfrac{\text{the treaties}}{c}$ than $\dfrac{\text{did he}}{d}$.

18. It is hoped that with the medical fee $\dfrac{\text{being withdrawn}}{a}$ and men $\dfrac{\text{can be tested}}{b}$ and $\dfrac{\text{finally accepted}}{c}$, a large number of people will $\dfrac{\text{come forward}}{d}$.

DIRECTIONS (Qs. 19 & 20) : Read the passage carefully to answer the questions.

Nature is an infinite source of beauty. Sunrise and sunset, mountains and rivers, lakes and glaciers, forests and fields provide joy and bliss to the human mind and heart for hours together. Everything in nature is splendid and divine. Everyday and every season of the year has a peculiar beauty to **unfold**. Only one should have eyes to behold it and a heart to feel it like the English poet William Wordsworth who after seeing daffodils said: "And then my heart with pleasure fills and dances with the daffodils".

Nature is a great teacher. The early man was thrilled with beauty and wonders of nature. The Aryans worshipped nature. One can learn the lessons in the vast school of nature.

Unfortunately the strife, the stress and the tension of modern life have made people immune to beauties of nature. Their life is so full of **care** that they have no time to stand and stare. They cannot enjoy the beauty of lowing rivers, swinging trees, flying birds and majestic mountains and hills. There is however, a cry to go back to village from the concrete and artificial jungle of cities. Hence the town planners of today pay special attention to provide enough number of natural scenic spots in town planning. To develop a balanced personality, one needs to have a healthy attitude which can make us appreciate and enjoy the beauty of nature.

There is other balm to soothe our tired soul and listless mind than the infinite nature all around us. We should enjoy it fully to lead a balanced and harmonious life, full of peace and tranquility.

19. Which of the following statements is not made in the passage about Nature?
    (a) Nature is an infinite source of beauty
    (b) Everything in nature is splendid and divine
    (c) Nature is a great teacher
    (d) The early man was scared of Nature

20. According to the author of the passage, Nature:
    (a) is the ultimate salvation of man
    (b) is the creator of this universe
    (c) brings uniformity in all seasons
    (d) is abundantly glorious and divine

SOLUTIONS

1. **(d)** Type – Pattern substitution (+1)

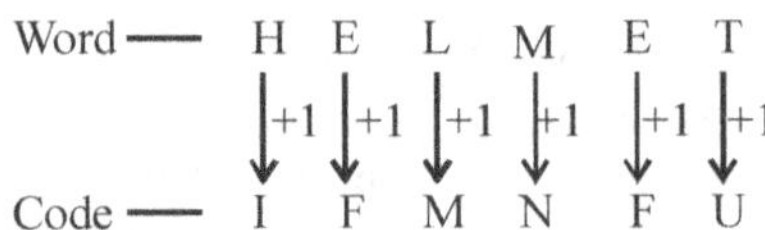

So, either F or B is facing A.

2. **(d)**

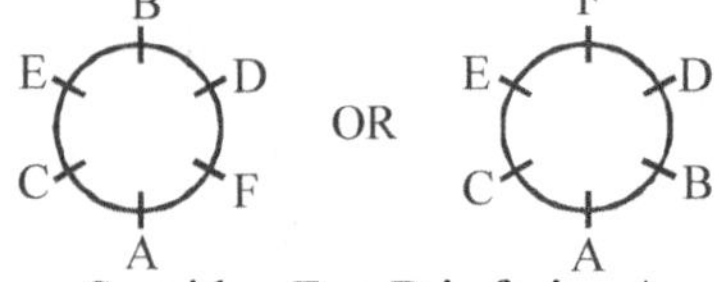

So, either F or B is facing A.

3. **(b)** C is facing D.

4. **(d)**

1. Mili $\xrightarrow[\text{(Sister)}]{}$ Ajay $\xrightarrow[\text{(Brother)}]{}$

   Vijay $\xrightarrow[\text{(daughter)}]{}$ Mehul

2. Sanjay $\xrightarrow[\text{(brother)}]{}$ Rahul

   There are two sets of relationship information given is incomplete and no relation can be established between the two sets.

5. **(d)** Interchanging (+ and ÷) and (2 and 4), we get :
   - (a) $4 \div 2 + 3 = 3$ or $5 = 3$, which is false
   - (b) $2 \div 4 + 6 = 1.5$ or $6.5 = 1.5$, which is false.
   - (c) $2 + 4 \div 3 = 4$ or $\dfrac{10}{3} = 4$, which is false.
   - (d) $4 \div 2 + 6 = 8$ or $8 = 8$, which is true.

6. **(a)** The movements of Raj are as shown in fig (X to Y, Y to A, A to B , B to C).

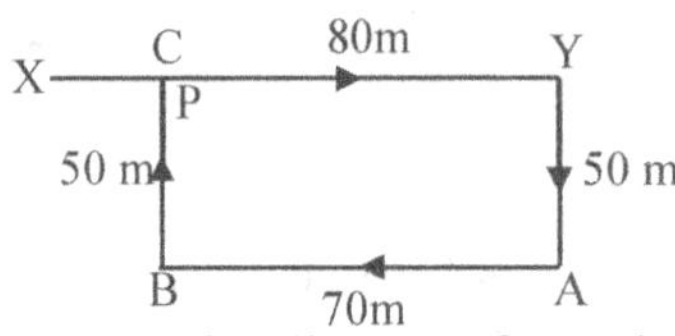

∴ Raj's distance from the starting point
$$= XC = (XY - YC) = (XY - BA)$$
$$= (80 - 70)\,m = 10\,m.$$

7. **(b)** We have $(56 + 15) - (22 + 8) = 41, (46 + 9) - (10 + 6) = 39$
   So, missing number $= (34 + 11) - (14 + 6) = 25$

8. **(b)**

9. **(a)** Arranging the words in alphabetical order, we have Random, Restrict, Robber, Rocket.
   So the word in the 2nd position is Restrict and the correct answer is (a).

10. **(a)** PLANET

11. **(b)** Classical music today is in need of patronage. Earlier, its patrons were the maharajas. Classical musicians were honoured in the royal courts. They were given all the support necessary to let their art flourish.

12. **(c)** Legitimate means legal or lawful, distinguished means eminent, and courteous means polite.

13. **(c)** 14. **(a)** 15. **(d)** 16. **(a)**

17. **(d)** he did

18. **(b)** men being tested
    The present (passive) participle, being tested ought to be used here to maintain the uniformity in the Sentence.

19. **(d)** The early man was scared of Nature.

20. **(d)** is abundantly glorious and divine.